ATHEISM FOR MUSLIMS

ATHEISM FOR MUSLIMS

A GUIDE TO QUESTIONING ISLAM, RELIGION AND GOD FOR A BETTER FUTURE

ADAM WADI

Contents

Part IV. Prophet Muhammad

Part V. The Prophets

Part VI. Science in Islam

Part VII. Women

Part VIII. The Modern World

Part IX. A Religion of Peace

About the author

Adam Wadi is a researcher in Islam and the psychology of religions, who advocates the importance of asking the right questions in life, to get the right answers.

Wadi teaches taking no assumptions as truths in order to understand ourselves better, understand each other better, and build a better world for future generations.

To be the first to receive news about Wadi's next book, sign up for exclusive access at www.about.me/adamwadi. Or, just say hello and tell him how the weather is where you are at adamwadi@protonmail.com

Introduction

"a lack of belief or a strong disbelief in the existence of a god or any gods" –
Merriam-Webster definition of 'atheism'[1]

I write this book as someone raised Muslim his entire life; Islam defined me as a man and human being in a way I wouldn't change for any other. To this day, I'm grateful to have been raised in a loving Muslim family. I received everything I needed in life from my parents, and I was fortunate enough to have my health as well. I believed it was God who took care of me and my family, He was the cause of all the happiness I was lucky enough to receive.

My entire extended family are Muslim too, and I loved all the occasions we got together to celebrate Eid, or to break our fast during Ramadan. Even when there was no particular occasion to celebrate, my mother and father always made the effort to go visit family across the country or across the world, so we would never forgot who we were, where we came from, and what was most important in life. It was fun to grow up with my cousins and to share the same experiences with them. It also felt great to have aunts and uncles who were more than relatives; they were a second set of parents.

I never experienced any discrimination or racism when I was growing up in a white, Christian community. I was aware I was the only Muslim, and the only ethnic boy in my school and social groups, but I was never made to feel inferior or embarrassed for being different in appearance and faith. I don't think my parents' generation were fortunate enough to have the same experience I did in a foreign country when they were my age.

I remember when I was around seven years old, I was in the car with my mother and we were on our way back home. We slowed down at an intersection and we had the right of way to go. But my mother paused and patiently waited for another car to come out and go ahead of us, even though she didn't need to. The man in the other car acknowledged my mother's courtesy and gestured a thanks towards her. My mother returned the gesture and we continued to drive on.

A few moments later I asked my mother why she let that man go ahead of us when we didn't need to stop for him. My mother smiled as she continued to drive. She then said "For most people in this town, we're the first Muslims

---

1. *Merriam-Webster. Accessed February 28, 2017. https://www.merriam-webster.com/dictionary/atheism.*

1

they'll ever meet, and we might even be the first people they've ever seen in their town who aren't white. This means we represent all the Muslims in the world for them. They're going to judge what all Muslims are like based on us and how we behave. We need to make sure they know we're good people and we're the same as them."

This is how I continued to live my life: to try to be as friendly and likable as I could since I was the Muslim all my friends would judge other Muslims by. Then, the planes hit the Twin Towers in New York on 11th September 2001.

That day changed everything for Muslims around the world. Suddenly we found ourselves on the back foot, justifying our religion and our beliefs. I remember in the following few days one of my friends came to me and asked why Muslims killed all those innocent people. I explained to him that those people aren't real Muslims, that's not what Muslims do. I believed that then, and I still believe that now. Muslims are good people, I know that with all my heart.

Muslims may be the most misunderstood people in the world. However, I also believe there are principles and ideologies from Islam that Muslims carry which don't help their cause, and that are worth questioning.

Since 9/11, a brighter spotlight has been placed on Muslims and Islam. However, 9/11 didn't cause me to question Islam, in fact, it made me committed to defending it from misjudgment. I was determined to prepare myself with the real facts about Islam so I'd be in a better position to explain my religion and beliefs to anyone who'd question them.

It all went well. But around 15 years later, things slowly started to turn.

Why this book exists

"The unexamined life is not worth living" – Socrates

Adam Wadi is not my name. I have decided to use a pen name to protect myself and my family. My intention is not to offend Muslims or insult the religion of Islam, my intention is to ask important questions I feel must be asked. But, I know Muslims will consider this book blasphemy.

In modern times, Islam has become a difficult topic to critique, so I would rather not put myself or my family in harm's way. Therefore, I've decided to use the pen name Adam Wadi to express myself without any inhibitions or fear of retribution. I know this has resulted in a more credible book so I make no apologies to those who consider me fake or cowardly for my decision. This book is not about raising awareness of myself, this book is about helping people by empowering them with knowledge.

The original decision to write this book came from a desire to deepen my knowledge of Islam and satisfy my own curiosities about the religion I still wanted to learn more about. At the time I was happy being a Muslim, and I had no idea where this exploration of Islam would take me.

Along my journey I came across many critiques of Islam, and religion in general. Ever since I was a teenager I had always been happy to challenge myself and my beliefs with further education. I believed further study of Islam and religion would make my faith stronger, not weaker, just like it had done in the past.

But as I went further down the rabbit hole, I began absorbing videos, articles and books by prominent atheists such as Christopher Hitchens and Richard Dawkins, some by scientists like astrophysicist Neil DeGrasse Tyson and neuroscientist Sam Harris, and even some by comedians, such as Bill Maher and Ricky Gervais, to name a few. These people and many others spoke about science, human behavior and language in a way I hadn't heard before. They made contrarian observations about things most of us accept as the 'gospel' truth, and they built them on the shoulders of giants such as Galileo, Darwin, Einstein, Feynman, Sagan and Hawking. But I didn't agree with all the statements some atheists made. For me it wasn't about getting rid of religion, but finding a common ground with religion.

Growing up, my parents always told me Islam wasn't about making life more difficult, in fact, it's the opposite: Islam exists to make everyone's life easier and better. My parents also told me Islam encourages questioning and reflection, it encourages the practice of free will and thought. I took this to heart. So over time, instead of accepting what I'd been told since I was a child at face value, I started to analyze everything on a deeper level.

The information I absorbed began a process of scrutinizing everything I knew about God. I'd always thought I knew the difference between what I was told to believe and what I actually believed, but that was naive of me. So from within, stirrings began. It didn't feel safe to share what I was thinking and feeling with my friends, and especially with my family, but it became harder and harder to justify why Islam is true. It wasn't so much an epiphany, but rather a slow and painful process of questioning. The answers to these questions conflicted with what I'd always believed, and it was these stirrings which gave rise to this book. I had gone through my Muslim-shaped rabbit hole, and on the other side I came out of it as an atheist.

I thought long and hard about all the information I'd processed to get to this point and it began to overwhelm me. To clear my head I knew it would be best to get it all out, so I started to put down on paper all the reasons why I didn't believe God exists anymore.

I scribbled notes about many different topics, anything that came to mind, and all the ideas that conflicted with my lifelong beliefs: cosmology, anthropology, and psychology of religion were a few. So many times I tried to find the reasons why; the justifications of why Islam said this or why we're told to believe that. My life would be so much easier had there been satisfying answers to the questions that kept arising. But I began to realize where this was heading. I was at a fork in the road. I was going in a different direction from the one my family had taken and the one my parents expected me to take. I became resistant to the road I'd been on, the Muslim road. It felt like I was physically changing, because I had changed.

I imagined the heartache it would cause my parents, my aunts and my grandmother, if I went where I was thinking of going. Many of them don't even know what the word atheism means. But would they even need to know and find out that I'm an atheist? Could I just fake it for the rest of my life? Could I write this book and publish it under a pen name so they'd never know it was me?

There were times I even thought to myself "What must God be thinking of me, of the thoughts I'm having and of what I'm doing? After everything He has given me." So deep was the fear and shame, I'd forgotten the notes I'd written and the knowledge I'd acquired about why I didn't believe in God. I couldn't stop speaking hypothetically to Him, as if I believed He was real again. I was even worried that when I continued to go to Friday prayers at the mosque with my father to keep up appearances, someone there would 'sense' there was a non-believer in the room praying among them. That they would look at me and notice something wasn't right about me.

The shame I carried when I first started to feel this way, the anxiety I had when I stopped praying because it suddenly felt empty and meaningless to me, and the guilt throughout the entire time of writing this book. I felt all these things because of fear. Religious fear is so deeply rooted into us at a young age, we panic that something terrible will happen if we disobey God. We tend to fear God's punishment just as much, if not more, than we crave his blessings. So even to this day, to reassure myself, I have to look through all the 50 chapter titles in this book to remind myself of how I came to the reasonable conclusion I now believe.

The shame and anxiety subsided, but the guilt, even now, is still here. How many people in my family will think I'm evil? I mean truly evil, since this book will be seen as the Devil's work. The shame it will bring upon my parents for the rest of their lives, forever asking themselves "What did we do wrong?" They'll believe their child is going to Hell, the ultimate failure for any religious parent.

It'll hurt my mother the most. I know she'll take all the blame and responsibility personally. It will crush her. It will break her heart. But what can I do? Should I have mercy on her, lie to her for the remainder of our lives together to save her from the pain? I've thought about it. Maybe I'm being obnoxious and self-righteous to think I have all the answers she needs to know. Maybe ignorance really is bliss. I've finished writing this book after a year and a half of beginning it and I'm still no closer to the answer. If I do decide to tell her, I only need her to know one thing: she did nothing wrong. My parents did nothing wrong. I am who I am.

Everything that has happened in my life has brought me to this point. Perhaps it was luck and chance, perhaps it was inevitable this perfect storm would occur. All I know is that I'm being authentic to myself, I'm doing what I believe is right in my heart. I don't need to pander to anyone who doesn't know anything about me as a man. I believe I'm a good person and I have good intentions. These are subjective and biased opinions I make of myself, but, I know every night I go to bed, I sleep easily and deeply, and every morning I wake up, I'm happy and grateful to be alive. I live my life excited about giving back to the world and helping people, this is the new meaning of my life which gives it purpose (I share more about my life after Islam in the part '*Life After Religion*').

I changed my mind several times on whether to write this book or not, and I know before it is published, I'll ruminate several more times on whether I'll tell my mother and father about it. But I realized writing this book wasn't just about being brave or overcoming my fears. At its core, it's about doing what I believe is the decent thing of helping my parents understand why I feel the way I feel. Writing these ideas down was the best possible way I knew of how to express all that information to them.

I've come to terms with the consequences of my actions and I still believe what I'm doing is for the greater good, even if it is at my own expense. I'm inspired by people throughout history who also did what they believed was for the greater good. These people changed the world for the better in a way I aspire to do, and even though they were ridiculed by society and treated like pariahs, humankind has benefited as a result. I look to Galileo with Heliocentrism, Darwin with evolution and Semmelweis with hand-washing as examples and sources of strength. I am in no way like any of these great people, but they knew what they were doing was important to them, and notably, they knew it was more important to others even though they were criticized for it. For me, *Atheism for Muslims* is about doing what I believe is right by humankind. I believe we must respect each other, always pursue truth and knowledge, and then share it with others. These are ideals which I believe are for the greater good and long term benefit of humanity.

I also believe it's important for the religious to understand why people don't believe in God. While it may be difficult for the religious to read arguments against God's existence, I believe it is important they at least try to understand how other people in society think and behave. I believe the empathy and understanding this can create will foster a more respectful society, and open a healthier dialogue between religious and non-religious people.

In today's world information is abundant. What we suffer from is a lack of constructive information, the kind that is to the point and straightforward to internalize. I couldn't find a concise, organized collection of critiques on Islam and God's existence, so I created my own. I wrote the book I wanted to read, the book I needed, and I knew if I was looking for such a book then others would be too.

I hope reading *Atheism for Muslims* will help you as much as writing it helped me. I've found it to be both therapeutic and cathartic. I hope it will lead more Muslims on a journey of self-discovery, regardless of where it takes them. I hope it will create more kind and open-minded people thus making the world a more tolerant place for humanity. We atheists and agnostics in the Generation Y and Z demographic in particular (I call us 'YZAs') are best placed to create the change we wish to see in the world. We have no allegiance to any religious dogma, therefore we can choose to actively cultivate an attitude of neutrality and equality to all people in the world, regardless of their religious beliefs. I hope I'll get to hear many more YZA voices in books like these, 'atheist confessionals'.

I wrote this book for my parents to help them understand why I believe what I believe.

I wrote this book to help other ex-Muslims who sought the information and answers I once sought.

I wrote this book to help Muslims understand why other people don't believe what they believe.

I wrote this book because the more knowledge we share, the more informed decisions we can make in our lives, and the better the world will be. I hope I find company with those who believe the same too.

How this book can help you

"Whenever you find yourself on the side of the majority, it is time to pause and reflect" – Mark Twain

Challenging religious dogma is a paradigm shifting moment. It liberates us since we begin to question why things are the way they are, and why other people do the things they do.

We used to challenge reality naturally when we were young. As children we asked "Why? Why? Why?" until our parents or teachers lost their patience. They would respond with "Because I said so" or ignore us if they couldn't answer our questions. The ability to ask questions is rooted in our genes; the more information we knew, the greater our ancestors' chances of survival were. Unfortunately this curiosity gets trained out of us by various authority figures as we grow up. We're ordered to do what we're told, obey the rules and stay in line. Our ability to ask questions, good, reasonable questions, becomes inhibited. But if we don't know how to ask the right questions, how can we hope to find the right answers about life?

Religious dogma is intimidating to challenge but we need to rediscover our ability to question it. Breaking down barriers to challenge an untouchable subject will empower us. It will enable us to develop the courage to start asking more good questions; questions about our societies, our media, and our governments. The rules these entities enforce may have existed for a particular reason in the past but many of them aren't relevant now. In fact, many may be detrimental to humanity's progression. To ask good questions we must have an open mind, and we must be willing to accept new information if it corrects our outdated one. Reason and evidence need to be the important tools used in the search for truth.

It's advantageous for humanity to have progressive religious beliefs because as we humans grow, we change, and so does the culture and society we live in. This symbiotic change allows people and religion to stay consistent with the reality we find ourselves in. If this didn't happen and religious beliefs remained rooted in the past, there would be no important changes throughout history, like women's rights and the abolition of slavery. Liberties like these and more defend our rights to be treated as equals, but they would never have happened if we had always stuck to the static religious beliefs civilizations had previously held. This is why it's important to have a healthy and inquisitive amount of skepticism about our lives and our societies.

It's important for me to say that though I don't practice Islam anymore, it doesn't mean I support every political or social action 'the West' makes, especially against a Muslim country. I believe we all have a lot to learn from each other and I feel fortunate to have had a seat on both sides of the table. It has equipped me with a unique perspective to write this book from. There is also a distinction between critiquing Islam and critiquing Muslims: the former criticizes an ideology and the latter criticizes human beings. This book is about the former, it is not about promoting any anti-Muslim sentiment. Ideologies (like Islam) can bring people apart, but communities (like Muslims) can bring people together. So while I disagree with Islam, it doesn't mean I carry any animosity towards Muslims. For example, I believe smoking is bad, but that doesn't mean I believe all smokers are bad people.

In addition, I disagree with people who wish to 'end' Islam or any other religion. Religionists make up roughly 6.5 of the 7.3 billion people in the world (of which Islam alone constitutes 1.7 billion followers), so to suggest we get rid of religion is unrealistic and unproductive.[1] The challenge humankind has always faced is to increase the tolerance and education of the religious and non-religious, thereby reducing the fear and discrimination people around the world face. This is more a practical way forward than 'ridding the world of religion'. People must be allowed their freedom of thought. This means people ought to be free to believe in whatever God or gods they wish to believe or not believe in. As long as those people are kind to themselves and others, people must be allowed to enjoy their liberties, their basic human rights. There are multicultural communities around the world living cooperatively with each other and they do this through diversity, not in spite of it.

It's possible to achieve this by respecting each other *and* actively challenging commonly held assumptions about the world we live in. Because regardless of whether people continue to believe in God or not, my ultimate hope above all is this: for people to make more conscious and informed decisions in their lives by reasoning from first principles.

Reasoning from first principles means looking at the fundamental facts of why we believe what we believe and why we do what we do.

1. Johnson, Todd M., Gina A. Zurlo, Albert W. Hickman, and Peter F. Crossing. Christianity 2015: Religious Diversity and Personal Contact. Report. Vol. 39. Series 1. South Hamilton: International Bulletin of Missionary Research, 2015. http://www.gordonconwell.edu/ockenga/research/documents/2IBMR2015.pdf.

Instead, what we often do in life (and especially with religion) is reason by analogy, meaning we assume what is true now must be true in the future. *Atheism for Muslims* is structured and reasoned from first principles rather than by analogy, meaning it takes no assumptions as truths. This means the fundamental concepts which religion and Islam are based on are analyzed and reconsidered independently on merit. Only once we've boiled things down to their fundamental facts, can we reason up from there.

I believe if we approach society from first principles we will develop a better perspective on understanding life and solving problems, rather than defaulting to seeing the present and future through the eyes of the past.

To our Mothers and Fathers

"I do not feel obliged to believe that the same God who has endowed us with senses, reason and intellect has intended us to forgo their use" – Galileo Galilei

To my mother and father,

I am eternally grateful for everything you've done for me. I'm thankful I was raised Muslim by two Muslim parents and that Islam is a part of my life, it helped me become the man I am today. It's not my intention to hurt you, although I know I will through this book in ways I can't even begin to imagine. But I can no longer pretend to follow something I don't believe in. I would be going through my entire life living a lie both to myself, and to you. Islam, like all religions, exists to provide guidance, but I don't believe Islam is guiding me in the right direction anymore.

Please know that I tried, I truly did, to believe in God and Islam. In this book, I'll do my best to explain how I got to this point in my life. I've written this book primarily for you both as I would never have been able to fully express myself, all my thoughts and rationales, just by speaking with you. Though, I will try to do that as well. My hope is that this book will provide both of you with an insight as to what's going on in my head, an insight into why I believe what I believe now. I explored Islam to the best of my ability, and it's here where I'll present it all in the clearest, most objective manner I could. I hope this experiment works.

I'm agnostic when it comes to the belief of whether or not there is a higher power out there, meaning I don't know if there is a being or presence guiding us and the universe. We're still limited in our abilities and knowledge of the universe, maybe we'll never know.

But, I'm an atheist when it comes to God, Allah. I don't believe He exists. If there is a higher power in the universe, I believe it's highly unlikely it's in the form of the Abrahamic God of Muslims, Christians and Jews. I can't prove He doesn't exist, but due to the information I'll share in this book, I believe there is such a low probability God exists that I choose to live my life as though He does not. This book will give you all the reasons as to why I believe this, and it will explain to you how I came to this point in my life.

I don't believe I have all the answers. I'm actually more aware than ever of how little I know about the world we live in. I know I can't be right all the time, no one can. But I believe I can at least try to be less wrong whenever possible.

Please know that although it might not look like it, I'm trying to help. I want to help you to understand me. If there is a God, then I'm sure He had a reason for making me the way I am and setting me on this path.

However, what I believe to be the truth has changed. I won't be practicing Islam anymore, but I also won't be disregarding the cultural traditions our family holds dear. This is my heritage, and I'm proud of it. It makes me who I am and I would never want to give that up.

What I'm trying to do with this book is to help Muslims make more informed decisions in their lives, to present them with information they may have never known otherwise. I also want to help other ex-Muslims (I can just imagine how repulsed you'll be by reading that word) by sharing my journey with them. I've read stories about ex-Muslims who get ostracized, fall into depression and become suicidal, all because of how their families have reacted to their decision.

This book is for all my sisters and brothers who couldn't put into words why they feel the way they feel, and why they believe what they believe. This book is for the ex-Muslims who need a way to tell their loved ones they're not a bad person for the thoughts they've had. They're still the same person, they just view the world in a different way.

It's not a decision I or any other ex-Muslim has taken lightly. We know the pain and ruptures it will cause in our families if we chose to tell them, or if they find out. Believe me when I say we've tried to find reasons to believe again, we've bargained with God Himself to show us He is real. We know life would be easier for us and for you if we believed He was. But it's impossible. We're not doing this to hurt you, we just can't believe what we don't believe. We know our families wanted something different for us; we can only hope they understand the journey we're on. We can only hope you're patient and kind with us, as you have been since we were babies, because we need you now just as we needed you then. Please don't abandon us.

Please understand Atheism for Muslims was not written to divert people away from Islam. I truly believe everyone is entitled to practice any religion they wish, as long as they're kind to themselves and others.

Though I now believe religion restricts humankind's progress in many ways, I also respect that it can provide many great qualities to someone's life. I just believe the ultimate choice ought to be with the woman or man.

This book uncovers the discoveries I made on my exploration for knowledge. I hope it helps those who are in need and are lost, just as I was. May they find dignity, wisdom and peace in their lives, regardless of what they choose to believe.

Mama and Baba, I'm sorry. I love you both with all my heart. I hope you will find the strength and love to forgive me for what I've done.

Adam Wadi

20th January 2017

Before we begin

1. WARNING – Only read this book if you're ready. If you're Muslim, I'm going to question everything you and your family believe about Islam, and it's better if you're ready for it. You may wish you'd rather not known the issues I raise, and have a great deal of anger towards me for writing such a book as you were happier in your life and relationships without it. This advice applies to any religious people. Although I'll be focusing on Islam, the first part '*Why Religion Works*' and the last part '*Life After Religion*' is applicable to anyone who believes in God or gods. This may sound like an excessive caution but it is not, I want to give a fair warning in advance. If you're not ready to live out the potential consequences from reading this book, please leave it until you are ready.

2. For my Muslim sisters and brothers, this will be a challenging book to read and it may take you a long time to complete. Be patient with yourself as there's a lot of content which will be difficult to process and digest. You may even go through the so called 'Five Stages of Grief' if you start to question your faith: denial, anger, bargaining, depression and (hopefully) acceptance.[1] I say this because losing a religion can be like losing a loved one, someone who has been there with you your entire life. Religion defines who we are as a person and with Islam, it's our entire identity. So to go through this rebirth is difficult. I've been through this process and it took me over a year to get to 'acceptance'. But everyone will experience it differently, everyone has their own journey to go through. I'm not implying every Muslim who reads this book will leave Islam, the opposite could happen for some people: their faith may be reaffirmed. But, there will be Muslims who'll find themselves questioning everything they knew. To those people I say please be patient and kind to yourself, it doesn't make you a bad person to have reasonable thoughts of doubt about Islam or God. Just because you are struggling, doesn't mean you are failing.

I would also say that as you're reading, you may come up with justifications for the arguments I've made. Please note that although the 50 chapters can be read independently in any order, it is the entire book which contains all the arguments, not just a few chapters or parts. So, to receive the complete

---

1. Kübler-Ross, Elisabeth, and David Kessler. On Grief and Grieving: Finding the Meaning of Grief through the Five Stages of Loss. London: Simon & Schuster, 2005.

reasoning of what *Atheism for Muslims* has to offer, please take the time to read the entire book.

3. I will refer to God as God throughout instead of what Muslims call God, Allah. First, this is to help all readers: Christians, Jews, atheists or otherwise. I want everyone to identify with the text in this book so I don't want people to feel disengaged by reading Allah as opposed to God. Second, I'm concerned if I use Allah it will unnerve Muslims. I don't want Muslims to read criticisms of Allah and then mentally block them out. Speaking from experience, this could happen due to the repulsion I felt every time I read blasphemy against Allah, such is the emotional and mental attachment to the word Allah by Muslims the world over. I believe this can be avoided by using the word God throughout this book instead which will help Muslim readers engage on a deeper level than had I used Allah.

4. The Quran is the only text which is indisputable to Muslims around the world. This is why I will base all my arguments on it. I will rely on the Quran as a source and refer to God as its author not because I believe it to be true, but because all Muslims must and do believe it to be true.

5. Translating the Arabic in the Quran is problematic, and most Muslims believe any translation is only an approximate interpretation. As a result, Islamic scholars judge each translation or interpretation of the Quran differently among themselves. There is no consensus on one translation or interpretation over another since Muslims agree the Quran is unequal in any other language. However, there are 1.7 billion Muslims around the world and the majority of them can't speak Arabic, never mind the Classical Arabic in the Quran which even native Arabic speakers often struggle to understand. This means most Muslims in the world rely on translations of the Quran. However there is no consensus among Muslim scholars on which English translation is best. So if you're unhappy with my choice, I encourage you to use your preferred translation, or the original text, alongside this book. A useful website to use is www.al-quran.info. It provides many language translations side by side so you can follow them while reading this book. To remain consistent, I will only use one translation throughout, '*The Koran Interpreted*', the 1955 translation by Arthur Arberry.[2]

Muslims reading this book may be unhappy with my choice of Arberry's

English translation, they may even dismiss this entire book as a result. But it's important to note that even interpretations of the Quran in its original form by reputable Muslim Islamic scholars causes disagreement among Muslims. So even if I'd used the original text of the Quran, there would still be dissatisfaction among Muslims due to its various interpretations. We can only do the best we possibly can, such is the difficulty in understanding the Quran. But there is valid reason as to why I have chosen Arberry's translation.

Arthur Arberry (1905-1969) was a British scholar of Persian, Arabic and Islam. He spent several years in the Middle East perfecting his Arabic and Persian language skills, serving as a professor of Classics at Cairo University. He also served as a professor of Persian at the University of London and professor of Arabic at Cambridge University, his alma mater. Arberry's translation was reprinted several times and it is the Quran of choice for many academics due to its clear and coherent English and the lack of prejudice in his interpretation. Arberry also made a special attempt to reproduce the rhythms and cadence of the Quran in his interpretation. Arberry's translation is regarded as an authoritative interpretation and with its title, *The Koran Interpreted*, we see his recognition that it is only an interpretation of the Quran. Arberry was aware any translation of the Quran has its limitations and I too have taken this into account while writing this book.

There are tens of English translations available and I considered many of the other most popular ones before dismissing them for various reasons. For example, Pickthall was dismissed due to its archaic prose. It, along with Muhammad Ali, were also both dismissed due to their bias against miracles like Prophet Muhammad's Night Journey. Both Pickthall and Muhammad Ali regarded these miracles as visions but most Muslim theologians argue these events in Prophet Muhammad's life should be taken literally.

Yusuf Ali's translation was originally the translation of choice by the Saudi religious establishment but it is now deemed to have dated language. The footnotes Yusuf Ali included are also considered to be anti-Semitic, so for these reasons I have dismissed it.

Hilali-Khan is the most widely distributed Quran in the English speaking world and it also carries the seal of approval from the University of Medina in Saudi Arabia. It replaced Yusuf Ali as the English translation of choice by the Saudi religious establishment, but there are concerns it reads more like a supremacist Muslim text. This is due to its anti-Semitic and anti-Christian connotations, as well as its militant interpretations. So I could use this Quran

2. Arberry, Arthur J. The Koran Interpreted. Oxford: Oxford University Press, 2008.

as it is the most widely distributed English translation and the Saudi religious establishment endorses it, it would make my arguments even stronger. But I selected a different translation because many Islamic scholars judge it to be steeped in Saudi Wahhabi theology. As a result, it has been criticized as a misrepresentation of Islam and the Quran.[3]

6. There is no Hadith cited in this book; only verses from the Quran are used to base all the arguments upon. Hadith are accounts which describe the words, actions and habits of the Prophet Muhammad. There are Hadith collections considered authoritative and authentic by most Muslims, but not all, particularly between Sunni and Shia. So although the Quran advises Muslims to follow the example of Prophet Muhammad, citing any Hadith would still provide some Muslims with a reason to refute any statements I make about these Hadith. This book will only refer to Hadith and the works of Islamic scholars (Tafsir) for historical context.

7. I will use CE (Common Era/Current Era) as an alternative to AD. AD signifies Anno Domini which is Latin for 'in the year of our Lord'. In addition, I will use BCE (Before Common Era/Current Era) as an alternative to BC. BC signifies 'Before Christ'. This is to remove the religious references implied when I cite historical dates.

8. *Atheism for Muslims* doesn't contain every argument possible. It also contains arguments Muslims or other religious adherents will dismiss as inaccurate. I can confidently say this in advance because when it comes to religion, it's impossible to achieve a consensus on anything. Of the arguments I do provide, I ask apologists to refrain from falling back on platitudes including "God knows best", "God works in mysterious ways", or "It's our fault for misunderstanding what God means". These clichés don't allow an opportunity for constructive discussion. On the contrary, they diminish our intellectual capacity for reasoning and analysis.

9. I recognize there are also positive aspects to Islam and religion in general, I

---

3. Mohammed, Khaleel. "Assessing English Translations of the Qur'an." Middle East Quarterly 12, no. 2 (Spring 2005): 58-71. http://www.meforum.org/717/assessing-english-translations-of-the-quran.

cover many of them in the chapter '*Why Religion Works*'. But I know there are many more I won't have covered. Before claims of bias are put forward, please note I wrote this book to provide a breadth of arguments on why atheists or agnostics may believe what they do about Islam and religion. There are other books which cover the benefits of Islam and religion and I recommend seeking out those books if you wish to review more of the other side of the argument.

10. I personally don't believe ex-Muslims need to make an all or nothing decision in their lives regarding their religion, life is rarely as black and white as that.

For example, I will still continue to fast during Ramadan. I do it because it makes me more grateful for the things I have in my life and I enjoy fasting with my family, rather than because a higher power tells me I must.

I still don't eat pork and never have done. I was raised avoiding it so the thought of eating it is unappealing to me. This doesn't affect my day to day life so I have no interest in starting to eat pork, ham, bacon or any other form of pig meat.

I don't gamble in any form and don't see any benefit in doing so as the house always wins.

I'll still say Inshallah (God willing), Alhamdulillah (Praise be to God) and other Arabic expressions with my family because it's a part of everyday Arabic language and I say it out of habit.

I sometimes drink alcohol to try the flavor of a drink, but since I've lived my life without alcohol, I'm disinterested in making it a part of my life. In fact, I'm thankful to Islam that I don't need nor desire alcohol, I've seen what it can do to the best of people.

I've also become more comfortable with my sexuality, I treat my body with respect and do the same to women's bodies as well. I believe sex is a natural part of life to be enjoyed in a healthy and consensual manner, so I'm unashamed to share my body with other women.

Having said all this, I must say those of us coming from Muslim backgrounds must be cautious. It'll be incredibly difficult for some of our closest friends and family to accept our new position on life, if we choose to tell them. We can't expect everyone to understand, and we may experience aggression, hostility or even threats upon our lives. It's up to us individually to decide how much we can share and to whom. I don't believe anyone can survive on their own, and it's unhealthy for us to isolate ourselves from people all our lives. So, we must do the best we can to maintain strong and respectful relationship with those we care about the most. For more information and support please see chapter 'Resources for ex-Muslims'.

These are my personal beliefs and decisions, and I take full responsibility for them. I shall continue living my life in the best way I believe possible. I will also continue to be a 'cultural Muslim/atheist Muslim'. This means taking part in Islamic celebrations and observing the culture and traditions with my family out of respect, or because I want to. I am no longer a practicing Muslim, but there are many customs I wish to keep. Since Muslim identity encompasses ethnic, cultural and religious components, the term atheist Muslim does not inherently entail a contradiction.

It's my choice how I choose to live with religion, and I believe it's your choice too.

PART I

Why Religion Works

"the service and worship of God or the supernatural" – Merriam-Webster definition of 'religion'[1]

In one form or another religion has been with humanity every step of our journey, and there's a reason why religion has become ubiquitous throughout humankind's history. It's important to understand why and how this happened since religion has shaped our world so comprehensively. It has influenced the behavior, ethics, social structures and laws of civilizations across the world for thousands of years.

Many of us have come to associate religion with our own identity. It defines who we are and how live our lives; it's our compass. Humans are naturally cautious and emotional animals, and as a result, we've developed a dependency on religion to reassure us. We feel as though we'd be insignificant or lost in the world without it. So much so that we happily believe the stories in our holy books, giving them the benefit of the doubt, though we know they couldn't have happened within the laws of our universe.

Perhaps more than ever we've begun to mistake the comfort and security religion gives us for happiness, rather than what it actually is, an operating system installed in us that we've been programmed to run. We believe we've chosen this operating system (religion), or that it's the best one available, but actually, circumstances mean most of us weren't given the choice of what was installed (indoctrinated) in us. But we've accepted it, and the idea of updating, rebooting or uninstalling it isn't something many of us consider or want to do.

History has shown time and again we're willing to sacrifice our intellectual integrity to protect our cherished beliefs (the age of the universe, theory of evolution, Noah and the flood) and this is because religious beliefs fulfill the psychological reassurances of the most basic human needs. This is one of the

---

1. Merriam-Webster. Accessed February 28, 2017. https://www.merriam-webster.com/dictionary/religion.

reasons why religions are so widespread throughout human history and the modern world, not because there's unanimous proof God or gods exists, but because our beliefs tap into our emotional desires. They sustain us, they give us something we can't get from anywhere else. Since we're also under the impression our religion has free will attached to it, then it appears as though the choice we've made is our own, and it's one we've made out of reason and logic.

But if we take a step back, we can play connect the dots with what initially looked like independent reasoning. If we approach our decisions based on first principles, we can reflect on why we believe what we believe. Do we consciously believe it, or was it influenced by our parents, our friends, or our society? Are we fully appreciating the influence our environment plays on our decision making, or are we taking the path of least resistance and disguising it as practicality?

If we zoom out even further and look at the entire history of human existence, we can see patterns. We can see throughout humanity every culture, in every location, in every point in time has developed some form of supernatural belief. This human behavior is so universal scientists argue belief in the supernatural may be an evolutionary adaptation by humans.[2] An evolutionary adaptation is something so helpful to an animal or plant, it causes its genes or species to thrive in comparison to others.

The evolutionary advantage of having supernatural beliefs in God is what we'll explore in this part. We'll look at why religion has thrived and the main benefits it provides people. We'll also review the most popular arguments for God's existence and provide a contrarian perspective.

2. Henig, Robin Marantz. "Darwin's God." The New York Times, March 4, 2007. Accessed October 31, 2016. http://www.nytimes.com/2007/03/04/magazine/04evolution.t.html.

1

People develop personal relationships with God

"Men create Gods after their own image" – Aristotle

Everyone has their own unique relationship with their God or gods, and no one else can ever understand the intricacies of this relationship. Our personal perceptions of God are built on a foundation of years of social and cultural influences. Even people who aren't religious have their own perspective on God, no matter how non-existent He may be to them. Everyone identifies with Him, Her or Them in their own unique way.

If you believe in God then your special relationship with Him proves His existence to you. But, it does nothing to prove His existence to anyone else. Their own relationship with God will determine how they feel about Him. This is because God is a subjective experience.

Someone's hairs on the back of their neck may stand from reading the Tanakh, Bible or Quran. Someone else may achieve a sense of inner peace from their daily practice of prayer. Another may hear voices or see visions which proves His existence to them. There are also ceremonies with music, incense, costumes and chanting, transporting people to another world (or another body) that proves God is real to them.

Any one of these experiences or others could prove God's existence to you. But, none of these encounters actually proves the existence of God. It only proves people can have a subjective experience of God. It proves the combination of the environment, the mindset, and chemical reactions in the brain can take people to another place they couldn't reach without religion.[1]

So it's important the religious understand that not everyone can believe in God just because they have a personal relationship, or had special experience

---

1. Swaab, D.F. "This Is Your Brain on Religion: Uncovering the Science of Belief." Salon, January 4, 2014. Accessed January 14, 2017. https://www.salon.com/2014/01/04/this_is_your_brain_on_religion_uncovering_the_science_of_belief/.

with Him; no matter how exceptional it may have been, or how much you believe God has helped you and others.

Religion works because everyone can have their own special relationship with God, a personal God: a deity who can be related to as a person rather than an impersonal authority. It opens up a unique connection between us and Him. But everyone has their own take on religion, so everyone has their own take on God. This means the reason you don't believe in other religions and other gods, is the same reason other people don't believe in your religion and your God. Many believers may not realize this, but if they did they may get a better understanding of why the extent of their belief in God doesn't account to much for other people, it only means something to them. So, if it only means something to them then they have to respect how other people feel about God's non-existence, just as they would want other people to respect how they feel about God's existence.

2

Religion fulfils basic human desires

"Religion. It's given people hope in a world torn apart by religion" – *Jon Stewart*

Religion gives its followers something they can't get from anywhere else, which is why it's a necessity for most people in the world. The most popular religions in existence today are the ones which have endured the test of time, fulfilling basic human desires effectively. They are the religions which have been able to integrate themselves fully into our lives and become a part of our identity. Religion creates this sense of belonging and purpose in people with the goal to achieving one outcome: submission.

Religions obtain their obedience and devotion from people using several methods, methods which are adopted by other entities in a similar fashion. For example, tribes like sports teams, businesses, countries or cults also wish to foster loyalty. These groups have the same goals as religion: to grow in strength through the support of their followers. We can see similarities when we compare religion with these other tribes and notice the human desires they both satisfy.

- Religions and sports teams both have a place of regular communal worship, for example, mosques and stadiums. People enjoy the feeling of being among a community of like-minded individuals striving towards a common cause because it helps them feel like they're part of a dependable tribe, and part of something bigger than themselves.
- Religions and countries both encourage compulsory ritual behavior, for example, the repetition of reciting prayers or national anthems. This helps develop a psychological attachment to the cause and regularly remind people where their loyalties lie.
- Businesses regularly take their employees on company retreats to unite everyone under one banner. These are similar to religious pilgrimages. Both unite followers of different colors, races and creeds

(and departments) from across the world at the same time every year. It allows everyone to come together and reaffirm why they do the things they do in their tribe.

- Fasting is a popular form of fostering mind control and manipulation, that's why it's a common practice in cults, as well as religions. Fasting creates docility and obedience among followers, promotes solidarity, and bonds followers since they're enduring the struggle together for a greater cause, whether it's Yom Kippur, Lent, or Ramadan.

These are some examples of how religion and other tribes promote loyalty among their followers. But to provide a more complete picture, let's approach this idea from a scientific perspective. Psychologist Steven Reiss PhD believes he has identified the 16 basic human needs people have, and, he believes religion is able to address them all:

1. **Acceptance** – the need to be appreciated
2. **Curiosity** – the need to gain knowledge
3. **Eating** – the need for food
4. **Family** – the need to take care of one's offspring
5. **Honor** – the need to be faithful to the customary values of an individual's ethnic group, family or clan
6. **Idealism** – the need for social justice
7. **Independence** – the need to be distinct and self-reliant
8. **Order** – the need for prepared, established, and conventional environments
9. **Physical activity** – the need for work out of the body
10. **Power** – the need for control of will
11. **Romance** – the need for mating or sex
12. **Saving** – the need to accumulate something
13. **Social contact** – the need for relationships with others
14. **Social status** – the need for social significance
15. **Tranquility** – the need to be secure and protected
16. **Vengeance** – the need to strike back against another person[1]

Reiss theorizes people are drawn to religion because it's able to satisfy all these 16 basic human desires. Religion is also able to cater to all types of people by

1. Reiss, Steven. The 16 Strivings for God: The New Psychology of Religious Experiences. Macon, GA: Mercer University Press, 2015.

providing these 16 psychological needs in a strong or weak form depending on what they need fulfilled.

For example, someone may have a strong basic desire for 'vengeance' so they may be attracted to the verses in holy books which speak of revenge. While another person may have a weak basic desire for 'vengeance' so they're only attracted to verses which speak of forgiveness and peace in the same holy book.

Or, someone may have a strong basic desire for 'social contact' so the opportunity to be involved with people in their community or place of worship is attractive to them. While another person may have a weak basic desire for 'social contact' so they're only attracted to the parts of religion they can practice in solitary contemplation at home, only visiting their house of worship once a week if they wish to.

Curiously, Reiss also observed that a strong basic desire for 'independence' pushes people away from religion and towards self-reliance. People who don't want to rely on anything (like God) are more likely to be atheists.

Tribes like sports teams, businesses, countries, cults and religions add value to people's lives; creating communities, facilitating friendships, and providing a purpose to work towards. However when it comes to religion, it's still not proof of an existence of God or gods. Religions are commendable when they impact their communities in a positive way and deliver great work to those in need. But these kinds of commendable acts are also carried out by secular communities and groups. Even sports teams and for-profit businesses provide financial and social support through their charities.

There's no proof here of a supernatural deity but there is proof that we don't need religion like we used to. We're now able to unite people and behave morally and charitably without religion and without God. What we've proven in the 20th and 21st century in particular is that when people are united behind a common goal, great things can be achieved. We only have to look at secular organizations like UNICEF or Médecins Sans Frontières for examples of this. There's no evidence to show God or gods have directly helped people, whereas there's a lot of evidence to show people have directly helped themselves and others. It's the people who take responsibility to make the world a better place that are the ones to do so. People may need the support, strength and belief that they can do it, something they feel they get from their religion, but it is within their capabilities the whole time. God or gods are like a placebo effect, albeit a powerful one.

The basic human desires religion satisfies are the result of its design and arrangement: religions are forged in a manner which fulfills our physical, emotional, mental and spiritual needs. But none of these are the exclusive domain of any religion, or religion in general. Basic human desires can be met, and even surpassed, through various secular methods (see part 'Life After Religion').

Religions have grown, evolved and adapted with us over thousands of years to be able to fulfill our needs better than ever before. There's a reason the religions we have now in the modern world are still in existence today: they're the ones which still fulfill our needs most effectively.

The question is whether people want to have their psychological needs fulfilled elsewhere. It's more effort to dispose of our religion and start from scratch; to go through the 16 basic human needs Reiss identified and tick them off as if it were a checklist. It doesn't work like that, but at least we can appreciate the appeals behind theology by looking at the cognitive science of religion.

Approaching religion using disciplines like anthropology, linguistics, neuroscience, philosophy and psychology helps us understand why and how religion has compelled billions of people today to believe in the supernatural. In fact, we should thank religion as it has helped us to understand ourselves better. We now know what needs religion fulfills, and we also know it's possible to have them fulfilled elsewhere without the associated mythologies and superstitions. It isn't religion's fault, it's just that humanity is starting to outgrow it. It's not you religion, it's us.

3

Everyone else believes in God

"Anytime I see a person fleeing from reason and into religion, I think to myself, there goes a person who simply cannot stand being so goddamned lonely anymore" – Kurt Vonnegut Jr.

Many people we know, trust and love may believe in God, including the family who raised us our whole lives, the friends who understand us better than everyone else, and even the role models and celebrities we admire and try to emulate. We've been conditioned to listen to these influential people and authority figures our entire lives. We do what our parents tell us, we learn what our professors teach us, we complete what our bosses give us, we obey what our government orders us, and we consume what our media feeds us.

This conditioning has been ingrained into our psyche since we were children. This means as adults, it's difficult to change our brain's pattern to question authority figures. We've always automatically assumed these authority figures know what's best for us or have our best interests in mind. Many times they do. But total reliance upon them can lead to intellectual laziness on our part.

As a society, we counter the threat of intellectual laziness by not believing everything we're told. We actively question information, attempt to understand it, and wait for things to be proven. Yet this is often not true when it comes to our religious beliefs. Our imams, priests, rabbis and parents make unbelievable claims about an all powerful being who watches over us, that created everything, and will put us all somewhere after we die. But even though many of these kinds of claims are fantastical, we often don't question them as much as would be reasonable to.

Now, in the 21st century, our ability to distinguish between what's true and what's false has never been more important. Our species has the capacity to destroy both our environment and itself, so we need to be able to solve the challenges we're facing, and not accept everything we're told at face value.

If we were to lose the skill of critical thinking in our personal lives (by not challenging religion), this may carry over to our social lives (by not challenging authority figures like politicians), leading to blind spots which reshape the way we view and interact with the world and everyone in it. But, if we're more conscious about scrutinizing the information we're presented with, it can help us to vet the 'truths' we're told to believe.

It's important to note that people we trust, like our parents, may not have been exposed to any kinds of doubts or difficult questions about their religion due to the environment they were raised in. Therefore they too may have blind spots about their faith, or blind spots about the authority figures they listened to in their lives like their teachers or parents (our grandparents). This goes to show belief in God in no way makes anyone less intelligent; external forces influence us all more than we realize. We all have blind spots, and therefore we must try to purposefully seek them out as much as we can in our lives.

This is challenging because it's not in our DNA to challenge authority figures; humankind didn't evolve with independent thinking as part of our self-preservation. The human brain didn't evolve to make us happy or fulfilled, it evolved to make us survive. We survived by fitting in with our tribe, staying in favor with leaders, and learning from elders. Then, the next generation were taught the same thing for their own self-preservation, slightly adapted to adjust for any changes. This is how we've come to live in societies where we all follow the same blueprint, because this is how we've always survived. This cycle then repeats itself generation after generation with people constantly reinforcing each other's religious beliefs in a self-perpetuating loop. With each round of mutual confirmation, the web of meaning tightens further, until we have no choice but to believe what everyone else believes.

We see this pattern appearing in our politics. For example, people often identify themselves as left wing or right wing, and then they adopt the beliefs of the left wing or right wing parties as a package. Even though it's a collection of different ideas: there's no correlation between a person's views on abortion and their views on taxation policy; they don't have any resemblance to each other as they're completely distinct issues. But they come in a package, and so people buy into that package of views and ideals instead of looking into each one on its own merit. This pattern occurs because it's easier to buy into a political party or religion, and identify and belong to a tribe of 'like-minded' people, than to be isolated and fighting for our views and our survival on our own.

To be on our own means questioning the core principles we've believed in our whole lives, which is frightening. It's scary because it could mean we're not only mistaken, but our friends and family may all be mistaken too. The world becomes a scarier place because of this new uncertainty. However, this doesn't have to be the collapse of our world as we know it, it can be the rebuild of the world as we see it.

We live in a unique stage of humanity's existence compared to the last 200,000 years of our Homo sapiens ancestors. For most of the world's population survival is much easier, we live in privileged societies in comparison to what most of humankind has previously had to endure. For most of us our primary purpose of survival is already taken care of, and then some. This means following the tribe and its beliefs for our self-preservation is not the necessity it used to be. It served us well when self-preservation and the protection of our families depended on extreme vigilance to all potential dangers (including God), but now we can safely take more risks in our professional and personal lives, and it won't always mean death or, just as bad for humans, social exclusion. We no longer need to believe what everyone else believes, just because they believe it. This isn't just because it's safer now to believe something different, but because they're just as likely to be wrong as any of us.

4

Religion provides social order

"When you grow up, you tend to get told the world is the way it is and your life is just to live your life inside the world. Try not to bash into the walls too much. Try to have a nice family life, have fun, save a little money. That's a very limited life. Life can be much broader once you discover one simple fact. And that is: Everything around you that you call life was made up by people that were no smarter than you. And you can change it, you can influence it, you can build your own things that other people can use. Once you learn that, you'll never be the same again" – Steve Jobs

We have much to thank religion for, it created order and structure where there was none before. It helped us alter our behavior so we could cooperate in larger groups, rather than focusing on the individual. For social animals like us, there are more benefits to being in an altruistic group than pursuing individualism. Being in a cooperative group increases everyone's chances of survival. This is true for countless animal species, whether they are tiny insects such as ants and bees, or large mammals such as elephants and whales.[1]

But religion is a secret weapon no other animal but humans possess. Religion has the ability to bring masses of unconnected and diverse people from across the world together under one banner. They may not look the same, live the same, or even speak the same language, but these people of faith can cooperate with each other. They can even meet each other peacefully every week in the same building on a Friday, Saturday or Sunday, all because they follow the same religion.

The stability religion gave human civilizations meant faith grew to be a pragmatic necessity to keep social order. Humans tens of thousands of years ago lived in much smaller groups than they have for the previous few thousand

---

1. Shermer, Michael. "Why Are We Moral: The Evolutionary Origins of Morality." In The Science of Good and Evil: Why People Cheat, Share, Gossip, and Follow the Golden Rule. New York: Times Books, 2004.

years. These groups started to grow larger with the first agricultural revolution (cultivating wheat) around 11,000 years ago. Human cultures transitioned from a nomadic lifestyle of hunting and gathering, to one of agriculture and settlement. But humans needed something to allow us to live in these larger groups without constantly fighting among each other, and a common religious belief may have been that key ingredient.[2]

Religions had authority because they instilled the belief that they're not man-made rules from the governing elite, but rather their rules were divinely inspired by a supernatural power beyond our capabilities of understanding. So who were we mere mortals to question the immortals, the gods?

There was also the belief that these supernatural powers were always watching us. So religion became an effective strategy to curb negative behavior in people. This tactic is still used today by parents. For example, some parents tell their children Santa Claus (God) is watching them all the time from the North Pole (Heaven) and he'll reward them with gifts (Paradise) on Christmas Day (Judgement Day), but only if they follow the rules all year (a lifetime) and if they're bad, they'll be punished with coal in their Christmas stocking (Hell). Though perhaps these children should be given more credit, every year their hypothesis of 'following the rules = reward' is proven. Unlike their parents hypothesis, 'follow the rules for a lifetime = unproven reward'.

The concept of a supernatural being like Santa Claus is humorous to us now, just like the concept of the tooth fairy or any of the Greek gods. So often the supernatural beliefs of one person, or one era, becomes the entertainment for another person, and another era. But a previous civilization's belief in the gods of Mount Olympus is no different to a belief in the God of modern day civilizations.

When groups of people become so certain of their beliefs it can result in groupthink: a psychological phenomenon where the desire for obedience in a group of people results in dysfunctional or irrational decision-making. This creates a groupthink mentality, and people reach decisions without considering other views. This is done by people suppressing dissenting viewpoints or by isolating themselves from external influences. All of this leads to a loss of independent thinking within the group and an 'illusion of invulnerability': the inflated certainty that right decisions have been made.[3]

So with regards to faith, religious groupthink gives us the impression we know with confidence we'll be rewarded if we perform certain acts, acts

2. Harari, Yuval Noah. Sapiens: A Brief History of Humankind. Random House UK, 2014.

3. Janis, Irving Lester. Groupthink: Psychological Studies of Policy Decisions and Fiascoes. Boston: Wadsworth, 2013.

which other people in our tribe or community are also performing. That social validation gives us the impression of certainty in our actions, however ill-guided it may be (Zeus granting Elysium, Santa delivering presents, a fairy giving money for teeth regardless of the exchange rate). In addition, since religions don't rely on data-based facts, followers can believe whatever they wish to with conviction. It doesn't matter what the beliefs and acts performed are, it's only important that everyone believes and does the same thing to maintain social order. This explains some of the implausible beliefs people can hold, and the unusual actions religious people often perform.

Having religious social structures also removes countless decisions from one's life. In today's world, we have more choices and opportunities than humanity has ever had before and it can lead to decision fatigue: the idea that people tend to make worse decisions after a long session of decision-making. It's for this reason impulse products like chocolates are placed close to the cash registers at supermarkets: we have less self-control at the end of a long time spent shopping. Being freed from responsibility and constant decision-making is appealing to us, and religion frees us from this burden.

When we're given something to refer to (permanently fixed instructions or rules) it's much easier to follow them than regularly make up our own, particularly if everyone else around us is following the same ones as well. The alternative is to risk social exclusion and constantly ask ourselves difficult questions about life; what we ought to be doing, what it all means, and if there's any point to it. Religion works so well because it helps us understand and make meaning of things on an individual and group level; a belief system providing a framework and reference point for putting everything into context.

If a religious framework makes sense at the time of origin and it's viable, it becomes accepted by more people. Once it has this social validation, it carries even more value and meaning so the number of followers grows. It begins to go viral. As the religion grows in size, if everyone is following it then everyone is using its reference point to play by the same set of rules, rewards and punishments. Thus the religion keeps everyone in line, the population's chances of survival increases, and human beings give their lives purpose and meaning.

Life becomes much more straightforward and effortless to us when we have a path laid out in front of us to take. There's no need to keep deciding what's moral and what's immoral because a reference book has told us what to believe. There's also no need to have an existential crisis as we're told what life is all about.

Being told when to go to a house of worship, and when and how to pray actually empowers people by providing familiarity and removing decision-making from their lives. It's beneficial because although a free-form life appears idyllic, it can often be paralyzing due to the continual paradox of choice (what should I do now?) and decision fatigue (what should I and can I eat?). In contrast, religion gives people structure and scaffolding to build their days around, allowing them to plan and execute their lives. It may appear paradoxical, but constraints can give people a greater sense of agency and feeling of freedom. It's this combination of stability and routine which is naturally alluring to the human psyche and, so far, religion has a monopoly on this product and is marketing it better than anyone else. Therefore the only decision that needs to be made for most people is which religion appeals to them the most.

The idea of delegating decisions to an all-seeing deity served another purpose in early human societies. When there were no courts of law, governments or police, there was no central authority to carry out punishments, restore law and order, and maintain justice. So in early human communities, group members had to make the decisions to convict and punish offenders. This caused disruptive consequences because the offender would have likely disagreed. The offender's allies and family also wouldn't have liked the punishment so they could develop a grudge. All this can lead to dangerous divides within a community. But if there is a god to be obeyed then the person convicting the offender is merely enforcing the divine law, so no rebuttals to the conviction or punishment would be valid.

In addition, as all-powerful deities are also all-seeing, selfish impulses harmful to the group are curbed because there's no escaping God's watchful eyes. This means people believed not only could their community punish them, but a supernatural being could also punish them in this life, or the next.

These are powerful deterrents which mustn't be underestimated, consequences like these didn't exist before religion. People generally respond to the right incentives, not the right intentions. It's this belief in justice (people getting their deserved fate after death) which can be one of religion's most appealing characteristics. The belief that God helps keep people accountable, providing a sense of balance, harmony or karma in the universe.

Our early-age ancestors once spread across the world seeking better lives, much in the same way we still do today. However there's a theory that the ones with religious belief systems survived because they were able to cooperate better together.[4] Over time these small bands of humans (cooperating better

---

4. Rossano, Matt J. Supernaturalizing Social Life: Religion and the Evolution of Human Cooperation. Report. Accessed November 2, 2016. http://www2.southeastern.edu/Academics/Faculty/mrossano/recentpubs/Supernaturalizing.pdf.

because of their shared religious beliefs) grew in size and power. They became chiefdoms, civilizations and states, and they had chiefs, kings and prophets playing the roles of both political and spiritual leaders, governing with their religion. It was these religions which helped the leaders maintain social and economic stability within their populations, and justify their political power through divine authority.[5]

These political and spiritual leaders played an important role throughout human history, and a lot of it has been negative since religious beliefs have caused abuse, discrimination and wars for thousands of years. But using religion has also helped the world advance in numerous ways, unifying humankind in the same way empires and the concept of money has.

The codes and laws regulating sovereign states, societies and communities are man-made, we've created their value out of nothing and assigned names and meaning to them all. But as these social structures became larger, the codes and laws keeping them together became more fragile. This is why religion has played such a crucial role for humankind. Religion gave these fragile societies a supernatural legitimacy that couldn't be questioned by humans. The codes and laws enforced are not a result of human greed or interference, they're ordained by a supreme authority, absolute in their power and knowledge. It doesn't matter what the beliefs are, or if the supreme supernatural authority even exists, as long as everyone believes in its value together (like they do with the concept of money) then it has purpose, meaning and influence.[6]

Religion has facilitated cooperation, discipline and conformity among empires for thousands of years and today there are political structures which still operate in the same way. There are nation states where a political authority is justified by divine sanction, and the most prominent of these in existence today are Islamic and Christian theocracies.

Islamic theocracies include nations which adopt Sharia as its basis for political laws exclusively, thus implementing the Islamic ruling system. Examples of the nations which have adopted Islam as the ideological foundation of state and constitution include Afghanistan, Iran, Mauritania, Pakistan, Saudi Arabia, and Yemen. The Christian theocracy is the office of the Bishop of Rome, the Pope. The Pope is the only person in the world who runs a sovereign state (Vatican City State) and a religion (the Roman Catholic Church) at the same time.

5. Shermer, Michael. "Why Are We Moral: The Evolutionary Origins of Morality." In The Science of Good and Evil: Why People Cheat, Share, Gossip, and Follow the Golden Rule. New York: Times Books, 2004.

6. Harari, Yuval Noah. Sapiens: A Brief History of Humankind. Random House UK, 2014.

We've now reached a tipping point in the history of humankind. Just like the universe, human knowledge is expanding faster as time progresses. Our understanding of planet Earth and our Homo sapiens ancestors is more accurate than ever before. Justice systems and human rights laws have developed so substantially that they're unrecognizable from the ones we had even 100 years ago. So let's ask, what purpose do religions serve in keeping social order, which cannot now be maintained by humans?

There's still value to be gained from religions for us and generations to come, after all, they're the accumulation of human experiences for thousands of years. For example, there's a law of reciprocity which is evident in various forms in almost every religion. It's known as the Golden Rule – to treat others as oneself would want to be treated.[7] This altruistic ideal is one of most endearing aspects of any religion.

But there are religions holding non-altruistic ideals which are also hindering us. Religious ideologies which withhold the rights of women and homosexuals, religious doctrines which declare the Big Bang Theory and Evolution as blasphemy, and religious creeds which condemn those who don't believe what's written in their holy books.

It's no surprise so many of these inflexible beliefs are prevalent in the world today as the majority of the 7.3 billion global population still holds beliefs based on ancient texts from thousands of years ago.[8] Religion is outdated because as human culture has updated and evolved, religion has not, because it can not. Religion has remained rooted in the same ideological principles and customs from ancient history, regardless of how irrational and bizarre they are now in the modern world. This is one way we as a species irrationally believe we are rational. Because as we've discussed, it doesn't matter what people believe in, as long as we all believed in it. This was enough to maintain social order and stability.

But religions are starting to slow us down with their unproven ancient beliefs, when rather we need to keep increasing our knowledge of the universe and everything in it with open-minded ideals. Instead of blaming people who don't believe what we believe, we need to practice tolerance, kindness and empathy. Just as important, we also need to approach what we're being told to

7. Epstein, Greg M. Good without God: What a Billion Nonreligious People Do Believe. New York: Harper, 2010. p.115.

8. Johnson, Todd M., Gina A. Zurlo, Albert W. Hickman, and Peter F. Crossing. Christianity 2015: Religious Diversity and Personal Contact. Report. Vol. 39. Series 1. South Hamilton: International Bulletin of Missionary Research, 2015. Accessed October 18, 2016. http://www.gordonconwell.edu/ockenga/research/documents/2IBMR2015.pdf.

believe in from first principles, to ask ourselves why we believe what we believe. It's not about destroying society, it's about living authentically.

Religion has historically provided social order that helped people cooperate better. But the price we paid is religion has also determined the goals of our cooperation. These are goals (and ethics) which were set thousands of years ago in ancient books. Many of them haven't been addressed since which is why they look archaic in modern society, conflicting with basic human rights and scientific discoveries.

So we may have cooperated better because of religion, but we've also only been serving religion's aims and interests. Our blind faith in religions has led our human efforts to frequently focus on the glory of supernatural beings like Zeus and Poseidon, Odin and Thor, Ra and Anubis, and the Abrahamic God of Jews, Christians and Muslims. This is all instead of solely focusing on improving the lives of real sentient beings, like humans and other animals.

Depending on our faith we may believe some, all, or no gods are fictional. But it doesn't matter which because any suffering or discrimination caused in the name of those gods was 100% real. This is why it's important to strive towards distinguishing between fiction and reality. Religions were so successful at keeping social order because people believed they had divine legitimacy. This is what made people conform, not question their political leaders, and foster an insular groupthink environment. So we can keep exclusively relying on religions to enforce goals and regulate humanity in the same way it did thousands of years ago. Or, we can adapt and find a middle-ground before the social order and structures religion creates does more harm than good to humanity in the next 10, 100 and 1,000 years.

5

Religion gives answers

"Essentially, almost all humans are born with a fear of the unknown. It casts a pall of anxiety which pushes us into the arms of religions and soothsayers and their made-up answers" – Mario Stinger

Whenever people had questions they needed answers to, religion was there to help out. Religion has the incredible ability to answer any questions about our life on Earth. Religion satisfies our desire to make sense of the world we live in. Whether the answers religion gives its followers are true or false isn't important, as long as an answer is given from a source they trust, religion will always help followers find meaning in things they don't understand.

It's human nature to try and understand everything which happens around us, and we adopt various kinds of reasoning to explain them. For some people God is often the first answer, without even looking any deeper for an explanation ("Why did I get hired for that job? God helped me"). But if people search for an answer and can't find one, then God can also become the last answer ("Why did that bus full of children crash? God has a reason and a plan"). It's become indoctrinated into us that God can become the answer for anything, and religion has the answers to all our questions.

This desire to understand life has been a part of our DNA for tens of thousands of years. Our brains are hardwired to seek answers and solutions because any knowledge gained would increase our ancestors' chances of survival. This is why people become addicted to the ubiquitous 24-hour media news coverage, even though most news is not worth tracking. We're not living in the most dangerous time in human history, we're living in the most fear-mongering time in human history. Our fear is easy to manipulate and mass media, insurance companies, pharmaceuticals and politicians know this; they know we're wired to respond to fear above everything else. Because if we miss an opportunity for abundance, life goes on; but, if we miss an important fear cue, life does not.

43

One way we've gained a sense of knowledge, power and control is by attributing a personality to inanimate objects, therefore crediting them with more importance than they actually carry. We give meaning to things which hold no influence because we crave any power over things we personally can't control. One of religion's main selling points is that it gives us this power. It helps us make sense of the world and feel in control, thereby increasing our chances of survival by instilling us with a sense of fortitude (however false this placebo effect may be).

Even today we still attribute a personality to inanimate objects which have none. For example, we beg traffic lights to stay green as we approach them closer, and we ask our keys where they've gone when we've misplaced them. This is what we do as human beings, and what we've always done as a species. It helps explain why people have worshiped the sun as a god, and why rain dances are performed. It's easy for us to look back at ancient religions now and find it whimsical that civilizations used to believe in those gods. Yet those same people today have no issue praying to an invisible God who not only controls the sun and the rain, but everything else as well. This isn't uncommon behavior as most people around the world perform habits believing it will influence something they have no control over. We just pick and choose whether to call it superstition or religious duty.

We believe if we perform a certain act (wear our football team's kit) then an event important to us will go in our favor (our football team will win). It gives us the impression we have power or influence over events which are out of our control. Religion operates in a similar matter. When believers perform habits (animal sacrifices, prayers, pilgrimages) they believe something important will go in their favor (a bountiful harvest, good health, entrance to Paradise). So to obtain this influence and control, historically we've turned to religion to empower us.

Let's look at another scenario. When a low probability event goes in someone's favor and they weren't expecting it to happen, how could they interpret it? If they don't understand how it happened then they won't have the answer, and if they follow a particular faith they may be inclined to believe it's an act of God, a 'miracle'. When we look at such surprises in isolation, it can look like an act of God since the likelihood of it occurring was so rare. But our lives consists of millions of insignificant events that happen everyday. When so many events happen all day, every day, for our entire lives, it's expected that some surprises will occur. God may be the easy answer, but it doesn't mean He's the correct one.

What's curious is that when rare but good surprises we don't understand happen, people attribute them to God. Like someone waking up after being in a coma for years. But bad things also happen which don't make sense to us and we can't always find a suitable answer for them. Like why a baby needs to die in childbirth along with the mother. In these instances, the religious may say it's God's will and it cannot be understood by us mere humans. But these are double standards, it must be one or the other:

> 1. Either good and bad things are attributed to God, therefore we don't give Him a pass on the bad things. If this is true, then why does a merciful God not just allow but actually cause so much pain and suffering in the world?
>
> 2. Or, we say His will can't be understood when good and bad things happen. If this is true, then how do we know if God has good intentions at all? After all, we can't understand His will so we don't know why both good and bad things happen. Therefore, we don't even know what God's intentions are to begin with.

Having God in their life empowers and reassures many people. This is especially true when it comes to the question of what happens after we die, since this question has tormented humankind for thousands of years. The fear of uncertainty surrounding death is one of the greatest fears existing in the human consciousness. So when a religion says they know what happens after death, we can imagine how powerful it would be to know that answer. To know that we'll be reincarnated, or that we're going to the greatest place ever for eternity, containing all the things and people we love. Is there a better way to invoke faithfulness than to tell people you have all the answers to all their questions?

But to believe in answers because they're the ones we like the most is a 'red herring'. The relevant issue at hand is still the question, does God even exist? So, even if people believe religion can provide us with life's answers, it still doesn't prove God's existence. He still exists the same amount, it hasn't changed.

But whether they're true or false, religion gives us the thing we humans crave: the answers to all our uncertainties about life. We never needed the answers to accurate, we just needed to believe in them.

6

God helps people

"The hands that help are better far than lips that pray" – *Robert G. Ingersoll*

People have depended on God for thousands of years, and while the religions may have changed over this time, our reliance on seeking help from a higher power has not. Even atheists at times look up to the skies at nothing in particular when seeking some reprieve (or looking to express gratitude), a habit inherited from our ancestors if nothing more. But this can be an argument some believers use against those who don't believe in God: they say atheists have never needed God's help like they have so it's no surprise they don't believe in Him. But, when they do need Him, then atheists will believe in Him or at least wish He was real.

This sentiment has been captured in the aphorism 'there are no atheists in foxholes'. It implies in times of extreme stress or fear (a foxhole) there will be no atheists because under extreme stress or fear (war, cancer, poverty) all atheists will believe in, or at least hope for, God's existence.

Of course, this argument doesn't prove God's existence, it only shows in times of high stress people can resort to desperate thoughts or actions. This is to be expected. In moments of suffering we would all be willing to do something, anything, to relieve ourselves of what we're enduring. We're only human. So if those who don't believe in God turn to Him and ask for His help in times of high stress, it still doesn't prove He exists.

However, it does recognize that tragedies like wars and diseases drive some people to a belief in God due to fear, and a desire to be released from that fear. It's for this reason deathbed conversions often carry no legitimacy. When someone is on their deathbed, they're at their weakest and most vulnerable so they'll likely turn to anything for help. Therefore they may turn to the only thing they believe has the power to help them in their final hour.

This vulnerable response towards God isn't based on any evidence or logic about faith, and it doesn't happen when the person is lucid and in control of their mental capacities. The decisions made by someone in a frightened and desperate mental state are more irrational than those made by someone who is in no danger, in a calm and relaxed mental state. These vulnerable responses are merely a result of chemical reactions in our brain which produce the emotions we feel when in mortal danger. A belief in God in times of need is more indicative of our human nature than it is of His actual existence.[1]

This is one of the reasons why there has been a trend towards secularization in North America, Western Europe, Australia and New Zealand. Not because people stopped believing in God, but because increasing economic prosperity in those areas reduced people's need for God for support and survival. In contrast, those living in less economically prosperous areas, such as countries in South America or Africa, are more inclined to 'need' God. Having belief in God helps them feel safer and more optimistic about their prospects and they may believe only God is able to help them and their family. Unfortunately, this also makes people from less economically developed areas more vulnerable to the indoctrination of religion.[2]

It's only concerning when people going through those difficult times actually rely on God alone to alter the tough situations they find themselves in, rather than taking the responsibility and initiative to physically affect it themselves whenever they can. Yes people need God's help, many of them in ways we can't even imagine or appreciate, but we need to be careful we don't rely on God more than we rely on ourselves. We need to be careful we don't leave everything in 'God's hands' when it's possible our own hands can make our world a better place.

1. Griffin, Andrew. "What Happens to You Just before You Die? Chemists Explain Exactly How Death Feels." The Independent, October 27, 2015. http://www.independent.co.uk/news/science/what-happens-to-you-just-before-you-die-chemists-explain-exactly-how-death-feels-a6710551.html.

2. Cox, Jeffrey. "Secularization and Other Master Narratives of Religion in Modern Europe." Kirchliche Zeitgeschichte 14, no. 1 (2001): 24-35. http://www.jstor.org/stable/43100018.

7

God answers prayers

"If you talk to God, you are praying; if God talks to you, you have schizophrenia" –
Thomas Szasz

Believing an omniscient (infinite knowledge), omnipotent (unlimited power) and omnipresent (present everywhere) supernatural being is in your corner is tempting. It can change us from a passive participant of life into an active individual. It's no surprise people around the world love their religion, who wouldn't want to feel empowered like this? Furthermore, once experienced, who would want to give it up, even if it's just a placebo effect? After all, if it's real in the individual's mind, then it exists in their own reality.

There's a tendency for the religious to believe that if something occurs in their favor which they prayed for, God did it or helped it to happen. Yet their only proof is anecdotal evidence and not empirical evidence others can verify. There's also an element of human psychology to take into account when considering these instances: confirmation bias. Confirmation bias means placing greater emphasis on the actions you want to occur, confirming your beliefs, and ignoring or rationalizing the times they didn't occur. In this context, it means a believer is more likely to remember all the times their prayers were 'answered' by God, rather than the countless times they weren't. It's a trap, and confirmation bias can give you a skewed image of reality.

Relying on prayers can also instill a detrimental attitude of passivity, instead of a proactive mindset and approach to life. When we have the ability to impact an event but we don't take responsibility for it, it reduces the chances of it going in our favor, and this can happen when we leave events in 'God's hands'. By relying on an outside agent like a god, spirit or saint, it limits the probability of the event occurring. For example, a child could have a medical issue, and her parents may decide not to seek professional help, only the help of God through prayer or by visiting a religious shrine (such as Our Lady of Lourdes in France). Obviously this is dangerous for the child and no one would advise any parent to do this. But this practice does happen and it is called faith healing, or ruqyah in Islam.[1] There has been no scientific evidence to support claims that faith healing has cured any physical ailments, and yet parents have refused medical care for their children based on religious grounds, leading to fatal outcomes.[2]

It's an exaggerated example as it's an uncommon occurrence in many religions, but the principle stands. However let's use another example. When a disaster occurs (environmental or man-made) the last thing that will help the victims is someone's prayers. This is possibly the worst way to help them. At least if someone did nothing, then they know nothing is going to happen. But to pray and believe one prayer is going to make a difference to the victims is unrealistic. The victims will likely be praying anyway. So to believe a god would need an extra prayer to convince him to help suffering people is a delusion of grandeur. Volunteering or donating are two obvious ways which are much more beneficial to the victims than a prayer.

It's one thing to say your thoughts are with them, this shows empathy, compassion and sorrow for what they're experiencing. But when people say "I'll pray for you" or "We're praying for them", it's a cop out. It's like someone saying to a friend "If there's anything I can do to help, let me know". Instead of being passive and thinking we've done what we can, we can be proactive and actually do something which helps the person in need. Otherwise, we'll think we've helped them because we offered our support, but we've actually done nothing at all for them.

We must be cautious of this passive mindset because it reduces the amount of action people take to help themselves and to help others. Instead, we can take full responsibility for our own lives and not rely on prayers. We can also be proactive and engaged when we want to help someone in need. This way we'll be working towards making what was an abstract prayer into an actionable reality, thus improving our lives and the lives of others around us. This is real self-empowerment.

There's a popular adage which says 'God helps those who help themselves', which is just a roundabout way of saying God isn't going to help you or others, so you'd better do it yourselves. The belief that 'God answers prayers' may help people feel better in their lifetime (short-term) but it's detrimental to humanity's

1. Kesvani, Hussein. "Why Are Some British Muslims Going To Faith Healers To Treat Mental Illness?" BuzzFeed, December 11, 2015. https://www.buzzfeed.com/husseinkesvani/why-are-some-british-muslims-going-to-faith-healers-to-treat?utm_term=.ugn9BgyyG#.ivMR7Nlle.

2. Wilson, Jason. "Letting Them Die: Parents Refuse Medical Help for Children in the Name of Christ." The Guardian, April 13, 2016. https://www.theguardian.com/us-news/2016/apr/13/followers-of-christ-idaho-religious-sect-child-mortality-refusing-medical-help.

progression (long-term). Belief in God or gods only helps when it inspires people to take positive action, which does indeed happen.[3] But when people are praying because they believe God answers their prayers and will take action for them if it's His will, then it reduces their capacity for making their world a better place.

3. Elgot, Jessica. "What The Huffington Post UK's Beyond Belief Series Taught Us About Faith."The Huffington Post, December 1, 2014. http://www.huffingtonpost.co.uk/2014/12/01/beyond-belief_n_6248360.html.

8

Religions evolve by natural selection

"We are all atheists about most of the gods that humanity has ever believed in. Some of us just go one god further" – *Richard Dawkins*

Religions have existed almost as long as humanity has and this is a testament to their appeal and sustainability. But the fact that there have been so many different religions says more about human nature than it does about the existence of any actual God or gods. In reality, our surviving religions today are a fraction of the religions which have ever existed on Earth. Religions are similar to animals in this regard, in that most are now extinct and what remains on Earth is the tiny minority.[1] It's survival of the fittest religions.

Like animals, religions have come and gone, and it has been from similar processes; natural selection and an element of chance. So like animals, the religions still alive today are the ones which have adapted effectively to survive. They've been the ones most effective at attracting and holding the allegiances of hundreds of millions of people. This, and some good fortune, is why religions have endured and thrived. It takes the right set of beliefs, at the right time, in the right environment, with the right leader, for a religion to prosper, rather like how Islam has done: it is now the fastest growing religion in the world.[2]

With 1.7 billion Muslims worldwide, Islam is the second largest religion in the world. Christianity, in all its denominations, is still the largest with 2.4 billion followers.[3] The religion of Islam has been able to prosper for a number of reasons. It has the ability to command unwavering obedience and loyalty from

1. Stearns, Beverly Peterson, and Stephen C. Stearns. Watching, from the Edge of Extinction. New Haven: Yale Univ. Press, 2000. pp 19-21.

2. Lipka, Michael, and Conrad Hackett. Pew Research Center. Why Muslims Are the World's Fastest-growing Religious Group. Report. April 23, 2015. http://www.pewresearch.org/fact-tank/2015/04/23/why-muslims-are-the-worlds-fastest-growing-religious-group/.

3. Johnson, Todd M., Gina A. Zurlo, Albert W. Hickman, and Peter F. Crossing. Christianity 2015: Religious Diversity and Personal Contact. Report. Vol. 39. Series 1. South Hamilton: International

its followers. It has a holy book unlike anything else people had ever seen. It had a focused and resolute leader in Prophet Muhammad. It has embedded itself into the everyday Arabic language of its followers, and it is able to adapt and spread throughout the world quickly and effectively.

However, there's a misconception about Islam that's prevalent, especially among Muslims. It's that Islam is the fastest growing religion in the world because people have seen 'the truth' in it; that people have been drawn to it and realized it's 'the one true religion'. Whereas in reality, Islam is the fastest growing religion in the world due to the high fertility rate of Muslims.

Muslims have the highest fertility rate of any religion in the world with an average of 3.1 children per woman. Christians are second with 2.7 children per woman. The Hindu fertility rate of 2.4 children per woman is similar to the global average of 2.5 children per woman. The Jewish fertility rate is below the global average, with 2.3 children per woman, but it's still above the global replacement level of 2.1 children per woman. Religions below the 2.1 children per woman replacement level are too low to sustain their populations, so they would require converts to their religion to grow or maintain their size.[4]

Research shows Islam's growth isn't due to converts finding 'the one true religion', it's entirely due to reproduction. The Muslim population is predicted to grow by 1.2 billion from 2010-2050. From these 1.2 billion Muslims, only 3.2 million will be because of conversions. This is 0.3% of the total growth. So 99.7% of the growth in Islam from 2010-2050 will be because of the high birth rate among the Muslim population.[5]

With more and more Muslims appearing in the world, it can be difficult not to believe in Islam when everyone around us believes it's true. After all, if billions of people believe in God they can't all be wrong can they? This idea, that a large group of people believing in something can make it true, is a logical fallacy. It's called *argumentum ad populum*. It's a false argument because the truth is still the truth even if no one believes it, and false claims are still false even if everyone believes them.

Regardless of how religions have grown and how many people believe in them, they've adapted in several ways throughout history. Some religions evolved to become less violent than they used to be (the Catholic Church),

Bulletin of Missionary Research, 2015. Accessed October 18, 2016. http://www.gordonconwell.edu/ockenga/research/documents/2IBMR2015.pdf.

4. Pew Research Center. The Future of World Religions: Population Growth Projections, 2010-2050. Report. April 2, 2015. http://www.pewforum.org/2015/04/02/religious-projections-2010-2050/.

5. Pew Research Center. The Future of World Religions: Population Growth Projections, 2010-2050. Report. April 2, 2015. http://www.pewforum.org/2015/04/02/religious-projections-2010-2050/.

while others evolved to become more aggressive (Islam, from its initial Meccan suras to its Medinan suras revealed in the Quran. See chapter '*Non-Muslims*'). Many religions have even given birth to new species of religions (denominations) to exploit new niches as they develop in society, increasing the genetic variation of the religion's gene pool and its chances of survival. Examples can be seen in most religions including Islam (Sunni and Shia), Christianity (Roman Catholic and Protestantism), Judaism (Orthodox, Conservative, Reform), Hinduism (Vaishnavism, Shaivism, Shaktism and Smartism) and Buddhism (Theravada, Mahayana and Vajrayana) to name a few.

It doesn't matter if those religions created an imagined reality, because an imagined reality can be perceived as an authentic reality to someone if everyone else around them believes in it too. But it doesn't change the truth which will continue to exist independently of anyone's beliefs, as it always has done. Due to the global population, more people now than ever in human history believe in God or gods. But while one may find strength and comfort in those numbers, it doesn't necessarily mean one has found truth in those numbers.

9

Everyone believes their God is the right God

"Suppose we've chosen the wrong God. Every time we go to church we're just making him madder and madder" – Homer Simpson

The religious are prone to over-emphasizing the authenticity of their religion, particularly in comparison to other religions. But more often than not, people believe in the god they believe, and practice the religion they practice, because of their environment. Most of us have (or had) the faith our parents and family held, or the faith our peers, school or society followed. These circumstances lead people to believe in the god they believe, out of all the hundreds of gods available to worship in the world today. If anyone of any faith had been born elsewhere, the chances are they'd believe in that native religion and God (or gods) just as devoutly. Whatever religion we follow (or followed), is because of relevant exposure, not divine fate, and most likely it is because of our parents.

Some religious people argue it's better to believe in God just in case. This is commonly known as Pascal's Wager, named after the 17th century French philosopher Blaise Pascal. He proposed it's safer to believe in God (he spoke of the Christian God at the time) because the pros outweigh the cons. The argument suggests that if God doesn't exist, then the believer will have limited losses from his life, but if God does exist, then that believer stands to receive unlimited gains (eternity in Heaven) and avoid unlimited losses (eternity in Hell).[1]

However this argument fails for two reasons. First, it falls on the premise we've even chosen the right god to believe in. Second, if there is an all-knowing God, He would know our true intentions. This means we must truly believe in the god we've chosen (or be punished for hypocrisy) and hope we've chosen correctly so he actually exists and we can reap the rewards. Or, we choose

---

1. Popkin, Richard H. "Blaise Pascal." In The Columbia History of Western Philosophy, p.353. New York: Columbia University Press, 2008.

the wrong god and will be punished for not believing in the right one. Or, it doesn't matter what god we choose or don't choose because none of them exist.

Let's assume there's at least one correct god to worship and let's decide we've chosen to believe in the Abrahamic God of Jews, Christians and Muslims. We've chosen this god because it represents the god that 56% of the 7.3 billion people in the world believe in.[2] So, we've chosen the god to believe in from the thousands of religions, faiths and belief systems in existence today, we now need to make sure we worship Him in the manner which pleases Him. Unfortunately, the ways to salvation with the Abrahamic God of Jews, Christians and Muslims aren't all the same. The Quran doesn't provide any help in this matter either. In one verse it says Jews, Christians and Muslims will all be taken care of by God. It's the same God (according to Muslims) so this would make sense.

> Quran 2:62 – Surely they that believe, and those of Jewry, and the Christians, and those Sabaeans, whoso believes in God and the Last Day, and works righteousness—their wage awaits them with their Lord, and no fear shall be on them, neither shall they sorrow.

But in another verse in the Quran it suggests believing in God may not be enough. We'd still need to worship Him in the correct way by choosing the correct religion.

> Quran 3:85 – Whoso desires another religion than Islam, it shall not be accepted of him; in the next world he shall be among the losers.

Therefore is picking the correct god out of the thousands available enough? Or do we need to pick the correct god and also worship Him in the correct way as well? No one can be sure, only a real god knows. So even though there's no consensus on what gets us into Heaven, it doesn't stop Judaism, Christianity and Islam exaggerating their knowledge that Heaven does indeed exist, and they know how to get us there.

Imagine if God does exist, and we've lived an honorable life of integrity, kindness, modesty and charity. But we worshiped the wrong god. Is it fair to be punished? Especially if we were never exposed to the 'correct' religion, just

---

2. Johnson, Todd M., Gina A. Zurlo, Albert W. Hickman, and Peter F. Crossing. Christianity 2015: Religious Diversity and Personal Contact. Report. Vol. 39. Series 1. South Hamilton: International Bulletin of Missionary Research, 2015. Accessed October 18, 2016. http://www.gordonconwell.edu/ockenga/research/documents/2IBMR2015.pdf.

as most people haven't been throughout history? There's no religion followed by more than half the people in the world. Meaning the majority of people in the world could potentially face punishment after death, maybe forever, because they picked the wrong religion out of the thousands which exist. The Quran would lead us to believe this is true in Islam, perhaps it's true in some other religions with their gods as well.

No religion has a monopoly on the truth, even if they all claim to do so. So when someone wonders why people don't believe in their god, it's for the same reason they don't believe in other gods. At the end of the day, no one can prove their God or gods is or are the correct ones, no matter how much they think they can with their holy books or anecdotal evidence. But if God or one of the gods does exist, we can only hope He, She or They are merciful, because picking correctly and worshiping correctly is a lottery we're all playing. But when the odds are this long in a lottery, there's a reason why people don't play it at all.

10

Books and faith are enough

"Faith is the effort to believe what your common sense tells you is not true" – Elbert Hubbard

When religious people have no more arguments to make for God's existence, they can always fall back on their faith. They may say something like "I don't need to prove God exists, I have faith", or "If you had faith, you'd know it was true", and "God can't be understood or proven, you just have to believe".

These are hypothetical answers, but faith is regularly used as an argument by the religious. However, when an appeal to faith is used as an argument, it's also an abandonment of reason. It signals no more logical explanations are left to give for their beliefs. It's a diversion from the realization that all their claims have been discredited and so the 'faith card' is used as a last resort argument.

This means theological discussions can quickly fall apart because anyone can use faith to support any claim they make, religious or otherwise. When someone says "I just believe", or "I have faith", it's as good as a parent telling their child "Because I said so". It avoids the issue entirely and provides no constructive material to continue with. Religious people need to be willing to discuss God's existence without solely relying upon their 'faith' in Him, otherwise it's futile to have a productive dialogue between the religious and non-religious.

This isn't a recent realization and there are many examples of how problematic pleas of faith can be. Perhaps the most famous in modern times is the Flying Spaghetti Monster, a thought experiment from 2005, created to protest the teaching of Intelligent Design in public schools in Kansas, USA. People who believe in Intelligent Design claim the universe is so incredibly complex, it must have been designed by a higher intelligent being rather than the process of evolution. The Flying Spaghetti Monster, as its name suggests, is a monster made of spaghetti which flies. The central belief behind the Flying Spaghetti Monster is that it's invisible, undetectable, and it created the universe.

There's no proof the Flying Spaghetti Monster doesn't exist and didn't create the universe, so this thought experiment pokes fun at the argument that there's no proof God doesn't exist and didn't create the universe. Therefore if faith is enough to warrant belief in God's existence, then faith is enough to warrant belief in the Flying Spaghetti Monster's existence.[1]

This thought experiment exposes the claim we're entitled to believe in anything we want as long as we have faith and until we're proven otherwise. Hence the absurdity (or non-absurdity) of the Flying Spaghetti Monster analogy. This thought experiment illustrates the argument that the burden of proof lies upon those who make non-believable and unfalsifiable claims, not the other way around. So it's with those who believe in God to provide proof of His existence, not those who don't believe in Him. Someone who believes in God may argue against this. But then as non-believers of the Flying Spaghetti Monster, it's up to them to prove it doesn't exist, rather than those who believe in the Flying Spaghetti Monster to prove it does exist.

The Flying Spaghetti Monster is a contemporary example of Russell's Teapot, an analogy coined after the British philosopher Bertrand Russell in 1952. He wrote if he were to claim a teapot is orbiting the sun somewhere between Earth and Mars, without offering any proof, he wouldn't expect anyone to believe him just because his claim can't be disproved.[2]

So if a book, like the Quran, is the word of God then it's up to the people making the claim to prove it. Muslims can insist it's the word of God because nothing like it exists and no one can ever reproduce anything like it. If so, Muslims can be directed to the Epic of Gilgamesh, the Vedas, the Upanishads, the Tao Te Ching, the Bhagavad Gita or the Buddhist Sutras to name a few. All are ancient masterpieces pre-dating the Quran, the likes of which never to be reproduced again. Like the Quran, some of them also claim to be divinely written (see chapter 'Equals of the Quran'). Even if Muslims wanted something globally accepted as inimitable masterpieces, then they can be directed to the works of William Shakespeare which also meets this criteria.

Religions have not just survived on faith, they've been able to thrive on it. Every religion relies upon the believer to take a leap of faith. No religion in history has ever proven their God or gods exist. Most religions point to signs of a higher power, such as a charismatic prophet or an enchanting book, but all

1. Henderson, Bobby. "About." Church of the Flying Spaghetti Monster. Accessed November 5, 2016. http://www.venganza.org/about/.

2. Russell, Bertrand. "Is There a God? [1952]." In The Collected Papers of Bertrand Russell, Vol. 11: Last Philosophical Testament, 1943–68, edited by John G. Slater, 547-48. London: Routledge, 1997. http://russell.mcmaster.ca/volume11.htm

still require believers to have faith. If a religion or God were true beyond doubt then it wouldn't ask us for faith since no faith would be necessary. For example, we don't say "I have faith gravity exists". We know gravity exists because it has been observed, tested, proven and its results replicated. But we can't say the same for any god, therefore faith is a prerequisite to any religion.

It's for these reasons the religious can't be surprised, upset or angry when people don't believe in their God, because faith is an opinion. It's fashioned from our upbringing, our environmental influences and the information we have at hand. There's nothing wrong with having faith in something. But we must remain mindful about where we put our faith, because misplaced faith can lead to misguided choices in life.

PART II

The Quran

The Quran, also written as Qur'an or Koran in English, is the religious text of Islam. Muslims believe it is a revelation from God, and it is the most revered piece of literature in the Arabic language. Muslims believe nothing like it can be, or will ever be, produced again because it's above the capabilities of humankind, now and forever.

Muslims believe the Quran was revealed to Muhammad by God who chose him as His prophet. The angel Gabriel (Jibril in Arabic) delivered the message of the Quran to Muhammad, on God's behalf. The Quran's revelation took place over a period of approximately 22 years. It began when Muhammad was 40 in 610 CE and concluded in 632 CE, the year of his death.[1] Muslims regard the Quran as a miracle of Muhammad and proof of his prophethood. When Muslims pray it is the Quran they recite in its original Arabic form.

According to Islamic tradition, companions of the Prophet Muhammad were scribes for him, writing down the revelations he received from the angel Gabriel. After Prophet Muhammad's death the scribes compiled the Quran, but these transcriptions had differences. This motivated the ruler of the Islamic empire at the time, Caliph Uthman ibn Affan, to put together a standard version of the Quran. It is this Quran (Uthman's Codex) which is considered to be the Quran known today.[2] Uthman was a companion of Prophet Muhammad, and he was also the Prophet's son-in-law twice, having married a second daughter of the Prophet after the first one died.[3]

The Quran shares narratives also recounted in Biblical scriptures. This is because Islam is an Abrahamic religion that builds upon the foundations of Judaism and Christianity which came before it. The Quran summarizes some

1. Brown, Daniel W. A New Introduction to Islam. Malden: Blackwell, 2005.

2. Leaman, Oliver. "Canon." In The Qur'an: An Encyclopedia. London: Routledge, 2010.

3. Ahmad, Abdul Basit, Aqeel Walkar, and Muhammad Ayub Sapra. Uthman Bin Affan: The Third Caliph of Islam. Riyadh: Darussalam, 2004.

of these narratives, goes into more depth in others, and also presents alternative interpretations of various events. The Quran is used with Hadith (words, actions and habits of Prophet Muhammad) to interpret Sharia law, the Islamic legal system. Both Hadith and Sharia law are discussed further in this book.

The interpretation of the Quran by Islamic scholars is called Tafsir. Tafsir is important because it provides contextual analysis and commentary of the Quran's 114 chapters. Each chapter in the Quran is called a 'sura' in Arabic. Each sura consists of verses, and each of these verses is called an 'ayah' in Arabic (although not grammatically correct in Arabic, when discussing sura and ayah in the plural throughout this book, they will be referred to as suras and ayahs).

This part will be discussed with the assumption that God exists, the Quran is His words, and Muhammad is His Prophet and Messenger. All Muslims believe this is true because the Quran tells them it is true. Since the Quran is the only text Muslims cannot and do not dispute, all the arguments in this part will be based upon the credibility of the Quran.

11

Equals of the Quran

"A man is his own easiest dupe, for what he wishes to be true he generally believes to be true" – Demosthenes

A significant assertion by the Quran is its claim no one can ever produce '*a sura like it*'.

> Quran 2:23-24 – And if you are in doubt concerning that We have sent down on Our servant, then bring a sura like it, and call your witnesses, apart from God, if you are truthful. And if you do not—and you will not—then fear the Fire, whose fuel is men and stones, prepared for unbelievers.

Muslims believe only something from beyond this world could have produced the Quran. God even says if men had help from other supernatural beings, they still wouldn't be able to produce a sura from the Quran. The Quran uses '*jinn*' to illustrate this point, which are one of God's three sapient creations, along with humans and angels.

> Quran 17:88 – Say: 'If men and jinn banded together to produce the like of this Koran, they would never produce its like, not though they backed one another.'

Presumably the inability to produce '*a sura like it*' applies to all the 114 suras of the Quran, even sura 108 al-Kawthar (Abundance) which is only three verses long.

> Quran 108:1-3 – Surely We have given thee abundance; so pray unto thy Lord and sacrifice. Surely he that hates thee, he is the one cut off.

But if we go back in time, we can find several literary masterpieces which pre-date the Quran, the like of which will ever be reproduced again. Though appraising which piece of literature is more transcendent than the other is subjective, there are literary masterpieces which would match, if not surpass, the Quran in stature for many people. These are sacred texts as epic and masterful as the Quran. It's vital Muslims have some awareness of these texts as it helps provide perspective on what humans can accomplish with language, and, it provides context to the Quran's claim of divinity. Such examples include, but are not limited to, the following six influential sacred texts:

1. The Epic of Gilgamesh – An epic poem from ancient Mesopotamia, it was written around 2100 BCE, 2,700 years before the Quran. The Epic of Gilgamesh tells the story of the quest for immortality amidst a great flood. It is one of the earliest surviving works of literature and what's particularly interesting is that it was written without any religious prompting. Yet, there are many parallels in its themes, plots and characters to the Hebrew Bible and as a consequence, to the Quran too.

There are stories in the Epic of Gilgamesh about Enkidu and Shamhat, which draw parallels to Adam and Eve. Enkidu is a man created from the soil by a god and he lives in nature among the animals. Enkidu is introduced to a woman, Shamhat, who tempts him to eat forbidden food, and he does. He then covers his nakedness and must leave that realm, unable to return as a punishment by the god. In addition, there is also a story in the Epic of Gilgamesh about a global flood which matches the flood story of Noah in Genesis and the Quran.

These two stories, about Enkidu and about the flood, were both written 2,700 years before the Quran. They are also from ancient Mesopotamia, which today roughly corresponds to most of Iraq, Kuwait, eastern parts of Syria, and included the regions along the Iran-Iraq and Turkish-Syrian borders.[1] So it's fair to say Abrahamic scriptures may have been influenced by previous texts like the Epic of Gilgamesh, and it certainly raises serious questions about the originality and authenticity of holy books like the Bible and the Quran.[2]

2. The Vedas – Vedas means 'knowledge' and they are four ancient Indian texts: Rigveda, Yajurveda, Samaveda, and Atharvaveda. The oldest one dates between

---

1. Foster, Benjamin R., and Karen Polinger Foster. Civilizations of Ancient Iraq. Princeton: Princeton University Press, 2009. p.6.

2. Dalley, Stephanie. Myths from Mesopotamia: Creation, the Flood, Gilgamesh, and Others. Oxford: Oxford University Press, 2008.

1500-1200 BCE, around 2,000 years before the Quran was revealed. They are the oldest forms of Sanskrit literature and the oldest writings of Hinduism. The individual verses are mantras and are comprised of hymns and prose. Just like the Quran, the Vedas are an ancient text believed to be divinely revealed.[3]

3. The Upanishads – The Upanishads were likely composed in India between 800-100 BCE, around 1,000 years before the Quran. Upanishads roughly means 'sitting at the feet of a teacher'. They are a collection of more than 200 philosophical texts and form the theoretical basis for Hinduism. Hindus consider the Upanishads to contain truths illustrating the concept of ultimate reality, Brahman. Although unique from the Vedas, the Upanishads are regarded as an extension of the Vedas by Hindus.[4]

4. Tao Te Ching – A classic Chinese text composed around 500 BCE, around 1,000 years before the Quran. According to tradition, a sage called Laozi wrote the Tao Te Ching. It contains 81 chapters, each composed in a flowing style of calligraphy. It is the fundamental text of both religious and philosophical Taoism, and it greatly influenced the schools of Confucianism and Chinese Buddhism. It covers issues such as advice for rulers as well as practical lessons for ordinary people.[5]

5. Bhagavad Gita – The Bhagavad Gita is a 700 verse scripture that is part of the Hindu epic Mahabharata. It was written between 400-100 BCE, around 800 years before the Quran. It spoke of a call for selfless action, and integrates dualism and theism into its text.[6] It had a profound affect on the leaders of the Indian independence movement, including Mohandas Gandhi who referred to it as his 'spiritual dictionary'.[7]

6. The Sutras – The Buddhist Sutras were first transmitted by Gautama Buddha between 100 BCE – 100 CE, around 600 years before the Quran. The scriptures

3. Flood, Gavin D. An Introduction to Hinduism. Cambridge: Cambridge Univ. Press, 2011.

4. Jones, Constance A., and James D. Ryan. Encyclopedia of Hinduism. New York, NY: Checkmark Books, 2008.

5. Chan, Alan. "Laozi." In Stanford Encyclopedia of Philosophy, edited by Edward N. Zalta. Stanford, CT: Stanford University, Metaphysics Research Lab., 2004. https://plato.stanford.edu/entries/laozi/.

6. Doniger, Wendy. "Bhagavadgita." Encyclopædia Britannica. Encyclopædia Britannica, March 5, 2015. https://www.britannica.com/topic/Bhagavadgita.

7. Minor, Robert Neil. Modern Indian Interpreters of the Bhagavadgita: Research Conference on Modern Interpreters of the Bhagavadgita: Papers. Albany, NY: State University of New York Press, 1986. p.88.

contain the Lotus Sutra, considered particularly noteworthy as it includes a sermon by Buddha to his followers teaching them the basis of Buddhism. Those who recite the Lotus Sutra are considered to receive good karma.[8]

It's possible to be in awe of literature without immediately inferring it has supernatural origins. Prophet Muhammad may have shown the rhymed prose of the Quran to people who'd never heard anything of its kind before (since the Quran didn't conform to the prose and poetry expressed in Arabian languages at the time), but the same would have happened to people who first heard the Epic of Gilgamesh, the Vedas, the Upanishads, the Tao Te Ching, the Bhagavad Gita or the Sutras. They too would have found them awe-inspiring, just as people still do today. But this doesn't automatically imply a god's involvement. If it did, then either one God had a hand in all of them or several gods played their parts. Either way, the Quran isn't the only unique literary masterpiece of ancient civilizations.

The Quran regularly claims something is true, just because it says it is true; it presupposes its premise which is a circular reasoning fallacy. For example, the Quran claims it is the word of God and no sura from it can be reproduced. It's the equivalent of believing 'this book is true, because it tells me it is true'. It's also similar to when people assert God is good and merciful, because God Himself says He is good and merciful. But the assertion God is good just means that God is approved of by God. It becomes a nonsensical argument to follow. Therefore the Quran can say no sura like it can ever be produced, but if someone tries or even succeeds, Muslims will still dismiss it because they believe what the Quran says about its inimitable perfection. So when the Quran calls itself perfect, Muslims believe it is perfect because they're told to believe it is perfect.

> Quran 6:114–115 – What, shall I seek after any judge but God? For it is He who sent down to you the Book well-distinguished; and those whom We have given the Book know it is sent down from thy Lord with the truth; so be not thou of the doubters. Perfect are the words of thy Lord in truthfulness and justice; no man can change His words; He is the All-hearing, the All-knowing.

However, the Quran can't call itself perfect due to the 'law of abrogation' (Naskh in Arabic). This law states later verses in the Quran can cancel out earlier

---

8. Williams, Paul. Mahayana Buddhism: The Doctrinal Foundations. London: Routledge, 2010.

verses if there is a contradiction.[9] The Quran explicitly acknowledges this and attempts to explain itself.

> Quran 2:106 – And for whatever verse We abrogate or cast into oblivion, We bring a better or the like of it; knowest thou not that God is powerful over everything?

> Quran 16:101 – And when We exchange a verse in the place of another verse and God knows very well what He is sending down — they say, 'Thou art a mere forger!' Nay, but the most of them have no knowledge.

The argument made by God here could be summarized as "I know what I'm doing, I know why I'm doing it and you don't, so don't question me". That a God must defend himself to humans is one thing, but that there has to be a law of abrogation says another about the Quran's 'perfection'.

> Quran 4:82 – What, do they not ponder the Koran? If it had been from other than God surely they would have found in it much inconsistency.

The Quran may be 'perfect' (according to itself), but apparently this doesn't mean God still can't change some of it through the law of abrogation, even though He says there's no changing His words.

> Quran 10:63-64 – Those who believe, and are godfearing — for them is good tidings in the present life and in the world to come. There is no changing the words of God; that is the mighty triumph.

In all the six ancient texts previously mentioned in this chapter, none of them have to defend their authenticity and quality. But within its verses, the Quran constantly defends itself from doubters, and it does so in a human and insecure manner. One would imagine a literary masterpiece could stand on its own to show it is a masterpiece, rather than continually having to say it is.

> Quran 10:37 – This Koran could not have been forged apart from God; but it is a confirmation of what is before it, and a distinguishing of the Book, wherein is no doubt, from the Lord of all Being.

9. McAuliffe, Jane Dammen. The Cambridge Companion to the Qur'ān. Cambridge: Cambridge Univ. Press, 2014.

We can agree it would be difficult to produce a sura like one in the Quran, but we must also ask if we would want to. The Quran is a difficult book for people to pick up and follow due to the complexity of the language, its nonlinear structure and the lack of continuity. In addition, the Quran's 114 suras don't have a thematic or chronological order: there is no beginning, middle and end. So depending on the length of the sura, each one can contain several topics which are skipped from one to the next with little hint or sign.

For example, sura 5, al-Ma'idah (The Table) is 120 ayahs (verses) long. It begins with some dietary guidelines for Muslims, which follows onto a reminder not to violate the rites of God. It goes back to more dietary guidelines, before reminding Muslims to settle disputes nonviolently. It then discuss non-believers and Islam, before going back to diet. It continues to talk about what else is good for Muslims, followed by what's good for women. There is a short part about losing faith and then a longer part about hygiene. The rest then consists of Biblical stories about Jews and Christians, before the sura finishes up with the rewards and punishments in store in the afterlife.

For anyone to reproduce a chapter from the ancient texts discussed would be a substantial feat, but to produce one from the Quran would be even more impressive. Not because the Quran is a superior text, but because the Quran makes it difficult to reproduce something of its kind for the wrong reasons. Perhaps the Quran does have no equals.

12

Inaccuracy of the Quran

"The greatest enemy of knowledge is not ignorance, it is the illusion of knowledge" –
Stephen Hawking

The Quran as we know it today didn't exist during Prophet Muhammad's time, though all the revelations came from only him. There were many scribes who wrote or memorized these revelations and this led to them being scattered around many places and onto many different materials.

The process of canonization of the Quran was completed about 20 years after Prophet Muhammad's death under the third Caliph, Uthman ibn Affan.[1] He was the leader of the Islamic empire from 644-656 CE. Caliph Uthman wanted a uniform Quran present throughout the Muslim world so he commissioned a committee to collect, compile and construct a standard copy of the text of the Quran.[2] This became the standard version of the Quran used by Muslims all over the world today.

The 7th century was a period of human history when as a society we were much less developed and literate than today. So we're asked to take a large assumption – that zero messages or meanings were changed in the Quran from the Prophet's death to the Quran's final compilation 20 years later.

Additionally, it was Prophet Muhammad's scribes who wrote down or memorized the revelations for him, Muslims' faith is built upon the accuracy of these scribes recordings and memorizations, and their honesty and integrity in keeping them perfect. This isn't impossible, but the passage of time and human fallibility must not be dismissed. Our memories fade with time, and they become more susceptible to mistakes.

It's possible many of the Prophet's scribes transmitted his message verbatim.

1. Leaman, Oliver. "Canon." In The Qur'an: An Encyclopedia. London: Routledge, 2010.

2. The Editors of Encyclopædia Britannica. "ʿUthmān ibn ʿAffān." Encyclopædia Britannica. Encyclopædia Britannica, July 20, 1998. https://www.britannica.com/biography/Uthman-ibn-Affan.

But it's also probable to suggest some could have relayed the information inaccurately, perhaps even knowingly. Those who relied on memorization and oral traditions alone were particularly at risk. Though they may have known the revelations by heart at the time and recited them regularly, it is still an unreliable method of transmission. Errors can arise, subtle changes can occur, and the substitution of words can all have a consequential impact on the Quran's final edit.

During his prophethood, Muhammad's scribes wrote his revelations down on many different materials including items like parchments, tablets, date palm leaves, thin stones and bones.[3] Scribes would had to have been diligent to protect all the materials from damage by dirt, sand, water, fire and time itself. So it would have been of paramount importance to store them safely, or at least transfer the texts onto new materials before the originals deteriorated. Otherwise the words on these materials would have been susceptible to corruption by damage, thus losing the true recitation of the message, or, replacing it from memory upon discovery of its degradation.

With all these variables, it's difficult to accept that the Quran as it is now is entirely error free from the revelations Muhammad received from Gabriel (an angel no one else ever heard or saw for the 22 years Muhammad was speaking to it). Also, none of the Quran was compiled by the man who actually received the revelations, nor did he give the final edit his endorsement.

What we're left with is taking a large leap of faith on the preservation of these materials 1,400 years ago, because 1.7 billion people today are relying on this supposed flawless transfer of information. It guides their entire way of life until they die. They're trusting every single material was found, collated and they all contained the correct revelations on them.

We'll never fully appreciate what life was like at the time of these revelations. We have no way of understanding the community psyches and cultural nuances, or the social dynamics Caliph Uthman or each of the Quran's scribes and orators experienced. But all this impacts their perception of the world, and their perception of the previous generations who came before them. As a result, they see the world with subjective eyes, with their own biases, just as we all do. So whenever there are questions of motive involved, as naturally biased individuals, we often pick the one which fits into our preferred narrative, just as Uthman, the scribes or orators may have done.

As far as we're aware, Prophet Muhammad didn't know about his impending death. However God would have known. It would have been

3. Tabā tabā i, Sayyid M. H. The Qur'an in Islam: Its Impact and Influence on the Life of Muslims. London: Zahra Publ., 1987.

logical to compile the complete collection of the Quran before the Prophet's death, so he could oversee it and confirm its legitimacy. The Prophet and God would surely have seen the benefit of this for all humankind, especially since the Quran claims previous messages from Judaism and Christianity became distorted. After all, this is the Quran's entire justification for existing in the first place: to correct the distortions people made in Judaism and Christianity.

> Quran 3:3-4 – He has sent down upon thee the Book with the truth, confirming what was before it, and He sent down the Torah and the Gospel aforetime, as guidance to the people, and He sent down the Salvation. As for those who disbelieve in God's signs, for them awaits a terrible chastisement; God is All-mighty, Vengeful.

> Quran 3:78 – And there is a sect of them twist their tongues with the Book, that you may suppose it part of the Book, yet it is not part of the Book; and they say, 'It is from God,' yet it is not from God, and they speak falsehood against God, and that wittingly.

For a book with divine origins, it doesn't have a divine conclusion. It's not an ideal process for something so crucial according to God and Prophet Muhammad. There is too much margin for human intervention and error if the Quran is indeed a divine message; the last one we're told we'll ever need or receive.

13

Ambiguity of the Quran

"Question with boldness even the existence of God; because, if there be one, he must more approve of the homage of reason than that of blindfolded fear" – *Thomas Jefferson*

Muslims consider the Quran's style to be beautiful, unique and ethereal. Many Muslims read the Quran and feel a sense of calm. When they recite it, they may feel a connection to something greater than this world. Hundreds of millions of Muslims across the planet enjoy reading the Quran. But, they all take different meanings from it.

The interpretation of the Quran by Islamic scholars is called Tafsir. Tafsir aims to explain the meanings of the 114 suras of the Quran. Islamic scholars also take into account the location each sura was revealed in: suras are either Meccan or Medinan suras depending on whether it was revealed before or after Prophet Muhammad's migration from Mecca to Medina.

Prophet Muhammad's migration from Mecca to Medina took place in 622 CE and is called Hijrah in Arabic. Hijrah was such a significant event that 622 CE marks the first year of the Islamic calendar. The Meccan suras revealed early in Muhammad's prophethood were more theological than his later Medinan suras. The early Meccan suras discuss the principles of faith such as the oneness of God and Judgement Day. The later Medinan suras are more legislative: outlining the social obligations Muslims must keep.[1]

Since the Quran was revealed, there have been hundreds of books of Tafsir from Islamic scholars, meaning hundreds of different Quranic commentaries exist all attempting to explain the Quran's verses. This goes to show the innumerable ways the Quran can be interpreted. Islamic scholars know the Quran better than anyone else, dedicating their lives to analyzing the Quran's

1. Robinson, Neal. Discovering the Qur'an: A Contemporary Approach to a Veiled Text. Washington, D.C.: Georgetown University Press, 2004.

linguistic style, its lesser known words, metaphors, parables, structure and meaning. They also refer to Hadith and Prophet Muhammad's life to acknowledge the context the verses were revealed in. Yet, there are numerous discrepancies among the most knowledgeable of Islamic scholars on the Quran's meaning. This means there's much less hope for non-scholars to grasp its message. It is both unfortunate and illogical to have humanity's eternal guidance book be so ambiguous in interpretation.

Perhaps it's no surprise the Quran can be interpreted in several ways, after all, it's a piece of literature and every piece of literature is a work of art. All artistic productions such as paintings, music or films divide opinion because their meaning is subjective. Even artistic masterpieces don't have a consensus on what its creator meant. So since the Quran is a work of art, this means it's open to interpretation, which is why the Quran is praised by some and criticized by others. Everyone reads the Quran and extracts different meanings from it. Therefore it's naive to expect people, even Muslims, from across the world, throughout various times in history, to interpret a piece of art, like the Quran, all in the same way.

One of the main reasons the Quran requires specialist interpretation is because of its language. It isn't written in the standard Arabic language in use today for writing and formal speech (Modern Standard Arabic), but rather a Quranic Arabic, more accurately known as Classical Arabic. Since the Quran was revealed in the 7th century the Arabic language has moved on, it has evolved and it is still updating over time as all languages do. For example, no one speaks Early Modern English, the language of William Shakespeare from 400 years ago. The same evolution has occurred with the Arabic language.

What's interesting about Arabic is that it isn't even the primary language for most Muslims. A study in 2010 showed that of the top five countries in the world with the highest Muslim populations, only one was an Arabic speaking country. Indonesia had 205 million Muslims and the official language is Indonesian (Bahasa). Pakistan had 178 million Muslims and its official languages are Urdu and English. India had 177 million Muslims and its official languages are Hindi and English. Bangladesh had 149 million Muslims and the official language is Bangla. Finally, Egypt with the fifth highest Muslim population in the world had 80 million Muslims and its official language is Arabic. Islam is now an Asian religion more than an Arab religion because as of 2010 there were 1 billion Muslims in South and Southeast Asia alone, and only 600 million Muslims in the Middle East, Africa, Europe and the Americas combined.[2]

So, most Muslims don't speak Arabic as their first language. Islamic scholars themselves have many interpretations of the Quran's Arabic, and for most of them Arabic *is* their first language. Therefore most Muslims in the world have little hope of deciphering the Quran in its original form, they must rely on the Tafsir and translations of others. So it's the Islamic scholars that tell the majority of Muslims what the Quran and their religion actually means. Presumably God knew this would happen, and yet He still chose Classical Arabic as the language of the Quran for all people, even though it hasn't been good enough to be actively spoken as an everyday language for over 1,000 years.

> Quran 41:3-4 – A Book whose signs have been distinguished as an Arabic Koran for a people having knowledge, good tidings to bear, and warning, but most of them have turned away, and do not give ear.

Islam now contains various denominations, branches, and types of schools of thought. They all stem from the same book, even though the Quran claims it is easy to follow and understand.

> Quran 16:89 – And the day We shall raise up from every nation a witness against them from amongst them, and We shall bring thee as a witness against those. And We have sent down on thee the Book making clear everything, and as a guidance and a mercy, and as good tidings to those who surrender.

Wars have been fought and blood has been shed between Muslims and non-Muslims, and between Muslims themselves, because of what's written in the Quran, and they are still happening today. A book easier to interpret wouldn't have led to this outcome. Conflicts like these arise due to various nuanced interpretations of the Quran and Islam all over the world. No religion is practiced in the exact same way by everyone, but a 'perfect' book from God could have made this more likely.

The Quran may carry a lot of beauty in its style and expression, but it doesn't exist to deliver style over substance. At the end of the day, the Quran's purpose is to be a guidance book for all people for all time. It's meant to impart wisdom and teach us how to grow spiritually. But when the linguistic style gets in the way of understanding the true message, then everyone suffers.

Even Prophet Muhammad himself had to explain the meanings of the

2. Grim, Brian J., and Mehtab S. Karim. The Future of the Global Muslim Population. Report. January 27, 2011. http://www.pewforum.org/2011/01/27/the-future-of-the-global-muslim-population/.

Quran to his followers because he knew it best. He had to reconcile expressions which appeared to contradict each other, he had to clarify any verses which were misunderstood, and he had to give indications of places or names which were not explicitly mentioned in the suras. There was confusion and questions about the Quran even at its time of writing. So it's no surprise we're still struggling with it today. If being present with Prophet Muhammad was a prerequisite to understanding the true meaning of the Quran, then there isn't much hope for the rest of us.

> Quran 5:15-16 – People of the Book, now there has come to you Our Messenger, making clear to you many things you have been concealing of the Book, and effacing many things. There has come to you from God a light, and a Book Manifest whereby God guides whosoever follows His good pleasure in the ways of peace, and brings them forth from the shadows into the light by His leave; and He guides them to a straight path.

It's impractical to stay true to a written work from over 1,000 years ago, it's illogical to believe it's flawless just because it says it is, and it's irrational to make consequential decisions based on it until the end of time when the most educated of Muslims can't even agree on all its messages. Decisions are made daily by 1.7 billion individuals, millions of organizations, and around 50 Muslims countries all based on the Quran, even though there is no consensus among Muslims to its entire meaning. If there was a consensus, then there wouldn't be such a disparity on how Muslims all over the world practice their faith.

No matter who reads the Quran, their upbringing will influence their interpretation of it. But this bias multiplies since the Quran can have innumerable interpretations. One would hope a book which promises salvation would be straightforward to follow. One would also imagine an omnipotent God would make it straightforward to follow, particularly if He wants His will to be obeyed correctly. Instead, a scenario exists where God may punish Muslims for incorrectly following His book, even though they did so to the best of their ability. I have sympathy for Muslims because the Quran itself even says some of its parts are ambiguous.

> Quran 3:7 – It is He who sent down upon thee the Book, wherein are verses clear that are the Essence of the Book, and others ambiguous. As for those in whose hearts is swerving, they follow the ambiguous part, desiring dissension, and desiring its interpretation;

and none knows its interpretation, save only God. And those firmly rooted in knowledge say, 'We believe in it; all is from our Lord'; yet none remembers, but men possessed of minds.

This does not appear to be the work of a divine or fair author.

14

Inadequacy of the Quran

"God used to be the best explanation we'd got, and we've now got vastly better ones. God is no longer an explanation of anything, but instead become something that would itself need an insurmountable amount of explaining. So I don't think that being convinced that there is no God is as irrational or arrogant a point of view as belief that there is" – Douglas Adams

During the 22 years the Quran was revealed, no one else heard or saw God, or the angel Gabriel, only Muhammad did. Though all other people are looked at with suspicion if they've claimed to have encountered God or an angel, Muslims don't dispute it with Prophet Muhammad due to the Quran. It's upon one man in human history and the words he presented, that 1.7 billion people believe his claim of encountering a supernatural being for 22 years.

But 22 years is a long time to put together a book, so one can wonder three things. First, if it needed to take this long. Second, if it took just the right amount of time. Or third, if it needed to take even longer. All can be argued, but all have their flaws.

First, the argument can be made it needed to take this long. The Quran contains a complex and extensive message to reveal, and matters of this importance can't be rushed. It also needed to take as long as 22 years because Muslims at the time raised several issues and questions which they needed guidance and answers to. They also needed to be reassured regularly so they'd keep their faith in Islam. Therefore revelations from the Quran were steadily revealed to coincide with the evolving social lives of Muslims 1,400 years ago. Much of what the Quran reveals is actually the result of responses to various incidents or events at the time. The Quran also announced revelations to support Prophet Muhammad, particularly during the difficult times he faced when challenges were made against him (this is an odd concept as it was Muhammad giving Muhammad support, since followers heard the Quran from him).

However, this is a sporadic and random manner of revealing divine revelations. It's as if the Quran was constructed out of a mixture of answers to questions people had at the time. The Quran was able to provide something for everyone throughout the Prophet's life, it's reactive rather than proactive by God. An omnipotent God would foresee all the questions people had and the issues they would face. In the Quran, God did anticipate some issues in advance and set guidelines for them, but, God still had to be continuously prompted to answer other questions or clarify His rulings, which is un-God-like since He creates the future. We can appreciate it's impossible or impractical to pass on the entire information in the Quran all at once. But responding to random requests of various people, having to constantly defend Himself, and regularly threatening those who don't believe in Him, all comes across as a Quran written by an appeasing and insecure author. One who wrote it in an inefficient manner unbefitting of an all-knowing deity.

But maybe it's the second of the three points mentioned, that the revelations of the Quran took as long as they needed to take. It was no more and no less than it needed to be because this is what God decided. So God being God, He knew when Prophet Muhammad would die, and indeed He let him die. Therefore the time when the Quran was fully revealed was when Prophet Muhammad died, as determined by God.

All Muslims believe the Quran is the word of God and as such, they believe the Quran as a book is infallible. Yet, there is so much information the Quran omits, information Muslims need to know to practice their faith. Muslims aren't even told how to pray or how to perform the Hajj pilgrimage, all this information is obtained outside the Quran in supplementary Islamic texts. So it's difficult to agree the Quran is complete and perfect.

In addition, many of the Quran's pages aren't actually helpful to humanity. These include rephrased, inconsequential fables already told in previous holy books, or the detailed rights of Prophet Muhammad, like who he can marry, which is only instructive to one person at a single period of time in human history.

This means Muslims have to rely on the Hadith (words, actions and habits of the Prophet) and Tafsir (interpretations of the Quran) to understand the Quran and provide enough information to practice their faith. Even though the Quran doesn't mention it needs supplementary texts or scholarly interpretation to understand it. In fact, it claims the contrary.

Quran 6:38 – No creature is there crawling on the earth, no bird flying with its wings, but they are nations like unto yourselves. We have neglected nothing in the Book; then to their Lord they shall be mustered.

Muslims are ordered to believe everything the Quran says. So if it says it's complete, easy to follow and contains all we need to know, then Muslims must believe it is true. Even though we know it is not.

Let's now look at the third and final point, that more time was needed to fully reveal the Quran. We can speculate that there were going to be more revelations but they only stopped because Prophet Muhammad died, or that there was never an end date in mind. Both of these speculations would suggest God's fallibility so they're often dismissed. But we were always going to need more information since it's human nature to ask questions and seek out information to aid our survival, it's how our species grows and develops.

We can't know God's intentions, but we can assume God knows everything that's going to happen. God knew Prophet Muhammad was going to die and when. God also knew we would still have more questions after his death, just as we have done. It's questionable whether the Quran or any self-proclaimed eternal guidance text can ever be complete. Humans are dynamic entities continuously evolving over time, just like our societies and cultures. It would be ambitious, if not impossible, for anything to claim it is perfect and has all the answers we would ever need. But this is what the Quran claims. We're expected to rely only on the issues faced in Muhammad's 22 year prophethood, 1,400 years ago, as guidance for all humanity, for the rest of time, even if into the future we've colonized other planets in our solar system (the Quran doesn't provide information as to where Muslims should pray towards on Mars).

The Quran didn't take too long, too short, or just the right duration of time to be revealed because none of these three would have created a perfect guidance document anyway. To create such a thing is impossible in the first place. Not all rulings and judgments are timeless as we'll explore later under the part 'The Modern World'. This is why laws change and are updated regularly, it's why over time slavery was abolished and women received the vote. To expect any piece of text to cover all the information we would ever need to know is a futile endeavor and for the Quran to not only claim it, but boast it, is conceited.

PART III

Hadith

Hadith are accounts describing the words, actions and habits of Prophet Muhammad. Hadith intend to provide supplementary information to Muslims not found in the Quran, for example, how and when Muslims must perform their five daily prayers. Hadith are the second most important source in Islam after the Quran. They are used to develop Islamic jurisprudence (Fiqh) and they are also used for understanding and interpreting the Quran (Tafsir).

In addition to Hadith, there are also Sunnah. Sunnah are accounts covering what Prophet Muhammad believed, implied or tacitly approved or disapproved of. Sunnah are the way of the Prophet, so to speak. Sunnah were originally recorded by Muhammad's companions in Hadith, which is why the use of the word Sunnah is often interchangeable with Hadith.

Hadith came into existence centuries after Prophet Muhammad's death. Hadith literature first began as spoken reports that were in circulation within the Muslim community after the death of Prophet Muhammad.[1] But Hadith were not compiled by a central authority, unlike the Quran which was compiled under the direction of Caliph Uthman. Caliph Uthman compiled the Quran as we know it today around 20 years after Prophet Muhammad's death, but the earliest reputable Hadith were consolidated over *200 years* after the Prophet's death; a considerable amount of time after Prophet Muhammad said, did or performed any of his acts.[2]

Hadith consists of two parts. The first is the text itself (matn in Arabic) describing Prophet Muhammad's words, actions and habits. The second is the chain of transmission that this text was communicated by (isnad in Arabic): a chronological list of all the narrators. Each narrator mentions who they heard that particular Hadith from, and this chain of transmission continues back until

---

1. Brown, Jonathan. Hadith: Muhammad's Legacy in the Medieval and Modern World. Oxford: Oneworld, 2011.

2. Leaman, Oliver. "Canon." In The Qur'an: An Encyclopedia. London: Routledge, 2010.

we reach the original text and narrator. Both the transmission's quality, and the reliability of the original source, determines a Hadith's authenticity. Muslim jurists and clerics classify Hadith into authentic (sahih), good (hasan) or weak (da'if) categories. There is no consensus between Sunni and Shia Muslims as to what are the authentic, good and weak Hadith.

Sunni Muslims regard six collections of Hadith to be the most reliable (Kutub al-Sittah). However, two in particular, the Two Sahihs, are deemed to be the most important:

> 1. 'Sahih Bukhari' compiled by Imam Bukhari. He died 870 CE, 238 years after the Prophet's death.
> 2. 'Sahih Muslim' compiled by Muslim bin al Hajjaj. He died 875 CE, 243 years after the Prophet's death.

Shia Muslims do not accept these two Hadith collections as trustworthy. Shia Muslims follow their Four Books (Kutub al-Arb'ah) of Hadith Collections:

> 1. 'Kitab al-Kafi' compiled by Muhammad ibn Ya'qub al-Kulayni. He died 941 CE, 309 years after the Prophet's death.
> 2. 'Man la yahduruhu al-Faqih' compiled by Muhammad ibn Babawayh. He died 991 CE, 359 years after the Prophet's death.
> 3. 'Tahdhib al-Ahkam' compiled by Shaykh Muhammad Tusi. He died 1067 CE, 435 years after the Prophet's death.
> 4. 'Al-Istibsar' also compiled by Shaykh Muhammad Tusi.[3]

This part will assess if Hadith are a reputable source to understand Islam or to live our lives by.

---

3. Nasiri, Ali. An Introduction to Hadith: History and Sources. MIU Press, 2013.

15

The Quran does not mention Hadith

"And what if I'm wrong? Well what if you're wrong about the other Gods? Followers of other religions are just as sure that their religion is the right one just as you are of yours. Anyone of them has the right to come up to say to me or you, what if you're wrong?" – Richard Dawkins

Hadith collections play a great deal of importance in Islam. Both Sunni and Shia sects consider Hadith as essential supplements to understanding the Quran and in creating Sharia law. The Quran also asks Muslims to follow the example of Prophet Muhammad, which is contained in the Hadith collections. But there is a contradiction here in that all mainstream sects use Hadith, yet neither the Quran nor Prophet Muhammad ever said Muslims needed a supplementary text.

> Quran 6:114-115 – What, shall I seek after any judge but God? For it is He who sent down to you the Book well-distinguished; and those whom We have given the Book know it is sent down from thy Lord with the truth; so be not thou of the doubters. Perfect are the words of thy Lord in truthfulness and justice; no man can change His words; He is the All-hearing, the All-knowing.

The Quran also demands us not to follow anything else but that which He delivered.

> Quran 7:2-3 – A Book sent down to thee — so let there be no impediment in thy breast because of it — to warn thereby, and as a reminder to believers: Follow what has been sent down to you from your Lord, and follow no friends other than He; little do you remember.

Quran 77:50 – In what discourse after this will they believe?

The majority of Muslims around the world refer to Hadith because they consider it a necessity, thereby contradicting what God claims in the Quran. This leaves us with two possibilities: either nothing is required as the Quran asserts; or, the Quran can't be seen as flawless since Muslims need the Hadith to interpret the Quran and follow the Prophet's example. We already know the former is false. So if it's the latter (which it is judging by the actions of most Muslims) then it raises questions about the Quran's divinity and credibility.

Modern day Muslims need Hadith. Without Hadith Muslims wouldn't know the specifics of the Five Pillars of Islam: the Shahada (profession of faith), Salah (prayer), Ramadan (fasting), Zakah (almsgiving) and Hajj (pilgrimage). The Quran presents the general principles of the Five Pillars of Islam, but without the details explained in Hadith they're just abstract concepts. Without Hadith, Muslims wouldn't know what the Shahada entails, how to perform Salah, the guidelines for fasting in Ramadan, how much to donate to charity for Zakah, or what the procedures are for Hajj. When the Quran can't help them (as it often cannot), Muslims either refer directly to Hadith or to the wisdom of Muslim clerics to guide them.

The Hadiths' credibility have been questioned by Arab scholars as early as the 9th century, when the first sahih (authentic) Hadith were published.[1] There are also groups of Muslims who reject the authority of all the Hadith collections entirely and they're often referred to as Quranists. Quranists believe using the Quran is enough by itself to derive all laws from since neither the Quran nor Prophet Muhammad mentioned Hadith as being required by Muslims. Quranists also question if a source recorded over 200 years after the Prophet's death can ever be truly reliable.[2]

The Quranists who argue against the Hadith do put forward a valid argument – if Muslims needed something supplementary which is so crucial, either God or Prophet Muhammad would have said so. Relying on texts created over 200 years after Prophet Muhammad's death does not appear to be something God or Prophet Muhammad planned or wanted.

Using Hadith appears to conflict with a central tenet of Islam: that the Quran is God's perfect word which is absolute. Yet if Muslims didn't use Hadith they wouldn't know how to pray, and therefore, Islam wouldn't be as we know

---

1. Hecht, Jennifer Michael. Doubt: A History; the Great Doubters and Their Legacy of Innovation from Socrates and Jesus to Thomas Jefferson and Emily Dickinson. New York: HarperCollins, 2004.

2. Robinson, Neal. Islam, a Concise Introduction. Washington, DC: Georgetown University Press, 1999.

it today. If Muslims do choose to use the man-made Hadith texts to perform Hajj or create Sharia law, what does it say about their thoughts on the Quran's perfection and God's requests of them? Unfortunately it's a no win scenario for Muslims: they're damned if they do, and damned if they don't.

16

Unreliability of Hadith sources

"We can judge our progress by the courage of our questions and the depth of our answers, our willingness to embrace what is true rather than what feels good" – Carl Sagan

Hadith have been passed on for generations to provide Muslims with information on how the Prophet lived his life and, consequently, how the Prophet wanted Muslims to live their lives. The first people to collect this information about the Prophet were his closest companions, who then conveyed it to others afterwards.

It worked something like this: one of the Prophet's companions would collect information about the Prophet. He would then pass it on by saying "I heard the Prophet say…" The person who heard this would then pass it on to the next person by saying "I heard a companion of the Prophet say, that the Prophet said…" The one after him would say "I heard someone say, that they heard a companion of the Prophet say, that the Prophet said…" and this continued until someone hundreds of years later finally decided to collect all these oral traditions into written form.

Muslim nations also use Hadith to form the basis of their country's Sharia law. But just as Sunni and Shia sects refer to different Hadith, so too do different Muslim states. For example, two countries may both be Sunni Muslim but they may choose to enforce different Hadith texts.

There are numerous collections of Hadith on a varied number of topics and each may support contrasting views on different matters. Therefore contradictions occur between different Muslims because of the Hadith texts they choose to follow. Islamic scholars don't deny false Hadith exist, but they do believe that through their work most of them have been disproved or eliminated. Yet this still means we're relying upon the work of a handful of men in ancient Arabia to determine what is authentic (sahih) Hadith and what isn't.

These handful of men in history dictate how almost 2 billion people live their lives today.

When Islamic governments create laws supported by Hadith, we hope the laws are worthy and commendable; and if most Muslims live their lives supported by Hadith, we hope their lives will be rich and fulfilling. Yet how likely are either of those two scenarios to happen if the Hadith is based upon corrupted information?

It's extremely challenging to orally maintain what Prophet Muhammad said or did verbatim for over 200 years. Prophet Muhammad and his companions took no steps to preserve the integrity of these oral traditions, unlike what they did with the Quran's revelations which were at least written down. So to expect the oral narratives to be accurate when nothing was collected over this time and people were more illiterate during 7-9th century Arabia is indeed a leap of faith. We also have to account for the fallibility of humans, we all have brains which are imperfect data taking and processing devices. For example, it only takes a few lines on a piece of paper to create optical illusions our brains can't compute.

We can compare the Hadith collections of Prophet Muhammad by using an analogy of a game played by children, commonly called the Telephone Game (or the less politically correct, Chinese Whispers). In the game one person begins by whispering a message to another person. This person then whispers it to the next person. This continues through the entire line of people until the last person receiving the message announces it to the entire group, often to amusing results because errors typically occur and accumulate in the retellings of the message. The errors are caused by messages inaccurately transmitted, mis-hearings, or individuals deliberately altering the message they heard. All this happens in a period of a few minutes with a handful of people.

People who play the telephone game are also trying their best to repeat the message accurately so the last person can get it right and everyone wins the game. There's little incentive for the participants to corrupt the message they're communicating. But the same can't be said for the narrators of Hadith texts. It's human nature to change stories and events to suit how we see the world. For instance, something we were told a year ago by our friend may carry an entirely different meaning to us today. A lot can happen in the space of a year which changes our perspective of the world and the people in it. Of course this is natural and always happens with the passage of time. The Quran itself claims this is what happened to the Jewish and Christian scriptures. In the Quran God says His original message became corrupted by people over the course of time.

Quran 2:75-79 – Are you then so eager that they should believe you, seeing there is a party of them that heard God's word, and then tampered with it, and that after they had comprehended it, wittingly? And when they meet those who believe, they say 'We believe'; and when they go privily one to another, they say, 'Do you speak to them of what God has revealed to you, that they may thereby dispute with you before your Lord? Have you no understanding?' Know they not that God knows what they keep secret and what they publish? And some there are of them that are common folk not knowing the Book, but only fancies and mere conjectures. So woe to those who write the Book with their hands, then say,'This is from God,' that they may sell it for a little price; so woe to them for what their hands have written, and woe to them for their earnings.

This is the reason for the Quran's existence, to correct the 'corrupted' Jewish and Christian scriptures. So it's likely something similar could have happened again to the Hadith.

It's impossible for any text, even the Quran, to cover every single specific aspect of life and how we should live it. Missing answers for new questions would occur as time and societies progressed. So, with Hadith, narrators may have taken it upon themselves to fill in these gaps, or to convey what they believed the Prophet intended. But over 200 years this would eventually lead to the narrator's pre-held prejudices or biases influencing their transmission of the message.

Human beings always prefer the stories which fit their narrative of the world. Throughout history we've always promoted the stories we prefer to tell and most often, we'll believe any story we're the hero of. But, if someone has their own personal hero it's likely they'll embellish the stories about her or him. So with the Prophet, it's plausible Muslims indulged in his sayings, actions and behavior, all leading to the enduring status he has today: the desire for all Muslims to emulate him, and his name becoming the most popular in the world with an estimated 150 million boys and men named Muhammad with all its spelling variations.[1]

But history is never just a single narrative, it's thousands of narratives. Whenever we choose to tell one, we're also choosing to silence the others. With

1. Dugan, Emily. "Most Popular Baby Names: The Top 20 Boys and Girls Names in England and Wales." The Independent, August 15, 2014. http://www.independent.co.uk/news/uk/home-news/most-popular-baby-names-the-top-20-boys-and-girls-names-in-england-and-wales-9671635.html.

Hadith, it only takes one source to drift slightly off course for the entire chain to veer in the wrong direction.

If we were to put the timescale of using Hadith into context, it would be as if we only relied upon oral transmissions of history for the past 200-300 years, around 7-10 generations. So imagine if our historical accounts of Beethoven, Napoleon and Thomas Jefferson were solely based on oral transmissions of their words and actions, and if our faith in the accuracy of these accounts fell to a handful of men who retraced the steps of what was said about them. If there was no consensus among historians as to what was authentic, good or weak information, then it would lead to some historical accounts being taught to some people, and other historical accounts being taught to others. It would result in information on Beethoven, Napoleon and Thomas Jefferson differing between populations, and by extension there would be different beliefs about Symphony No.5 in C minor, the French Revolution and the Declaration of Independence. We would never know for certain what is true and what is not.

So, no matter how 'authentic' Hadith may be, there's still an element of doubt about its accuracy. Placing one's entire trust in its reliability, as Muslims and Islamic governments do with Sharia law, isn't rational. Especially when the Telephone Game is played over hundreds of years.

PART IV

Prophet Muhammad

Muslims acknowledge Prophet Muhammad as the last Prophet sent by God for humanity, and the Quran as God's message sent through Prophet Muhammad to restore His message. Muslims believe the previous Abrahamic religions, Judaism and Christianity, had altered God's message and the Quran is the only divine book God will protect from corruption until Judgement Day. During his Prophethood, Muhammad formed the basis of Islam and united Arabia into a single Muslim polity using his teachings, actions and the Quran.

Recognizing Prophet Muhammad as a Messenger of God is an essential requirement in Islam. It's within the Shahada, the Islamic proclamation of faith.

> lā ʾilāha ʾillā-llāh, muḥammadur-rasūlu-llāh
> There is no god but God. Muhammad is the messenger of God

However, Muslims don't worship Prophet Muhammad, only God. Muslims don't believe Prophet Muhammad was of any relation to God nor that God has any son or equal.

Within Islam, Prophet Muhammad's behavior represents the highest ideal for human conduct: to imitate the Prophet is to behave how God wants us to live. Prophet Muhammad is not seen as God's Messenger for any specific people or region, but for all humanity. Muslims also believe Islam is a faith that has always existed, over time it was gradually revealed to humanity by a number of prophets, but it was Prophet Muhammad who delivered the final and complete revelation of Islam.

This part will look into the claims of Prophet Muhammad's reputation as a just and moral man, and his standing as a role model for all Muslims until the end of time.

17

Prophet Muhammad the illiterate man

"I respect faith, but doubt is what gets you an education" – Wilson Mizner

God decided to reveal the Quran to a 40 year old man named Muhammad, in a cave in the Arabian desert, through an angel called Gabriel. Muhammad is widely accepted by Islamic scholars to have been illiterate at the time.

> Quran 7:156-157 – And prescribe for us in this world good, and in the world to come; we have repented unto Thee.' Said He, 'My chastisement — I smite with it whom I will; and My mercy embraces all things, and I shall prescribe it for those who are godfearing and pay the alms, and those who indeed believe in Our signs, those who follow the Messenger, 'the Prophet of the common folk, whom they find written down with them in the Torah and the Gospel, bidding them to honour, and forbidding them dishonour, making lawful for them the good things and making unlawful for them the corrupt things, and relieving them of their loads, and the fetters that were upon them. Those who believe in him and succour him and help him, and follow the light that has been sent down with him — they are the prosperers.'

> Quran 29:48-49 – Not before this didst thou recite any Book, or inscribe it with thy right hand, for then those who follow falsehood would have doubted. Nay; rather it is signs, clear signs in the breasts of those who have been given knowledge; and none denies Our signs but the evildoers.

In *Quran 7:156-157* God refers to Muhammad as '*ummi*' in Arabic, which Arberry translated as '*the Prophet of the common folk*'. The word '*ummi*' is traditionally interpreted by Muslim scholars as 'illiterate', but some have also interpreted it as meaning ignorant of the previous holy books from Christianity and Judaism.[1]

Muhammad became the self-proclaimed Messenger of God and His last Prophet, with the Quran as proof of his status since no illiterate person could have produced its verses. Nonetheless, Muhammad was constantly doubted about who he claimed to be. Both during and after his life, critics claimed Muhammad was either schizophrenic or epileptic, and that he was having hallucinations or seizures, not divine revelations. However these allegations have been largely rejected by modern Islamic scholars since Prophet Muhammad had to have been in full possession of his mental faculties to be the active political, military and religious leader that he was until his death.[2] But these weren't unreasonable claims since history is littered with people who claimed divinity and made unexpected 'holy' proclamations and visions. However, Prophet Muhammad's conviction and the Quran he recited set him apart from the others, and it is upon the words which came through him that Muslims believe his genuineness and follow Islam.

From previous Abrahamic scriptures we know God likes to whisper to only one man in secret. Rather than remove any and all doubt about Him and His existence by announcing it to the world through all the methods available to Him. Instead, we're told to accept His will from Muhammad, an illiterate 40 year old man who heard an angel in a cave in ancient Arabia and continued to speak to it for 22 years while no one else could hear or see it. God chose to do all this in secrecy, and the only explanation we're offered is that we don't understand His ways.

Many Muslims claim Muhammad's illiteracy as proof of the Quran's authenticity and his prophethood, but there are a few issues associated with these claims. First, Muhammad's illiteracy meant he didn't know how to read or write. It doesn't necessarily mean he didn't know Jewish and Christian stories from previous scriptures (though varying interpretations of 'ummi' claim otherwise). Muhammad was also a merchant who would have encountered many different people throughout Arabia on his travels. He is known to have had an honest and friendly character which, if true, would have meant he was able to build a rapport with many different kinds of people. Muhammad could

1. Al-Tabari. The Commentary on the Qur'ān. Edited by Wilferd Madelung and Alan Jones. Oxford: Oxford University Press, 1990.

2. Watt, W. Montgomery. Muhammad: Prophet and Statesman. London: Oxford University Press, 1961. p.19. See also Freemon, Frank R. "A Differential Diagnosis of the Inspirational Spells of Muhammad the Prophet of Islam." Epilepsia 17, no. 4 (1976): 423-27. doi:10.1111/ j.1528-1157.1976.tb04454.x.

have conversed with them and learnt a lot about their customs, cultures and religions.

Second, producing the Quran while being illiterate does not necessarily correlate as a miracle. In fact there are masterpieces of literature predating Prophet Muhammad that were also "written" by illiterate people in rhymed prose and dictated to scribes. Famous examples are *The Iliad* and *The Odyssey* by the classical Greek poet Homer, both are world renowned literary masterpieces. They were dictated in the 8th century BCE, predating the Quran and Prophet Muhammad by around 1,300 years.[3] They were dictated, not only because Homer himself was illiterate, but because he was also blind. Yet this blind man dictated the combined total of more than 27,000 lines of *The Iliad* and *The Odyssey*; two masterpieces of literature the like of which are unlikely to be reproduced again.[4]

Another example of a commonly held literary treasure is *Paradise Lost* by John Milton. Written in 1667, *Paradise Lost* is an epic poem with over 10,000 lines of verse about the Biblical fall of man. Milton composed and dictated *Paradise Lost*, and he too was not just illiterate, but blind as well. Milton composed verses of his poem and memorized them, he then dictated them to friends and assistants who transcribed it for him.[5]

Too often the religious are quick to attribute events or abilities as miracles from God. But we must distinguish between perceived miracles from God and the accomplishments of naturally gifted people. Some individuals are skilled orators, speaking with influence and delivering captivating speeches. Others may be gifted writers, composing exquisite prose and poetry. Perhaps Prophet Muhammad possessed some of these talents. Muslims may then say these talents were gifts from God, they may also say the same for Homer's or Milton's gifts. But if we start attributing every talent to God, then we're subjectively analyzing the capabilities of human beings. We're not approaching their talents and these questions from first principles to seek out an explanation as to how they were able to produce such masterpieces.

We must try to the best of our abilities to objectively evaluate if one man in history and his story with an angel is trustworthy enough to base our entire 80 or so year lives on. Correlation does not imply causation: any correlation

3. Altschuler, Eric Lewin, Andreea S. Calude, Andrew Meade, and Mark Pagel. "Linguistic Evidence Supports Date for Homeric Epics." BioEssays 35, no. 5 (2013): 417-20. doi:10.1002/bies.201200165.

4. Fox, Robin Lane. The Classical World: An Epic History from Homer to Hadrian. New York: Basic Books, 2006. p.19.

5. Greenblatt, Stephen, and Meyer Howard. Abrams. The Norton Anthology of English Literature. New York: Norton & Company, 2013.

between impairment (illiteracy) and producing great artistic work (the Quran) does not immediately imply supernatural involvement (God).

If we keep attributing everything to God or falling back on 'God works in mysterious ways' it limits our potential and intellectual capabilities, and these are weak mindsets to adopt in our lives. It also greatly underestimates the inherent abilities of humans and our potential as a species on Earth. It has been proven throughout human history we're capable of accomplishing extraordinary things, all without the attribution of a god.

18

Prophet Muhammad's successor

"We must question the story logic of having an all-knowing all-powerful God, who creates faulty Humans, and then blames them for his own mistakes" – Gene Roddenberry

In 632 CE Prophet Muhammad died after falling ill. Though he was ill for several days and a prophet for 22 years, he gave no instructions for a successor. There is also no information from the Quran on Muhammad's succession. None of Prophet Muhammad's sons survived into adulthood so hereditary succession was not an option. Consequently, there were many disagreements about who should guide Muslims in the years after Prophet Muhammad's death.

The leader wouldn't be a prophet, as Muhammad is the final Prophet from God, but rather a Caliph, a leader of the entire Muslim community (ummah in Arabic). It was decided a Caliph would be elected based on merit, his knowledge of the Quran, and knowledge of Prophet Muhammad. However there was no consensual agreement. This divided the Muslim community at the time which consisted of many tribes in Arabia under a single Muslim polity. This disagreement is the reason Sunni and Shia branches of Islam first came into existence. Currently, modern day Islam does not have a Caliph.

After Prophet Muhammad's death Abu Bakr was eventually confirmed as the first Caliph by the heads of the Muslim community at the time. This was done by *shura*, a process of consultation among Muslims. Abu Bakr was Muhammad's father-in-law and trusted aide. Sunni Muslims believe that Abu Bakr was the rightful successor to Prophet Muhammad, and they make up approximately 87-90% of the global Muslim population. The other approximate 10-13% of the Muslim population are Shia.[1] The Shia majority countries are Azerbaijan, Bahrain, Iran and Iraq. Shia Muslims believe Ali ibn

---

1. Pew Research Center. Mapping the Global Muslim Population. Report. October 7, 2009. http://www.pewforum.org/2009/10/07/mapping-the-global-muslim-population/.

Abi Talib is the proper successor to Prophet Muhammad. Ali was Muhammad's son-in-law and cousin. Shia Muslims argue Prophet Muhammad appointed Ali as his successor a few months before he died at a speech the Prophet gave at Ghadir Khumm, near the city of al-Juhfah in present day Saudi Arabia. Sunni Muslims agree Prophet Muhammad told the audience to hold Ali in high regard, but they disagree he declared Ali as his successor. So while the Sunni branch of Islam stipulates that a Caliph should be elected on merit by Muslims, followers of Shia Islam believe a Caliph should be an Imam chosen by God from Prophet Muhammad's direct descendants, Ahl al-Bayt (People of the House).

We would suspect Prophet Muhammad didn't want his Muslim community to become divided, nor would an omnipotent God want his final message to humankind to become corrupted. Yet neither of them did something as simple as to give instructions for what was to happen after Prophet Muhammad's death. God and Prophet Muhammad must have known a dispute would happen with no guidance on succession since the Muslim community weren't told what was the right thing to do. This oversight has led to needless bloodshed among the Muslim community for over a thousand years, and continues till this day in the Middle East. Curiously, the Quran actually acknowledges Muslims may dispute and fight amongst each other.

> Quran 49:9-10 – If two parties of the believers fight, put things right between them; then, if one of them is insolent against the other, fight the insolent one till it reverts to God's commandment. If it reverts, set things right between them equitably, and be just. Surely God loves the just. The believers indeed are brothers; so set things right between your two brothers, and fear God; haply so you will find mercy.

However these verses also don't provide any clear guidance for Muslims. Sunni and Shia Muslims would judge each other to be the '*insolent*' one since there is no way of knowing otherwise. Therefore Sunni and Shia Muslims will keep fighting each other in the hope that one '*reverts to God's commandment*'.

All this miscommunication appears counter-intuitive to what a chosen Prophet would want to happen to his followers. Perhaps Prophet Muhammad was too conceited to appoint a successor? Or maybe he was fearful that if he did leave instructions for one, a mutiny may occur putting his leadership and life at risk?

But what about God? He must have known this dispute would happen. If this was deliberate by God (as we can assume all His actions are), judging on the past 1,400 years of violence, it appears irresponsible and reckless.

What's disillusioning is Islam exists solely to correct the corruptions of the previous holy scriptures.

> Quran 5:12-16 – God took compact with the Children of Israel; and We raised up from among them twelve chieftains. And God said, 'I am with you. Surely, if you perform the prayer, and pay the alms, and believe in My Messengers and succour them, and lend to God a good loan, I will acquit you of your evil deeds, and I will admit you to gardens underneath which rivers flow. So whosoever of you thereafter disbelieves, surely he has gone astray from the right way. So for their breaking their compact We cursed them and made their hearts hard, they perverting words from their meanings; and they have forgotten a portion of that they were reminded of; and thou wilt never cease to light upon some act of treachery on their part, except a few of them. Yet pardon them, and forgive; surely God loves the good-doers. And with those who say 'We are Christians' We took compact; and they have forgotten a portion of that they were reminded of. So We have stirred up among them enmity and hatred, till the Day of Resurrection; and God will assuredly tell them of the things they wrought. People of the Book, now there has come to you Our Messenger, making clear to you many things you have been concealing of the Book, and effacing many things. There has come to you from God a light, and a Book Manifest whereby God guides whosoever follows His good pleasure in the ways of peace, and brings them forth from the shadows into the light by His leave; and He guides them to a straight path.

Yet after all this, there are two distinct branches within Islam: Sunni and Shia. They have differences in their religious practices, traditions and customs stemming from this single disagreement over Prophet Muhammad's successor. Sunni and Shia Muslims have been fighting among each other, tearing communities apart, for over a thousand years. Modern day sectarian violence among Muslims continues today in Lebanon, Iraq, Pakistan, Saudi Arabia, and Yemen to name a few countries. Tensions have intensified most recently in Syria: leading to the Syrian Civil War, the formation of the self-styled Islamic State of Iraq and Syria/the Levant (ISIS or ISIL) and their genocide against Shias, and the resulting refugee crisis in the 21st century.

It's difficult to believe the Quran is from God if it and His Prophet fall short on their entire *raison d'etre*.

19

Prophet Muhammad's Night Journey

"Forgotten were the elementary rules of logic, that extraordinary claims require extraordinary evidence and that what can be asserted without evidence can also be dismissed without evidence" – Christopher Hitchens

Prophet Muhammad's Night Journey is called Isra and Mi'raj in Arabic. It's the story of a journey Prophet Muhammad took from Mecca to Jerusalem (roughly 1,500 km each way) in a single night. On this journey Prophet Muhammad also went to Heaven and back, and while there he met many prophets and God. The Night Journey occurred around the year 621 CE, roughly 12 years into Muhammad's prophethood. Islamic scholars have judged Isra and Mi'raj as both a physical and spiritual journey undertaken by the Prophet.[1] It's described in detail in various Hadith, but only in one ayah in the Quran: sura 17 al-Isra (The Night Journey).

> Quran 17:1 – Glory be to Him, who carried His servant by night from the Holy Mosque to the Further Mosque the precincts of which We have blessed, that We might show him some of Our signs. He is the All-hearing, the All-seeing.

In the introduction to *Atheism for Muslims* it was stated that the Quran would be the only source of all the arguments to follow. So although the specific details of the Night Journey are in the authentic Hadith collections, not the Quran, the remembrance of this journey is a significant event in the Islamic calendar. It is celebrated and observed every year by Muslims as Lailat al-Mi'raj. Many Muslims offer extra prayers on this night, and some Islamic countries decorate their cities with lights and candles to commemorate it. So Prophet Muhammad's Night Journey carries a great deal of importance in Islam, and it even has a

1. Martin, Richard C. Encyclopedia of Islam and the Muslim World. New York: Macmillan Reference USA, 2004.

sura in the Quran named after it. Therefore the Night Journey's legitimacy is worthy of being discussed.

Isra and Mi'raj are two parts of the Night Journey. The Isra part of the journey begins with Prophet Muhammad in Masjid al-Haram in Mecca, the most sacred mosque in Islam. Masjid al-Haram surrounds the Kaaba which Muslims all over the world face when they pray. While the Prophet was in the mosque, the angel Gabriel came to him and brought Buraq. In Islamic mythology Buraq is a heavenly steed of the prophets: a white horse-like animal with wings. Muhammad mounted Buraq, and Buraq flew him '*to the Further Mosque*' which is generally agreed to have been Masjid al-Aqsa in Jerusalem. While Muhammad was there, he performed prayer.

The second part of the journey is called Mi'raj, which means ladder in Arabic. From Jerusalem, Buraq then took Prophet Muhammad to the Heavens where he toured all of its seven stages. During Muhammad's tour of the seven Heavens he spoke with previous prophets of God and Islam (seven Heavens is a concept pre-dating Abrahamic religions, see chapter '*Origins of the universe*'). These included Abraham, Moses, John the Baptist and Jesus. Muhammad was then taken to a holy tree in the seventh Heaven called Sidrat al-Muntaha. It was there God instructed Prophet Muhammad that Muslims must pray fifty times a day to Him. However, Moses told Muhammad this would be too difficult for Muslims, so Moses told Muhammad to go back to God and ask for a reduction. Muhammad did so until God reduced the daily prayers to five times a day. After this, Buraq flew Prophet Muhammad back to Mecca, completing his Night Journey from Mecca to Jerusalem, to the seven Heavens, and back again to Mecca all in one night – on a flying horse.[2]

There were no witnesses to Prophet Muhammad's Night Journey so it's another extraordinary event in Islam with unsubstantiated evidence. The only proof we have is one man's word (Hadith), and a single vague ayah in the Quran. But this is enough for most Muslims and Muslim scholars to say the Night Journey was a physical event which took place, not merely a spiritual or allegorical event.

What's quite impressive is that Prophet Muhammad even managed to get God to change his request of Muslims to perform fifty prayers daily for him, rather than the five prayers Muslims are accustomed to now. As if God Himself didn't know how much time and energy investment it would be for Muslims to pray fifty times a day, and He had to be corrected by a human. Though perhaps

2. Mahmoud, Omar. "The Journey to Meet God Almighty by Muhammad—Al-Isra." In Muhammad: An Evolution of God, p.56. Bloomington, IN: AuthorHouse, 2008.

Prophet Muhammad returned home as a hero since he negotiated with God for the benefit of all Muslims, and God came across as merciful and compassionate for agreeing to it.

It's a difficult story for non-Muslims (and some Muslims) to accept as reality, but if it's in the Quran, Muslims must believe it is fact. Though there's no way of knowing what's to be taken as metaphorical in the Quran. Since Muslims must and do believe it is the word of God, they must take it all literally as events having occurred, occurring, or that will occur. Another example of a story about the Prophet Muhammad which is difficult to accept as reality is when he allegedly split the moon in sura 54, al-Qamar (The Moon).

> Quran 54:1-2 – The Hour has drawn nigh: the moon is split. Yet if
> they see a sign they turn away, and they say 'A continuous sorcery!'

Many Islamic scholars say this event was a miracle performed by Prophet Muhammad: he literally split the moon.[3] Others claim Prophet Muhammad performed no miracles, that the Quran itself is the only miracle of his prophethood (though riding a white horse to Heaven and back does seem somewhat miraculous, enough so that it gets acknowledged as a public holiday), so they interpret the splitting of the moon as a metaphorical event. While another group of Islamic scholars say the verses about the moon splitting is a reference to what will happen on Judgement Day: the moon splitting will be a cataclysmic sign of the end of the world.[4]

The Quran's ambiguity doesn't help, and neither does the lack of any evidence of the events occurring. But at the end of the day Muslims will have to choose for themselves what stories to believe in since there is no universally agreed upon answer. But as humans, this is what we do anyway. We favor the narratives we most want to believe in. We do it with our personal relationships, we do it in our office politics, and we do it with our perception of national and global affairs. After all, that's all religion is, people choosing the stories they most want to believe in whether they are true or not.

3. Muslim, Sahih. Translation of Sahih Muslim. International Islamic University Malaysia. Sahih Muslim, Book 39: The Book Giving Description of the Day of Judgement, Paradise and Hell (Kitab Sifat Al-Qiyamah Wa'l Janna Wa'n-Nar). Translated by Abdul Hamid Siddiqui. November 17, 2005. http://www.iium.edu.my/deed/hadith/muslim/039_smt.html. Book 39, Number 6725

4. Mourison, Robert G. "The Portrayal of Nature in a Medieval Qur'an Commentary." Studia Islamica, no. 94 (2002): 115. doi:10.2307/1596214.

20

Prophet Muhammad's self-serving rules

"The most heinous and the most cruel crimes of which history has record have been committed under the cover of religion or equally noble motives" – *Mohandas Gandhi*

A lot of the Quran speaks to Prophet Muhammad alone, laying out what is and isn't permissible for him. In Prophet Muhammad's mind everything he revealed was true, and the conviction in which he shared the message of Islam proved compelling to other people too. But in many instances the rules regularly, if not always, favored Prophet Muhammad. The most noticeable examples of this are found in the relationships he had with his wives.

It is generally agreed by most Muslim scholars that in his lifetime Prophet Muhammad had a total of 11 wives.[1] Although, this number is considered higher by some Islamic historians.[2] The wives of Prophet Muhammad are held in high esteem within Islam and Muslims refer to them as 'mothers of the believers.'

> Quran 33:6 – The Prophet is nearer to the believers than their selves; his wives are their mothers. Those who are bound by blood are nearer to one another in the Book of God than the believers and the emigrants; nevertheless you should act towards your friends honourably; that stands inscribed in the Book.

The concept of polygyny in Islam (a man having more than one wife) will be discussed further in the chapter '*Women and polygyny*'. Polygyny wasn't an uncommon practice among Arabs, especially with nobles and leaders in 7th

---

1. "Marriages of the Holy Prophet." Al-Islam.org. Accessed January 25, 2017. https://www.al-islam.org/life-muhammad-prophet-sayyid-saeed-akhtar-rizvi/marriages-holy-prophet.

2. "List of Muhammad's Wives and Concubines." WikiIslam. February 28, 2016. https://wikiislam.net/wiki/List_of_Muhammads_Wives_and_Concubines.

century Arabia. However in Islam polygyny is restricted to four wives for each Muslim man as long as he treats all his wives equally.

> Quran 4:3 – If you fear that you will not act justly towards the orphans, marry such women as seem good to you, two, three, four; but if you fear you will not be equitable, then only one, or what your right hands own; so it is likelier you will not be partial.

So how was Prophet Muhammad allowed to have more than four wives at the same time? Let's begin answering this question by starting with his first wife, Khadijah.

Muhammad married Khadijah when he was 25 years old, 15 years before his prophethood began. Khadijah was 40 years old, wealthy, and Muhammad's employer at the time. He stayed monogamous to her until she died 25 years later.[3] Then, from the age of 50 until his death 11-12 years later, Prophet Muhammad married another 10 women. This is a significant contrast for a man who had only one wife for 25 years. Only Prophet Muhammad's power, authority and perhaps fame could have allowed him to manage such a feat. But according to Islamic belief, there are four logical reasons Prophet Muhammad was allowed to have so many wives:

> 1. To help widows. Remarriage was difficult in a society which emphasized virgin marriages and many widows were without a provider as their husbands died in battle.
> 2. To create family bonds with significant Muslim families. Muhammad had family bonds with all the first four Caliphs. Muhammad married the daughters of Abu Bakr and Umar, while Uthman and Ali married Muhammad's daughters.
> 3. To spread his message of Islam by uniting different Arabian tribes through marriage. Creating such alliances met the larger needs of the Muslim community.
> 4. To ease his wives' responsibility of conveying his private acts of worship. It's suggested having several wives provided more opportunities for people to learn about Prophet Muhammad. The wives who lived with him and observed him could then teach others what they had learnt about him.[4]

3. Esposito, John L. Islam: The Straight Path. New York: Oxford Univ. Press, 1998.

4. Anwar Al-Awlaki. The Life of the Prophet Muhammad (Makkan Period). Enjoyislam.com. Accessed February 28, 2017. http://www.enjoyislam.com/lectures/AnwarAlAwlaki/ LifeOfMohammad.html. CD 5 - Important Events

Therefore we can speculate that Prophet Muhammad's marriages were based upon politics, compassion or maybe even love.

In a book for all the people of the world, God found the time to outline who one man may marry.

> Quran 33:50 – O Prophet, We have made lawful for thee thy wives whom thou hast given their wages and what thy right hand owns, spoils of war that God has given thee, and the daughters of thy uncles paternal and aunts paternal, thy uncles maternal and aunts maternal, who have emigrated with thee, and any woman believer, if she give herself to the Prophet and if the Prophet desire to take her in marriage, for thee exclusively, apart from the believers — We know what We have imposed upon them touching their wives and what their right hands own — that there may be no fault in thee; God is All-forgiving, All-compassionate.

In the Quran, God also regularly produced revelations which justified Prophet Muhammad's actions – his marriage to Zaynab bint Jahsh is an example of this. Zaynab was originally the wife of Zayd ibn Harithah. Zayd was an ex-slave whom Muhammad adopted as his own son. Pre-Islamic practices would have frowned upon Muhammad's marriage to Zaynab because an adopted son was seen as the same as one's actual blood-related son. So to marry your adopted son's ex-wife would have been wrong. It would have been seen as the equivalent of marrying your blood-related son's ex-wife.[5] However, a timely revelation appeared to clear up this matter. It stated that when adopted sons *'have accomplished what they would'* of their wives, then their adoptive fathers can marry their now ex-wife.

> Quran 33:37 – When thou saidst to him whom God had blessed and thou hadst favoured, 'Keep thy wife to thyself, and fear God,' and thou wast concealing within thyself what God should reveal, fearing other men; and God has better right for thee to fear Him. So when Zaid had accomplished what he would of her, then We gave her in marriage to thee, so that there should not be any fault in the believers, touching the wives of their adopted sons, when they have accomplished what they would of them; and God's commandment must be performed.

5. Watt, W. Montgomery. Muhammad: Prophet and Statesman. London: Oxford University Press, 1961.

This timely self-serving revelation appears to reflect Muhammad's desires rather than God's will. It even names 'Zaid' (Arberry's spelling of the name Zayd) *directly* in the holy Quran itself.

There are other prophets in Islam which aren't even named in the Quran, and there is only one women in the entire book mentioned by name: Mary, mother of Jesus. There is so much God hasn't clarified about the world and universe which would benefit everyone forever. Yet in the Quran Prophet Muhammad gets 'a pass from God' on someone he wants to marry and, just to make sure this was clear, Zaid himself is explicitly named.

This isn't the only instance of a revelation in the Quran favoring only Prophet Muhammad: here's an ayah which actually threatens Prophet Muhammad's wives if they're disobedient to him. It warns them by claiming God will give Prophet Muhammad a better wife in exchange for them if they are disobedient to the Prophet.

> Quran 66:5 – It is possible that, if he divorces you, his Lord will give him in exchange wives better than you, women who have surrendered, believing, obedient, penitent, devout, given to fasting, who have been married and virgins too.

Through the Quran, God also says the Prophet can treat his wives as he sees fit, putting off one or setting aside another should he so wish. This is in contrast to other Muslim men who are told to treat all their wives equally if they chose to marry more than one.

> Quran 33:51 – Thou mayest put off whom thou wilt of them, and whom thou wilt thou mayest take to thee; and if thou seekest any thou hast set aside there is no fault in thee. So it is likelier they will be comforted, and not sorrow, and every one of them will be well-pleased with what thou givest her. God knows what is in your hearts; God is All-knowing, All-clement.

But in case other Muslims were to question Prophet Muhammad's actions towards the women he chooses to marry, another self-serving revelation appears to let him know God says it's okay.

> Quran 66:1 – O Prophet, why forbiddest thou what God has made lawful to thee, seeking the good pleasure of thy wives? And God is All-forgiving, All-compassionate.

When the day comes that Prophet Muhammad passes away, it's made clear no one can remarry his wives as this would be seen as '*a monstrous thing*' in the eyes of God. There's no verse in the Quran to instruct Muslims on who succeeds the Prophet of Islam after his death, but there is a verse to tell all of humanity that no one is allowed to marry his wives after him.

> Quran 33:53 – O believers, enter not the houses of the Prophet, except leave is given you for a meal, without watching for its hour. But when you are invited, then enter; and when you have had the meal, disperse, neither lingering for idle talk; that is hurtful to the Prophet, and he is ashamed before you; but God is not ashamed before the truth. And when you ask his wives for any object, ask them from behind a curtain; that is cleaner for your hearts and theirs. It is not for you to hurt God's Messenger, neither to marry his wives after him, ever; surely that would be, in God's sight, a monstrous thing.

We can also see in *Quran 33:53* that if you are in the Prophet's house for a meal, you're told not to linger afterwards for any '*idle talk*'. Apparently the Prophet is too polite to say so, therefore God says it for him, and now Prophet Muhammad doesn't come across as rude.

With these revelations in mind, we can only hope that we're not coming across as rude when we ask if they're truly for the benefit of all humankind, or are just kind to one human.

21

Prophet Muhammad as a role model

"What we call 'morals' is simply blind obedience to words of command" – *Havelock Ellis*

Muhammad is not just a Prophet to Muslims, he is also the greatest human being to have ever walked the Earth. He's held as the ideal role model for all people. So much so that his sayings (Hadith) and practices (Sunnah) are followed by most Muslims. Though they're not in the Quran, Muslims follow Prophet Muhammad's example because God tells them to.

> Quran 4:80 – Whosoever obeys the Messenger, thereby obeys God; and whosoever turns his back – We have not sent thee to be a watcher over them.

According to God, Prophet Muhammad knows best regarding all matters of the Quran and Islam, which is why God also granted Prophet Muhammad the ability to create new laws.

> Quran 7:156-157 – And prescribe for us in this world good, and in the world to come; we have repented unto Thee.' Said He, 'My chastisement — I smite with it whom I will; and My mercy embraces all things, and I shall prescribe it for those who are godfearing and pay the alms, and those who indeed believe in Our signs, those who follow the Messenger, 'the Prophet of the common folk, whom they find written down with them in the Torah and the Gospel, bidding them to honour, and forbidding them dishonour, making lawful for them the good things and making unlawful for them the corrupt things, and relieving them of their loads, and the fetters that were upon them. Those who believe in him and succour him and help

him, and follow the light that has been sent down with him — they are the prosperers.'

As well as being the head of the Muslim community, Prophet Muhammad was also a military leader. Taking the context of the time into account, Prophet Muhammad's use of warfare wasn't unusual to Arab custom. Nor was it unusual in comparison to previous Abrahamic prophets, many of whom also believed God gave them permission to use violence and force to overcome opponents.

However during Islam's early years, Prophet Muhammad and all Muslims preached pacifism and tolerance. Muslims were few in numbers in comparison to other religions at the time and so didn't wield much influence. But as the Prophet's followers grew in number, their ability to spread the word of Islam became stronger. Years passed and Prophet Muhammad's ability to spread Islam through the manpower at his disposal grew more powerful, and a tolerance for non-Muslims began to decline.

This transition is seen in the Quran through God's own words. Islam was founded in Mecca; it was a time when Islam was nascent and largely unknown. The Meccan suras revealed were theological and pacifistic which made sense as no one knew anything about Islam or the Quran; there was no power to wield over pagans, theists and other Arabian tribes.

But by the time Prophet Muhammad and all Muslims migrated to Medina, the community was larger and more developed. This migration occurred 13 years into Muhammad's prophethood. During their time in Medina, the Muslim community grew further to no longer be in a minority position as they had been in Mecca. Medinan suras reflected this as they became more legislative than the previous Meccan suras, and they also began to express an aversion to non-Muslims (discussed in more detail in the chapter 'Non-Muslims').

Early in Muhammad's prophethood, the battles fought were seen as self-defense. But as Muhammad's prophethood progressed, battles began to be waged to consolidate his position and spread the word of Islam in Arabia. This ideology of spreading Islam has continued with some Muslims long after Prophet Muhammad's death.

Other religions have also been guilty of spreading their message through force and violence, but Islam is one of the few religions to have it laid out by God in His ideology and through His Prophet, the role model for all humankind.

Quran 9:33 – It is He who has sent His Messenger with the guidance and the religion of truth, that He may uplift it above every religion, though the unbelievers be averse.

Critics of Islam claim the ideological desire to spread it through non–Muslim countries still occurs today, and one of the motivations for Islamic terrorists is that they're attempting to emulate their Prophet's actions. However, it's only a minority of Muslims who are deciding to interpret his actions and the Quran as justification for militant action. The overwhelming majority of Muslims regard Islamic terrorists who kill innocent people as criminals. However, there must be something in Islam which provides this minority of Muslims the rationale to carry out terrorist acts. It isn't something we see from other modern day religions on the same global scale anymore (see chapter 'Terrorism').

The sources of Prophet Muhammad's character are mostly Islamic traditions from those who were close to him; there's no definitive source which defines him. But even if there was, not everyone would see him in the same way. Even today many see Prophet Muhammad as their role model, the Prophet of a religion of peace; while others see him as a dangerous historical figure, a charlatan and a warmonger. It all depends on which perspective he's viewed from. For example, when Alexander III of Macedon spread his empire 2,400 years ago, many people suffered and died. But 2,400 years was so long ago that it's difficult to appreciate the tragic element of those deaths. So much so that he's not known as Alexander III of Macedon anymore: he's Alexander the Great. He's been lauded for his achievements. Such is the subjective nature of remembering someone in the past: one person's liberator or freedom fighter, is another's oppressor or terrorist. There isn't a single person in history that everyone on Earth will agree was 'perfect'. There will never be a person that everyone agrees was 'good' or 'moral'. That's because these terms are vague and subjective for each individual human being; it all depends on their perspective. So when a man from 1,400 years ago is never to be questioned or challenged, it can lead to negative consequences in contemporary society. A clear example of this is Prophet Muhammad's marriage to Aisha.

Most Islamic scholars agree Aisha was 6 or 7 years old at the time of her marriage to Prophet Muhammad, with the marriage becoming consummated when she reached puberty at around 9 or 10 years of age.[1] So Prophet

---

1. Armstrong, Karen. Muhammad: A Biography of the Prophet. San Francisco: HarperSanFrancisco, 1993. See also Brown, Jonathan. Misquoting Muhammad: The Challenge and Choices of Interpreting the Prophet's Legacy. London: Oneworld, 2014. pp.143-44. See also Spellberg, Denise A. Politics, Gender and the Islamic Past: Legacy of A'isha Bint Abi Bakr. Columbia U.P., 1996.

Muhammad would have been around 53 years old when he consummated his marriage with his 10 year old wife.

Immediate reactions Muslims and other Islamic historians have to critics of this marriage is that it's taken out of context: marriages between older men and young girls were customary at this time in Arabia. So Prophet Muhammad marrying a prepubescent girl wasn't considered improper by his contemporaries, even if he was in his 50s.[2] In fact, the marriage of adults to minors wasn't a practice exclusive to Arabia, it's been common in many continents, cultures and civilizations throughout ancient times.[3]

This may be so, but there are still two issues here. First, that a man in his 50s would be sexually interested in a girl as young as 6 or 7 years old, and be sexually active with a girl as young as 9 or 10 years of age. These kinds of acts are not just perverse to us today, they're widely regarded as criminal acts and one of the worst things anyone can do to a child.

Which brings us to our second issue: that people can claim Prophet Muhammad with his ancient practices can always be a role model. This logically can't work due to constantly changing morals, societies and laws. Throughout human history every culture has had its own typical beliefs, norms and values, and these are always in flux. Cultures transform in response to changes in their environment, or by interactions with neighboring cultures.

The world has changed a lot since 7th century Arabia, and what may have been a suitable practice 1,400 years ago doesn't constitute a suitable practice now, and forever. But if Prophet Muhammad did it, then to dispute it would be to go against him and the word of God. This is inconceivable if you want to be a devout Muslim.

> Quran 33:36 – It is not for any believer, man or woman, when God and His Messenger have decreed a matter, to have the choice in the affair. Whosoever disobeys God and His Messenger has gone astray into manifest error.

But this issue really starts to take hold when governments enforce Sharia and base their laws solely on the Quran and the Hadith. This has resulted in many Islamic countries having no legal age of consent (only banning sexual relations which are outside of marriage) which has allowed child marriages to still occur with girls as young as 9 or 10 years old, like Aisha.

Muslim countries with marriage-based ages of consent include

---

2. Turner, Colin. Islam: The Basics. London: Routledge, 2011.

3. Armstrong, Karen. Muhammad: Prophet for Our Time. London: HarperPress, 2006. p.167.

Afghanistan, Iran, Kuwait, Libya, Maldives, Oman, Pakistan, Qatar, Sudan, Saudi Arabia, Yemen, and the UAE.[4] So these countries may never discard child marriages. If they did, it might imply they disagree with Prophet Muhammad's marriage to Aisha, and this would be un-Islamic.

A UNICEF report has also shown the top five countries in the world with highest observed child marriage rates, Niger (75%), Chad (72%), Mali (71%), Bangladesh (64%), Guinea (63%), are all Muslim majority countries.[5] All Muslim countries may ban sexual relations outside of marriage, but with puberty (the only age-based restriction for sexual intercourse), and parents' consent, child marriage is still permissible in some Muslim countries around the world. Naturally this has raised concerns with many international child welfare organisations. UNICEF has stated:

> "Justified as an accepted norm with social and financial benefits, child marriage has little or no benefit for the young girls themselves, who are more vulnerable to domestic violence, more likely to be uneducated, at greater risk of contracting HIV/AIDS, and more likely to bear children before they are physically ready."[6]

Child marriages also occur outside of Muslim countries, but it's likely that without the precedence set by Prophet Muhammad, the practice of child marriages would be less prevalent in the modern Islamic world. Particularly when Muslim majority countries like Saudi Arabia and Yemen have stopped attempts to reform laws banning child marriages on the basis that such a ban would be un-Islamic.[7] Or, when a Muslim majority country like Malaysia passes laws allowing the practice of child marriages between Muslims.[8]

4. "Highest and Lowest Ages of Consent." AgeOfConsent.net. Accessed November 21, 2016. https://www.ageofconsent.net/highest-and-lowest.

5. UNICEF. Media Centre. "In Mali, Child Marriage Is a Death Sentence for Many Young Girls." News release. Unicef.org. Accessed February 28, 2017. https://www.unicef.org/wcaro/english/media_5120.html.

6. UNICEF. Media Centre. "In Mali, Child Marriage Is a Death Sentence for Many Young Girls." News release. Unicef.org. Accessed February 28, 2017. https://www.unicef.org/wcaro/english/media_5120.html.

7. "Deep Divisions over Child Brides." IRIN, March 28, 2010. http://www.irinnews.org/feature/2010/03/28/deep-divisions-over-child-brides. See also "No Minimum Age for Marriage of Girls – Grand Mufti." Arabian Business, December 22, 2014. http://www.arabianbusiness.com/no-minimum-age-for-marriage-of-girls-grand-mufti-576044.html.

8. Barr, Heather, and Linda Lakhdhir. "Time to Ban Child Marriage in Malaysia." Human Rights Watch, April 29, 2016. https://www.hrw.org/news/2016/04/29/time-ban-child-marriage-malaysia.

The issue with Islam is that there's zero room for flexibility. But it doesn't have to be a question on Prophet Muhammad's morals or character, it can be a reflection on his acts which were culturally acceptable at the time and aren't anymore in contemporary society. Many religions are still facing the issue of trying to remain relevant in modern day society. It could be said that Christianity, to some extent, is attempting to carry a more flexible stance on certain issues. For example, the introduction of female priests and a more relaxed approach to homosexuality than those previously held. Unfortunately in Islam, these principles aren't open to discussion for most Muslims (see part 'The Modern World').

So Muslims can objectively and rationally assess which of Prophet Muhammad's sayings, habits or actions are worthy to uphold in contemporary society, and which have become outdated. Or, they can remain stubbornly resistant to change while the rest of the world looks on in concern.

PART V

The Prophets

Belief in the 25 prophets mentioned in the Quran is one of the six articles of Islamic faith. The other five are belief in God, the angels, the divine books, Judgment Day and God's predestination.

Prophets are those chosen by God to send His message to a people in a language they can understand. All the prophets in Islam have been men (despite half the population of the world at any time in human history being female). The Quran considers the men chosen as prophets to be the most virtuous of all human beings.

> Quran 4:69 – Whosoever obeys God, and the Messenger — they are with those whom God has blessed, Prophets, just men, martyrs, the righteous; good companions they!

Though only 25 prophets are named in the Quran, God says He sent many other prophets and messengers, who weren't mentioned by name, to every nation that existed on Earth.

> Quran 16:36 – Indeed, We sent forth among every nation a Messenger,; saying: 'Serve you God, and eschew idols.' Then some. of them God guided, and some were justly disposed to error. So journey in the land, and behold how was the end of them that cried lies.

> Quran 40:78 – We sent Messengers before thee; of some We have related to thee, and some We have not related to thee. It was not for any Messenger to bring a sign, save by God's leave. When God's command comes, justly the issue shall be decided; then the vain-doers shall be lost.

Not every prophet began to prophesy from birth: some were from the cradle such as Jesus, some were as a child like John the Baptist, and others were later in adulthood such as Muhammad.

Many prophets mentioned in the Jewish and Christian scriptures reappear in the Quran. For example, Adam is the first human being in Christianity and the first prophet in Islam as well. The Quran's stories of the prophets vary from those told in Judaism and Christianity. The prophets are also described with Arabic names in the Quran, Noah is Nuh, Abraham is Ibrahim, Moses is Musa, and Jesus is Isa to name a few. However we shall continue to use the English names throughout.

Muslims believe all prophets in Islam, even Adam, Moses and Jesus, are all Muslims. This is due to the definition of the word Muslim: one who submits to God's will. Muslims believe all prophets are Muslims themselves because they all taught the same message of the Oneness of God and the Day of Judgement. Muslims believe Muhammad is the last of all the prophets and it is he who has delivered God's final message.

Since we've discussed Prophet Muhammad in a separate part, this part will look at the other five prominent prophets in Islam, from Adam to Noah, Abraham, Moses and finally Jesus. The accounts of each of these prophets are all detailed in the Quran throughout various suras. This part will be analyzing the legitimacy of each of the prophet's stories.

I must repeat once more that I don't believe in the stories of the prophets in the Quran, but Muslims must literally believe they occurred, and the majority do, since they believe the Quran is *the* word of God. Some Muslims may choose to read the stories as solely metaphorical or allegorical as opposed to literal, but there's no indication of this instruction in the Quran or from Prophet Muhammad. So since the Quran repeatedly states belief in the prophets is essential, Muslims have no choice but to take the literal word of what God says about them in the Quran.

Therefore I will base my arguments on what is in the Quran because all Muslims must believe the Quran to be true. If they do not believe the stories of the prophets in the Quran are true, then the validity and integrity of what else the Quran says diminishes as a result.

22

Adam

"God is Perfect: Perfect beings do not experience anger or surprise towards a sequence of events they knew of in advance" – John Kelly Ireland

According to the Quran, the story of the first prophet of Islam is also the account of how all humans came into existence on Earth. We'll look at the origins of the universe and evolution later in the part *'Science in Islam'*, where we'll discuss the empirical scientific evidence which conflicts with the Abrahamic account of human origin. But for now, let's focus on the Quran's story of Adam.

The Quran tells Adam's story many times, although this is not surprising as repetition is a familiar pattern in the Quran. In one account, we're told God made him from dust when He just said *'Be'* and then Adam was there.

> Quran 3:59 – Truly, the likeness of Jesus, in God's sight, is as Adam's likeness; He created him of dust, then said He unto him, 'Be,' and he was.

Yet in another account, God says he makes Adam from clay, not dust.

> Quran 17:61 – And when We said to the angels, 'Bow yourselves to Adam'; so they bowed themselves, save Iblis; he said,, 'Shall I bow myself unto one Thou hast created of clay?'

In the 'clay' account, when God created Adam he asked the angels to bow down to His creation. They all did except Iblis/Shaytan (the Devil/Satan), so God asks Satan why he didn't bow down to Adam. Satan says he refuses to bow down to Adam who is made of clay, when he is superior as he's made of fire.

> Quran 7:11-12 – We created you, then We shaped you, then We said to the angels: 'Bow yourselves to Adam'; so they bowed

themselves, save Iblis — he was not of those that bowed themselves. Said He, 'What prevented thee to bow thyself, when I commanded thee?' Said he, 'I am better than he; Thou createdst me of fire, and him Thou createdst of clay.'

God didn't need to ask Satan this question since God already knows everything. Nonetheless God did ask and He was unhappy with Satan's disobedience. So God cast Satan out of Heaven. Satan, now more upset, told God he'd do everything he can to misguide humankind until the Day of Judgement; thus proving humankind's inferiority and justifying his act of defiance towards God. For some reason, God gave Satan permission to do this.

> Quran 7:13-18 – Said He, 'Get thee down out of it; it is not for thee to wax proud here, so go thou forth; surely thou art among the humbled.' Said he, 'Respite me till the day they shall be raised.' Said He, 'Thou art among the ones that are respited.' Said he, 'Now, for Thy perverting me, I shall surely sit in ambush for them on Thy straight path; then I shall come on them from before them and from behind them, from their right hands and their left hands; Thou wilt not find most of them thankful.' Said He, 'Go thou forth from it, despised and banished. Those of them that follow thee — I shall assuredly fill Gehenna with all of you.'

God then gives Adam a 'wife' to be with (she is not named in the Quran as Eve but is generally believed by Muslims to be called Eve). God later puts Adam and Eve into the Garden of Paradise and tells them they're free to enjoy it. But God tells them they're not to eat from the fruits of a particular tree. However Satan tricks Adam and Eve into tasting the fruit of the forbidden tree (even though Satan had been cast out of Paradise, he managed to get back in behind an omnipotent God's back). Taking no responsibility Himself, God punishes Adam and Eve (humans which He made fallible in the first place) for disobeying Him by casting them out from Paradise and onto Earth.

> Quran 7:19-25 – 'O Adam, inherit, thou and thy wife, the Garden, and eat of where you will, but come not nigh this tree, lest you be of the evildoers.' Then Satan whispered to them, to reveal to them that which was hidden from them of their shameful parts. He said, 'Your Lord has only prohibited you from this tree lest you become angels, or lest you become immortals.' And he swore to them, 'Truly, I am for you a sincere adviser.' So he led them on by delusion; and when

they tasted the tree, their shameful parts revealed to them, so they took to stitching upon themselves leaves of the Garden. And their Lord called to them, 'Did not I prohibit you from this tree, and say to you, "Verily Satan is for you a manifest foe"?' They said, 'Lord, we have wronged ourselves, and if Thou dost not forgive us, and have mercy upon us, we shall surely be among the lost.' Said He, 'Get you down, each of you an enemy to each. In the earth a sojourn shall be yours, and enjoyment for a time.' Said He, 'Therein you shall live, and therein you shall die, and from there you shall be brought forth.'

God then leaves a warning to us, the '*Children of Adam*', by warning us not to be tempted by Satan again just like our 'parents' Adam and Eve were.

> Quran 7:26-27 – Children of Adam! We have sent down on you a garment to cover your shameful parts, and feathers; and the garment of godfearing — that is better; that is one of God's signs; haply they will remember. Children of Adam! Let not Satan tempt you as he brought your parents out of the Garden, stripping them of their garments to show them their shameful parts. Surely he sees you, he and his tribe, from where you see them not. We have made the Satans the friends of those who do not believe.

It's peculiar this situation arose in the first place as why would God want His angels to bow down to Adam? God has always preached His Oneness and that there should be no worshiping of anything else but Him.

> Quran 4:48 – God forgives not that aught should be with Him associated; less than that He forgives to whomsoever He will. Whoso associates with God anything, has indeed forged a mighty sin.

Yet God asks the angels to bow down to Adam, as if it's Adam who they are submissive to and should be obedient towards. It's also odd why someone like Satan would even be in Paradise in the first place since God would have known what Satan can do and would do. Having human emotions of surprise and anger is the opposite of a God-like reaction to these series of events. God may be perfect, but it appears He has created a world and humans in it which causes Him nothing but frustration and anger. How can something God-like be continually surprised, disappointed and proven wrong with how things have worked out with his prophets? Surely a god only needs one attempt to get everything right?

In addition, Satan's incentive to Adam and Eve to eat from the forbidden tree is that they'll become like the angels, or immortal (*Quran 7:19-25*). But as we've already read, it's the angels who bow down to Adam. So in God's eyes, Adam and humans are more favored than the angels. Therefore it's illogical Adam would want to 'downgrade' to an angel, even if they are immortal, if God favors humans more. God even reinforces the point that Adam is superior to them, and that God knows things about Adam the angels do not.

> Quran 2:30-34 – And when thy Lord said to the angels, 'I am setting in the earth a viceroy. 'They said, 'What, wilt Thou set therein one who will do corruption there, and shed blood, while We proclaim Thy praise and call Thee Holy?' He said, 'Assuredly I know that you know not.' And He taught Adam the names, all of them; then He presented them unto the angels and said, 'Now tell Me the names of these, if you speak truly.' They said, 'Glory be to Thee! We know not save what Thou hast taught us. Surely Thou art the All-knowing, the All-wise.' He said, 'Adam, tell them their names.' And when he had told them their names He said, 'Did I not tell you I know the unseen things of the heavens and earth? And I know what things you reveal, and what you were hiding.' And when We said to the angels, 'Bow yourselves to Adam'; so they bowed themselves, save Iblis; he refused,and waxed proud, and so he became one of the unbelievers.

With all the inconsistencies in Prophet Adam's story, it's important to ask, do we truly believe this is how human beings came into existence on this planet? That we all came from a clay man (or a dust man, it's unclear), and that this man lived in Paradise with his 'wife' before being banished to Earth for eating from a tree, and from there the entire species of Homo sapiens evolved?

> Quran 4:1 – Mankind, fear your Lord, who created you of a single soul, and from it created its mate, and from the pair of them scattered abroad many men and women; and fear God by whom you demand one of another, and the wombs; surely God ever watches over you.

The importance of Prophet Adam's story is self-evident by the number of times it is repeated in the Quran. It's not meant to be a symbolic story. Therefore if Muslims have any doubts regarding the authenticity of Prophet Adam's story, then why believe any other prophets' stories, or why believe anything else the Quran says?

23

Noah

"It's 90 degrees in the shade in Jerusalem. Where did Noah get two penguins and two polar bears from?" – Sir David Stevens

Many of the stories religions tell have been told for thousands of years by previous civilizations. Religions have grown and evolved with each other throughout history, leading to some religions borrowing myths from each other, and some religions adopting and sharing customs with each other. For example, flood myths are some of the most popular stories told throughout human history, pre-dating Islam, Christianity and Judaism. This is likely where the Abrahamic religions got their inspiration from, rather than any divine source.[1]

An example of the earliest flood myth comes from the Epic of Gilgamesh, an epic poem from ancient Mesopotamia written around 2100 BCE.[2] It contains a story about a great flood and a hero (called Utnapishtim) who saved his family and many animals by putting them in a large boat.[3]

Another flood myth is in an epic Akkadian tradition written around 1600 BCE. It contains a story about a great flood and a hero (called Atra-Hasis) who saved his family and many animals by putting them in a large boat.[4]

Yet another flood myth is in the ancient Hindu text the Shatapatha Brahmana written around 700 BCE.[5] It contains a story about a great flood and

1. Cline, Eric H. From Eden to Exile: Unraveling Mysteries of the Bible. Washington, D.C.: National Geographic, 2007.

2. Dalley, Stephanie. Myths from Mesopotamia: Creation, the Flood, Gilgamesh, and Others. Oxford: Oxford University Press, 2008.

3. Rosenberg, Donna. World Mythology: An Anthology of the Great Myths and Epics. Lincolnwood, IL: NTC Pub. Group, 1994. pp.196-200.

4. Finkelstein, J. J., W. G. Lambert, and A. R. Millard. "Atra-Hasis: The Babylonian Story of the Flood." Journal of Biblical Literature 88, no. 4 (1969): 477. doi:10.2307/3263801.

5. Bremmer, Jan N. The Strange World of Human Sacrifice. Leuven: Peeters, 2007. p.158.

a hero (called Manu) who saved his family and many animals by putting them in a large boat.[6]

So since the flood myth was such a popular story to share, the Abrahamic religions also have their own version. In the Quran, Noah is a prophet tasked with saving wicked people who were plunging into sin. God wanted Noah to preach to his people to make them abandon idolatry and worship only Him. Noah preached God's message with great effort, but he couldn't convince his people to change their ways.

> Quran 7:59-63 – And We sent Noah to his people; and he said, 'O my people, serve God! You have no god other' than He; truly, I fear for you the chastisement of a dreadful day.' Said the Council of his people, 'We see thee in manifest error.' Said he, 'My people, there is no error in me; but I am a Messenger from the Lord of all Being.' I deliver to you the Messages of my Lord, and I advise you sincerely; for I know from God that you know not. What, do you wonder that a reminder from your Lord should come to you by the lips of a man from among you? That he may warn you, and you be godfearing, haply to find mercy.'

So God told Noah not to concern himself with preaching to his people anymore as no one else was going to listen to his message who hadn't already submitted to Him. As a result, God decided the best thing to do is to get Noah to build a colossal boat, an ark, so God can drown all the nonbelievers while the believers were safe from the flood in their ark.

> Quran 11:36-39 – And it was revealed to Noah, saying, 'None of thy people shall believe but he who has already believed; so be thou not distressed by that they may be doing. Make thou the Ark under Our eyes, and as We reveal; and address Me not concerning those who have done evil; they shall be drowned.' So he was making the Ark; and whenever a council of his people passed by him they scoffed at him, He said, 'If you scoff at us, we shall surely scoff at you, as you scoff and you shall know to whom will come a chastisement degrading him, and upon whom there shall alight a lasting chastisement.'

---

6. Klostermaier, Klaus. A Survey of Hinduism. Albany, NY: State University of New York Press, 2007. p.97.

From the Quran's account of events, it seems the nonbelievers didn't have much of a reason to believe Noah, they only had his word. People had a right to be skeptical as many men in ancient times claimed they had a divine power or had spoken to one. Not all these men could be telling the truth, so people had to be wary to distinguish between those who are lying and those who they believed were telling the truth. God could have easily proven to all the people that Noah was telling the truth or that He existed. But instead God decided to kill them, all because they didn't believe in Him when they weren't given a valid reason to do so in the first place.

> Quran 23:23-28 – And We sent Noah to his people; and he, said, 'O my people, serve God! You have no god other than He. Will you not be godfearing?" Said the Council of the unbelievers of his people, 'This is naught but a mortal like yourselves, who desires to gain superiority over you. And if God willed, He would have sent down angels. We never heard of this among, our fathers, the ancients. He is naught but a man bedevilled; so wait on him for a time. He said, 'O my Lord, help me, for that they cry me lies.' Then We said to him, 'Make thou the Ark under Our eyes and as We reveal, and then, when Our command comes and the Oven boils, insert in it two of every kind and thy, family — except for him against whom the word already has been spoken; and address Me not concerning those who have done evil; they shall be drowned. Then, when thou art seated in the Ark and those with thee, say, "Praise belongs to God, who has delivered us from the people of the evildoers."

As the Quran states, Noah built the ark with the capability of holding two of every kind (of animal) and his own family. God saves all the animals in the ark and Noah's family, all except one of Noah's sons who believed he could survive the flood by going to the top of a mountain.

> Quran 11:40-47 – Until, when Our command came, and the Oven boiled, We said, 'Embark in it two of every kind, and thy family — except for him against whom the word has already been spoken and whosoever believes.' And there believed not with him except a few. He said, 'Embark in it! In God's Name shall be its course and its berthing. Surely my Lord is All-forgiving, All-compassionate.' So it ran with them amid waves like mountains; and Noah called to his son, who was standing apart, 'Embark with us, my son, and be thou not with the unbelievers!' He said, 'I will take refuge in a

mountain, that shall defend me from the water.' Said he, 'Today there is no defender from God's command but for him on whom He has mercy.' And the waves came between them, and he was among the drowned. And it was said, 'Earth, swallow thy waters; and, heaven, abate!' And the waters subsided, the affair was accomplished, and the Ark settled on El-Judi, and it was said: 'Away with the people of the evildoers!' And Noah called unto his Lord, and said, 'O my Lord, my son is of my family, and Thy promise is surely the truth. Thou art the justest of those that judge.' Said He, 'Noah, he is not of thy family; it is a deed not righteous. Do not ask of Me that whereof thou hast no knowledge. I admonish thee, lest thou shouldst be among the ignorant.' He said, 'My Lord, I take refuge with Thee, lest I should ask of Thee that whereof I have no knowledge; for if Thou forgivest me not, and hast not mercy on me, I shall be among the losers.'

After the flood, Noah began preaching again. Presumably it went better than before as God had actually shown some proof of his existence to Noah's people (if any survived to witness God's existence). God must also have been delighted with Noah as his prophet since He let Noah live to be 950 years old.

Quran 29:14 – Indeed, We sent Noah to his people, and he tarried among them a thousand years, all but fifty; so the Flood seized them, while they were evildoers.

Stories can live long before and long after the people, languages and civilizations that shared them. As time passes, it can become more difficult to distinguish between what's myth and what's reality. For Prophet Noah, his story in the Quran is one which has already been told for thousands of years. Taking all this (and the likelihood of a man building a boat large enough to hold two of every animal and living to be 950 years old) into account, there's little to suggest any of Noah's story in the Quran is either original or true. Which is why instead of the religious reflecting upon their stories to fit reality, they change reality to fit their stories.

24

Abraham

"The most dangerous aspect of religion is its tendency to glorify the absurd and justify the abhorrent" – Stifyn Emrys

Abraham is an important prophet in Islam, Christianity and Judaism. He's seen as a prominent example of being faithful and devout to God. Abraham played an important role for Muslims as they believe he set up and reformed the Kaaba in Mecca.

> Quran 2:127-128 – And when Abraham, and Ishmael with him, raised up the foundations of the House: 'Our Lord, receive this from us; Thou art the All-hearing, the All-knowing; and, our Lord, make us submissive to Thee, and of our seed a nation submissive to Thee; and show us our holy rites, and turn towards us; surely Thou turnest, and art All-compassionate;

Furthermore, an important day in the Islamic calendar, Eid al-Adha (the Festival of the Sacrifice), is celebrated every year by Muslims to commemorate Abraham's willingness to sacrifice his son for God. Muslims slaughter an animal to eat in God's name, just as Abraham did. The story of this willingness to self-sacrifice is a reminder to Muslims of the importance of obedience to God.

In the Quran, Abraham has a dream and in it God tells him to sacrifice his son Ishmael. So Abraham tells his son Ishmael what he dreamt and asks him what he thinks of it. Ishmael responds to his father by telling him he's willing to be sacrificed, if that's what God desires. Abraham is about to kill his son for God, but God intervenes. God tells Abraham he doesn't need to sacrifice his son anymore, he has passed the test and proven his obedience to Him. There's no mention in the Quran of Abraham's son being replaced with an animal, only '*a mighty sacrifice*'. The name of Abraham's son is also not given, but it's presumed to be Ishmael as the ayahs following mention the birth of Abraham's other son, Isaac.

> Quran 37:100-112 – My Lord, give me one of the righteous.' Then We gave him the good tidings of a prudent boy; and when he had reached the age of running with him, he said, 'My son, I see in a dream that I shall sacrifice thee; consider, what thinkest thou?' He said, 'My father, do as thou art bidden; thou shalt find me, God willing, one of the steadfast.' When they had surrendered, and he flung him upon his brow, We called unto him, 'Abraham, thou hast confirmed the vision; even so We recompense the good-doers. This is indeed the manifest trial.' And We ransomed him with a mighty sacrifice, and left for him among the later folk 'Peace be upon Abraham!' Even so We recompense the good-doers; he was among Our believing servants. Then We gave him the good tidings of Isaac, a Prophet, one of the righteous.

Abraham is seen as the first prophet to be asked to make the ultimate sacrifice for God. Abraham passed God's test because he had the will to sacrifice his own son at God's command. It's this willingness to self-sacrifice which demonstrated Abraham's devotion and submission to God.

Muslims speak to God everyday and ask Him for many things. Some Muslims may say God speaks back to them, God has done things for them, or they've had signs which indicate what God wanted them to do. So what if someone dreamt God spoke to them, and He asked them to do something which proved their obedience to Him, perhaps something dangerous that affected other people's lives? After all, this is what happened to Abraham. What if the celebrated story of Abraham's willingness to sacrifice his son for God sets a precedent for Muslims, Christians and Jews? What if killing someone is not forbidden (haram in Arabic) if it's for the benefit of God since He asked them to do so?

It's curious why the willingness to murder your innocent child is admired by Muslims, Christians and Jews, especially since this request only occurred to Abraham in a dream. Other believers may have dreams in which they think they've been told by God to kill their children, does that make it justified if they do? How can we prove God didn't speak to them when the believers say He did? There have been mothers who have murdered their children because God told them to do it.[1] It's a story that has occurred enough times to prompt

Huffington Post to have a 'God Told Me to Do It' news sub-section on their website.[2]

Though God commanded Abraham to prove his obedience and he did, the ends don't justify the means. In the cold light of day, it's a cruel trick to play on a father and his child, particularly by a God supposed to be benevolent. Why God needs the satisfaction of pushing a parent to the edge of murdering his son is unknown, but it's sadistic. These acts don't appear to be the qualities of a fair-minded and compassionate God, but rather an insecure and troubled God. Yet every year Muslims celebrate Eid al-Adha; and the trauma God put Abraham through.

1. "Mom Who Said She Killed on God's Orders Acquitted." CNN, April 3, 2004. http://edition.cnn.com/2004/LAW/04/03/children.slain/.

2. "God Told Me to Do It." The Huffington Post. Accessed January 25, 2017. http://www.huffingtonpost.com/news/god-told-me-to-do-it/.

25

Moses

"People everywhere enjoy believing things that they know are not true. It spares them the ordeal of thinking for themselves and taking responsibility for what they know" –
Brooks Atkinson

Within Islamic tradition Moses is particularly revered by God. This is because God spoke with Moses directly, rather than through an angel as He had done with many other prophets. Moses is also recognized within Islam as having received the revelation of the Torah, although this is not explicitly stated in the Quran.

> Quran 6:154 – Then We gave Moses the Book, complete for him who does good, and distinguishing every thing, and as a guidance and a mercy; haply they would believe in the encounter with their Lord.

In Islam, the Torah is considered to be one of the holy revealed scriptures, repeating and confirming what's within the Quran. However Muslims don't see Moses as a prophet who introduced a new religion, but a prophet who taught and practiced the religion of his predecessors, confirming the prophets and scriptures that came before him while preaching the Oneness of God. Just like Prophet Muhammad, Prophet Moses was also a military leader, lawmaker and the head of his community.

Moses' importance is self-evident within the Quran: he's the most mentioned person in the holy book. But as is customary with the Quran, it's often the same narratives repeated, with little new information added to each retelling. One can't help but feel God could have put forward more useful information in the Quran, rather than the same story retold several times.

Most of Moses' stories in the Quran involve a supernatural element, with none supported by any evidence of having occurred. A well known story of the

Abrahamic religions is Moses' time in ancient Egypt. It was there he grew into a prophet and performed and witnessed miracles: the Burning Bush (Biblical name) and turning his staff into a snake.

> Quran 28:29-32 – So when Moses had accomplished the term and departed with his household, he observed on the side of the Mount a fire. He said to his household, 'Tarry you here; I observe a fire. Perhaps I shall bring you news of it, or a faggot from the fire, that haply you shall warm yourselves.' When he came to it, a voice cried from the right of the watercourse, in the sacred hollow, coming from the tree: 'Moses, I am God, the Lord of all Being.' 'Cast down thy staff.' And when he saw it quivering like a serpent, he turned about retreating, and turned not back. 'Moses, come forward, and fear not; for surely thou art in security.' Insert thy hand into thy bosom, and it will come forth white without evil; and press to thee thy arm, that thou be not afraid. So these shall be two proofs from thy Lord to Pharaoh and his Council; for surely they are an ungodly people.'

Bringing forth the 'Plagues of Egypt' to the Pharaoh's people.

> Quran 7:130-133 – Then seized We Pharaoh's people with years of dearth, and scarcity of fruits, that haply they might remember. So, when good came to them, they said, 'This belongs to us'; but if any evil smote them, they would augur ill by Moses and those with him. Why, surely their ill augury was with God; but the most of them knew not. And they said, 'Whatsoever sign thou bringest to us, to cast a spell upon us, we will not believe thee.' So We let loose upon them the flood and the locusts, the lice and the frogs, the blood, distinct signs; but they waxed proud and were a sinful people.

Parting a sea (generally acknowledged to have been the Red Sea).

> Quran 26:60-67 – Then they followed them at the sunrise; and, when the two hosts sighted each other, the companions of Moses said, 'We are overtaken!' Said he, 'No indeed; surely my Lord is with me; He will guide me.' Then We revealed to Moses, 'Strike with thy staff the sea'; and it clave, and each part was as a mighty mount. And there We brought the others on, and We delivered Moses and those with him all together; then We drowned the others. Surely in that is a sign, yet most of them are not believers.

Finally, introducing the Ten Commandments (Biblical name).

> Quran 7:144-145 – Said He, 'Moses, I have chosen thee above all
> men for My Messages and My Utterance; take what I have given
> thee, and be of the thankful.' And We wrote for him on the Tablets
> of everything an admonition, and a distinguishing of everything: 'So
> take it forcefully, and command thy people to take the fairest of it. I
> shall show you the habitation of the ungodly.

Many of us are familiar with this story from our childhood, but we may have
never actually taken the time to consider the plausibility of them. The only
supporting evidence for these claims are a collection of writings in ancient
books. No doubt they're engaging and memorable stories which have been told
for thousands of years, but it doesn't necessarily mean they happened.

Too often we blindly accept these stories as a part of our religion without
seriously considering their legitimacy. I know this is true because I was one of
those people. I practiced my faith, but did so on autopilot, preoccupied with
what had happened in the past and what will happen in the future after death,
without consciously considering why I believe what I believe in the present.

This isn't a surprise as people who have been raised in a religious household
as I was often hear or learn the same things passed on for generations in families.
It manifests into what's known as the Illusory Truth Effect: the tendency
to believe information is correct after consistently repeated exposure. This
can turn a religious home into an echo chamber: a place where different or
competing views are censored or underrepresented. Therefore religious stories
are not as rigorously questioned as they ought to be. We all believe we have
many more pressing matters in our lives to concern ourselves with. But, what's
more important than deciding how we choose to live our lives, what we choose
to believe about our world, and what we choose to base all the decisions of our
lives upon?

While his adventures in Egypt is a well known story of Moses', there's another
in the Quran less commonly told. Sura 18 al-Kahf (The Cave) contains a story
of Prophet Moses and an unidentified figure. In Hadith the unidentified figure
is named as Khidr, so we'll use this name as opposed to 'unidentified figure'.[1]

Khidr is a man so knowledgeable that God instructs Moses to learn from
him (even though Khidr is not identified as a prophet in the Quran, only one

1. Wheeler, Brannon M. Moses in the Quran and Islamic Exegesis. London: Routledge, 2009.

of God's servants). Upon meeting Khidr, Moses asks if he can accompany him so he can learn directly from him. Khidr agrees but on one stipulation: Moses doesn't question his actions until Khidr wishes to explain himself.

> Quran 18:65-70 – Then they found one of Our servants unto whom We had given mercy from Us, and We had taught him knowledge proceeding from Us. Moses said to him, 'Shall I follow thee so that thou teachest me, of what thou hast been taught, right judgment.' Said he, 'Assuredly thou wilt not be able to bear with me patiently. And how shouldst thou bear patiently that thou hast never encompassed in thy knowledge?' He said, 'Yet thou shalt find me, if God will, patient; and I shall not rebel against thee in anything.' Said he, 'Then if thou followest me, question me not on anything until I myself introduce the mention of it to thee.'

Khidr then goes on to do what appears to be three strange things: he sinks a boat, kills a child, and fixes a wall for free in a city where he and Moses were treated with hostility. After each of the three actions, Moses can't help but ask Khidr why he did them.

> Quran 18:71-77 – So they departed; until, when they embarked upon the ship, he made a hole in it. He said, 'What, hast thou made a hole in it so as to drown its passengers? Thou hast indeed done a grievous thing.' Said he, 'Did I not say that thou couldst never bear with me patiently?' He said, 'Do not take me to task that I forgot, neither constrain me to do a thing too difficult.' So they departed; until, when they met a lad, he slew him. He said, 'What, hast thou slain a soul innocent, and that not to retaliate for a soul slain? Thou hast indeed done a horrible thing.' Said he, 'Did I not say that thou couldst never bear with me patiently?' He said, 'If I question thee on anything after this, then keep me company no more; thou hast already experienced excuse sufficient on my part.' So they departed; until, when they reached the people of a city, they asked the people for food, but they refused to receive them hospitably. There they found a wall about to tumble down, and so he set it up. He said, 'If thou hadst wished, thou couldst have taken a wage for that.'

Khidr decides to part with Moses since Moses has broken their agreement of not questioning his actions. But before Khidr leaves, he explains himself. The boat belonged to poor people and had it been operational, a King would have stolen it further down the water. The child was killed because he was a non-believer who may cause his devout parents a lot of grief in the future. So it was better to kill him, and as a replacement, God will provide the parents with a purer son with better conduct. As for the wall, he built it because it is covering a hidden treasure and two orphan boys will find this treasure later in life.

> Quran 18:78-82 – Said he, 'This is the parting between me and thee. Now I will tell thee the interpretation of that thou couldst not bear patiently. As for the ship, it belonged to certain poor men, who toiled upon the sea; and I desired to damage it, for behind them there was a king who was seizing every ship by brutal force. As for the lad, his parents were believers; and we were afraid he would impose on them insolence and unbelief; so we desired that their Lord should give to them in exchange one better than he in purity, and nearer in tenderness. As for the wall, it belonged to two orphan lads in the city, and under it was a treasure belonging to them. Their father was a righteous man; and thy Lord desired that they should come of age and then bring forth their treasure as a mercy from thy Lord. I did it not of my own bidding. This is the interpretation of that thou couldst not bear patiently.'

Let's now consider the morals this story from the holy Quran imparts. Khidr was a man so knowledgeable that he was effectively able to to see into the future. God Himself holds Khidr in such high regard that he asks one of his most favored prophets to spend time with him.

Regarding the second of the acts, the murdered boy, Khidr states in the Quran 'we were afraid he [the boy] would impose on them [the parents] insolence and unbelief'. So the child hadn't done anything wrong yet, but he may in the future cause his parents grief. The wise and revered Khidr decides it is best to kill this disobedient child now, rather than give him the opportunity to learn and become a devout believer. In return, God will exchange this child with a better one for the parents. This is the reward for killing a mischievous boy.

We're already aware God doesn't appear to have any issues with innocent children being murdered. Ishmael, the son of Abraham, was going to be sacrificed to please God (see chapter 'Abraham'), but this time a child has actually been killed. It's odd because God made this child, and yet He has him killed as he's a 'faulty model' so to speak. God then decides it's best to replace this faulty model He made with a better one for the parents.

This troubling story of Prophet Moses and Khidr could be interpreted as an example of an honor killing in the Quran. Honor killings are acts still committed in small pockets of a few Muslim countries. An honor killing, or shame killing, is the murder of a family member by another member of that family. It's often male family members or community individuals targeting and attacking women. This is due to the murderer's belief that the victim has brought, or will bring, shame and dishonor to the family, community or Islam. This shame or dishonor could be delivered in many ways: being in a relationship disapproved of by the family, having premarital sex, refusing to enter an arranged marriage, dressing and behaving inappropriately, engaging in homosexual activities, renouncing Islamic faith, and even by becoming the *victim* of rape.

An example of a honor killing occurred in July 2016 when 26 year old Pakistani Qandeel Baloch (real name Fauzia Azeem) was strangled to death by her brother as she slept in their family home in Multan, Pakistan. This was a high profile honor killing as Ms Baloch was a 'social media celebrity' in Pakistan with a large number of followers on her Facebook, Twitter and YouTube accounts. She was a controversial figure in Pakistan as her divisive and provocative publicity stunts conflicted with the country's conservative values, making her a target of misogynistic abuse and threats. Ms Baloch had previously written to Pakistani security officials requesting protection as she'd received threatening phone calls and had her personal details posted online, including a scanned copy of her passport. Ms Baloch was popular among many young Pakistanis for her refusal to censor her behavior, and just hours before her death she wrote on Facebook:

> "I believe I am a modern day feminist. I believe in equality...I am just a women [sic] with free thoughts, free mindset and I love the way I am."

Her death sparked an outpouring of grief and rage, reigniting the debate about honor killings in Pakistan.[2]

However, the acts Ms Baloch carried out are only interpreted by a minority of Muslims as worthy of a fatal punishment. It's important to note that this behavior has not received approval from any Islamic scholar, either in the medieval or modern era.[3] Muslim organizations and Muslims themselves regularly condemn honor killings and view them as an un-Islamic practice.[4]

2. Marszal, Andrew. "Pakistani Social Media Star 'murdered by Her Brother' in Apparent Honour Killing." The Telegraph, July 16, 2016. http://www.telegraph.co.uk/news/2016/07/16/pakistani-social-media-star-murdered-by-her-brother-in-apparent/.

Yet, although this practice occurs worldwide, and it's argued it comes from cultural not religious origins, most honor killings in the world are Muslim-on-Muslim. Sikhs and Hindus do sometimes commit such murders, but a study in 2010 has shown that 91% of the perpetrators worldwide from 1989-2009 were Muslims.[5]

Khidr wasn't a family member of the boy he murdered, but Khidr was a member of the Islamic community, and he was acting in what he believed were the best interests of the boy's parents. His actions are also supported by God, who sent Moses to him to learn from. Unfortunately the story God tells in the Quran about Moses and Khidr may have set a dangerous precedent: promoting an unhealthy mindset among Muslims and giving them license to act with disregard for human life. In spite of what God and the Quran believes about Khidr, these are not the wise morals we must all adopt.

3. Brown, Jonathan. Misquoting Muhammad: The Challenge and Choices of Interpreting the Prophet's Legacy. London: Oneworld, 2014. p.180.

4. Esposito, John L. What Everyone Needs to Know about Islam. Oxford: Oxford University Press, 2011. p.177.

5. Chesler, Phyllis. "Worldwide Trends in Honor Killings." Middle East Quarterly 17, no. 2 (Spring 2010): 3-11. http://www.meforum.org/2646/worldwide-trends-in-honor-killings.

26

Jesus

*"No miracle has ever taken place under conditions which science can accept.
Experience shows, without exception, that miracles occur only in times and in
countries in which miracles are believed in, and in the presence of persons who are
disposed to believe in them"* – Ernest Renan

Muslims believe God revealed a new scripture, the Gospel, to Jesus, and the
Gospel validated the Torah, previously revealed to Moses.

> Quran 5:46 – And We sent, following in their footsteps, Jesus son
> of Mary, confirming the Torah before him and We gave to him the
> Gospel, wherein is guidance and light, and confirming the Torah
> before it, as a guidance and an admonition unto the godfearing.

Muslims also don't believe Jesus (Isa in Arabic) was the Son of God as Christians
do, nor do Muslims believe Jesus is the Lord. Muslims believe there can only be
one Lord and that is God Himself.

> Quran 5:17 – They are unbelievers who say, 'God is the Messiah,
> Mary's son.' Say: 'Who then shall overrule God in any way if He
> desires to destroy the Messiah, Mary's son, and his mother, and all
> those who are on earth?' For to God belongs the kingdom of the
> heavens and of the earth, and all that is between them, creating what
> He will. God is powerful over everything.

For Muslims, calling Jesus the Son of God is haram (forbidden) as Jesus was just
a man and God has no equal. In fact in the Quran, God questions Jesus about
this and Jesus says to God he never said such a thing.

> Quran 5:72-73 – They are unbelievers who say, 'God is the Messiah,
> Mary's son.' For the Messiah said, 'Children of Israel, serve God, my

Lord and your Lord. Verily whoso associates with God anything, God shall prohibit him entrance to Paradise, and his refuge shall be the Fire; and wrongdoers shall have no helpers.' They are unbelievers who say, 'God is the Third of Three. No god is there but One God. If they refrain not from what they say, there shall afflict those of them that disbelieve a painful chastisement.

Quran 5:116-117 – And when God said, 'O Jesus son of Mary, didst thou say unto men, "Take me and my mother as gods, apart from God"?' He said, 'To Thee be glory! It is not mine to say what I have no right to. If I indeed said it, Thou knowest it, knowing what is within my soul, and I know not what is within Thy soul; Thou knowest the things unseen I only said to them what Thou didst command me: "Serve God, my Lord and your Lord." And I was a witness over them, while I remained among them; but when Thou didst take me to Thyself, Thou wast Thyself the watcher over them; Thou Thyself art witness of everything.

In addition, Muslims don't believe Jesus died on a cross, but Muslims do believe Jesus deceived his enemies and ascended to Heaven. Islamic tradition also states Jesus will return to Earth near Judgement Day, bringing justice to the world and defeating the Antichrist/False Messiah.[1]

Quran 4:155-159 – So, for their breaking the compact, and disbelieving in the signs of God, and slaying the Prophets without right, and for their saying, 'Our hearts are uncircumcised' — nay, but God sealed them for their unbelief, so they believe not, except a few — and for their unbelief, and their uttering against Mary a mighty calumny, and for their saying, 'We slew the Messiah, Jesus son of Mary, the Messenger of God' — yet they did not slay him, neither crucified him, only a likeness of that was shown to them. Those who are at variance concerning him surely are in doubt regarding him; they have no knowledge of him, except the following of surmise; and they slew him not of a certainty — no indeed; God raised him up to Him; God is All-mighty, All-wise. There is not one of the People of

1. Muslim, Sahih. Translation of Sahih Muslim. International Islamic University Malaysia. Sahih Muslim, Book 41: Book Pertaining to the Turmoil and Portents of the Last Hour (Kitab Al-Fitan Wa Ashrat As-Sa'ah). Translated by Abdul Hamid Siddiqui. November 17, 2005. http://www.iium.edu.my/deed/hadith/muslim/041_smt.html. Book 41, Number 7023

the Book but will assuredly believe in him before his death, and on the Resurrection Day he will be a witness against them.

Just like Moses, Jesus is mentioned more times in the Quran than Muhammad. But unlike Muhammad, Jesus performed many miracles: he speaks as a baby, breathes life into a clay bird, heals the blind, heals the lepers and resurrects the dead.

> Quran 5:110 – When God said, 'Jesus Son of Mary, remember My blessing upon thee and upon thy mother, when I confirmed thee with the Holy Spirit, to speak to men in the cradle, and of age; and when I taught thee the Book, the Wisdom, the Torah, the Gospel; and when thou createst out of clay, by My leave, as the likeness of a bird, and thou breathest into it, and it is a bird, by My leave; and thou healest the blind and the leper by My leave, and thou bringest the dead forth by My leave; and when restrained from thee the Children of Israel when thou camest unto them with the clear signs, and the unbelievers among them said, "This is nothing but sorcery manifest."

Mary, Jesus' mother, gave birth to Jesus even though she was a virgin. Naturally, Mary's virginity was questioned, but as a baby, Jesus speaks up to defend his mother.

> Quran 19:27-35 – Then she brought the child to her folk carrying him; and they said, 'Mary, thou hast surely committed a monstrous thing! Sister of Aaron, thy father was not a wicked man, nor was thy mother a woman unchaste.' Mary pointed to the child then; but they said, 'How shall we speak to one who is still in the cradle, a little child?' He said, 'Lo, I am God's servant; God has given me the Book, and made me a Prophet. Blessed He has made me, wherever I may be; and He has enjoined me to pray, and to give the alms, so long as I live, and likewise to cherish my mother; He has not made me arrogant, unprosperous. Peace be upon me, the day I was born, and the day I die, and the day I am raised up alive!' That is Jesus, son of Mary, in word of truth, concerning which they are doubting. It is not for God to take a son unto Him. Glory be to Him! When He decrees a thing, He but says to it 'Be,' and it is.

Another unusual talent the Quran claims Jesus had was the ability to know what people ate and what items they kept in their homes. This seems more of a party trick than an ability of divine importance. It's likely if people weren't convinced of Jesus' divinity when he spoke as a baby, or when he resurrected the dead, then knowing the contents of their stomachs and homes probably isn't going to compel them either.

> Quran 3:45-49 – When the angels said, 'Mary, God gives thee good tidings of a Word from Him whose name is Messiah, Jesus, son of Mary; high honoured shall he be in this world and the next, near stationed to God. He shall speak to men in the cradle, and of age, and righteous he shall be.' 'Lord,' said Mary, 'how shall I have a son seeing no mortal has touched me?' 'Even so,' God said, God creates what He will. When He decrees a thing He does but say to it "Be," and it is. And He will teach him the Book, the Wisdom, the Torah, the Gospel, to be a Messenger to the Children of Israel saying, "I have come to you with a sign from your Lord. I will create for you out of clay as the likeness of a bird; then I will breathe into it, and it will be a bird, by the leave of God. I will also heal the blind and the leper, and bring to life the dead, by the leave of God. I will inform you too of what things you eat, and what you treasure up in your houses. Surely in that is a sign for you, if you are believers.

Jesus had many followers and the most devout were his disciples, known in the Quran as the Apostles. There's a story in the Quran of the Apostles who ask Jesus to ask God to send them a table laden with food. This is to put their hearts at rest (and presumably their stomachs too) regarding Jesus' claims of who he says he is (as though his track record of incredible unrealistic feats weren't satisfactory for those most devout to him). Nonetheless, for some reason, almighty God obliges to these men's simple whims and delivers to them a table of food from Heaven.

> Quran 5:112-115 – And when the Apostles said, 'O Jesus son of Mary, is thy Lord able to send down on us a Table out of heaven?' He said, 'Fear you God, if you are believers. They said, 'We desire that we should eat of it and our hearts be at rest; and that we may know that thou hast spoken true to us, and that we may be among its witnesses.' Said Jesus son of Mary, 'O God, our Lord, send down upon us a Table out of heaven, that shall be for us a festival, the first and last of us, and a sign from Thee. And provide for us; Thou art the best of providers.' God said, 'Verily I do send it down on you;

whoso of you hereafter disbelieves, verily I shall chastise him with a chastisement wherewith I chastise no other being.'

According to the Quran, Jesus also took the time to foretell the coming of another prophet, with Muslims attributing the name '*Ahmad*' in *Quran 61:6* to Prophet Muhammad.

> Quran 61:6 – And when Jesus son of Mary said, 'Children of Israel, I am indeed the Messenger of God to you, confirming the Torah that is before me, and giving good tidings of a Messenger who shall come after me, whose name shall be Ahmad.' Then, when he brought them the clear signs, they said, 'This is a manifest sorcery.'

However it's no surprise this prophecy wasn't in any Jewish or Christian scriptures. What occurs here is a circular reasoning fallacy: the Quran attempts to validate itself, by using itself to validate itself. It's a weak argument to use and an illogical train of thought to follow. For example, if people started to believe every book or person was holy just because that book or person said it was holy, the world would be a confusing place.

For the acts Jesus performed we would need substantial evidence for such unsubstantiated miracles. A book produced at a time when miracles are said to have occurred does not mean the miracles actually occurred; it can mean the book was produced at a time when people were more likely to believe miracles occurred.

Civilizations 1,400 years ago were more impressionable and uninformed about the world than we are today, so it would be unfair to criticize them for believing in miracles they read in a book. But these people passed on their beliefs to their children, and this pattern continued for generations up until today. Now, we have many educated adults who believe in miracles because they read about them in an ancient book their parents told them to believe.

Muslims, Christians and Jews may wonder why people don't believe in their God and holy books. Well, it's for the same reason Muslims, Christians and Jews don't believe in other religions' ancient stories. Like the ancient stories about the Greek Gods Zeus and Hades, or the Norse Gods Odin and Thor, and the Egyptian Gods Ra and Anubis. They don't believe them because they are ancient stories told to extinct civilizations which have no consistent evidence to support their claims. Just like the stories of the prophets in the Quran.

PART VI

Science in Islam

Muslim mathematicians, astronomers, geographers and scientists have made significant contributions to humankind's knowledge of the world. Many of these Muslims were motivated by Islam: they sought to explain and solve issues raised by the Quran and Hadith. Muslims developed algebra (from the Arabic word al-jabr) to help solve Islamic inheritance laws. Muslims made developments in geography, astronomy, spherical trigonometry and spherical geometry to determine the direction of prayers, times of prayers, and dates of the Islamic calendar.[1] The Quran influenced all these positive scientific developments.

But there are also Muslims who try to present the Quran as a source of scientific knowledge, trying to prove that it has made scientific predictions. They've attempted this by retrofitting proven scientific research back into the Quran, looking for any verse which could potentially have foretold a scientific discovery. It's in this manner that some Muslims try to prove the Quran's divinity since no human could have known this information at the time, only a supernatural being like a God. The Quran is often used liberally this way to confirm science's findings, rather than Muslims using the Quran to provide any scientific discovery (of which there have been none).

Scientific thought and knowledge previously blossomed in Islamic communities. Muslims produced advancements in numerous fields of science to the benefit of civilizations all over the world. But contemporary Islam has seen its once prevalent curiosity and thirst for science diminish. This has led to believers lacking a basic scientific understanding about the world we live in, because they use their holy books as their main source of knowledge. This misunderstanding can manifest itself when members of a religious community blame events like earthquakes and floods on sinfulness in the world, rather than viewing them as a natural phenomena unaffected by human moral behavior.

1. Gingerich, Owen. "Islamic Astronomy." Scientific American 254, no. 4 (April 1986): 74-83. doi:10.1038/scientificamerican0486-74.

With regards to Islam, we've begun to see a decrease in Muslim contributions to science: a disproportionately small output in relation to Islam's 1.7 billion population.[2] This scientific output can be measured in many ways; the numbers of Muslim research scientists and engineers relative to population size, the annual expenditure on research and development by Muslim countries, the citations of articles published by Muslims in international science journals, and the lack of Muslim Nobel Laureates in the sciences comparative to population size. Such indicators suggest the global Muslim community is trending towards a more insular interpretation of Islam, yet, this would be in stark contrast to the Islamic civilization of the Middle Ages that was open to foreign ideas and scientific development.

This part will look at the scientific claims the Quran makes about how the world and humans were created, and critiques them alongside current scientific knowledge on the universe's origins and humankind's evolution. We will also analyze the scientific discoveries Muslim scholars attribute to the Quran and determine if there is any credibility to their claims.

2. Johnson, Todd M., Gina A. Zurlo, Albert W. Hickman, and Peter F. Crossing. Christianity 2015: Religious Diversity and Personal Contact. Report. Vol. 39. Series 1. South Hamilton: International Bulletin of Missionary Research, 2015. Accessed October 18, 2016. http://www.gordonconwell.edu/ockenga/research/documents/2IBMR2015.pdf.

27

Evolution

"I would rather be the offspring of two apes than be a man and afraid to face the truth" – *Thomas Henry Huxley*

Let's travel back in time from the present day and attempt to take stock of the significant events that have come before us. This will help provide context about our place in the universe, and about the entire breadth of time which has passed for us to be here in this moment, reading this book.

When presented with this information we sometimes ignore it, distracting ourselves from such existential thoughts as we begin to grasp our insignificance and morality. It often leads to anxiety in some people, which is both understandable and normal. The facts of reality can become too immense and intense for our brains to process. Nonetheless, we must always try to do the best we can, and we must always try to further our education about the planet we live on.

So, in 60 steps, let's begin our abridged travel back in time and see how science explains it all began.[1] All the dates below are from 2017, the year this book was originally published, and the tilde character (~) will be used where appropriate to signify 'approximately'.

1. 7 years ago – Arab Spring begins

2. 9 years ago – Barack Obama's presidency of the United States of America begins

3. 10 years ago – First iPhone released by Apple, launching the smartphone era

---

1. Urban, Tim. "Putting Time In Perspective - UPDATED." Wait But Why (blog), August 22, 2013. http://waitbutwhy.com/2013/08/putting-time-in-perspective.html. See also Harari, Yuval Noah. Sapiens: A Brief History of Humankind. Random House UK, 2014.

4. 28 years ago – Fall of the Berlin Wall. Cold War ends

5. 31 years ago – Chernobyl disaster

6. 48 years ago – Neil Armstrong becomes the first man on the moon

7. 62 years ago – US Civil Rights Movement begins

8. 72 years ago – End of World War 2

9. 99 years ago – End of World War 1

10. 103 years ago – First commercial airplane flight

11. 105 years ago – Titanic sinks

12. 131 years ago – First car

13. 141 years ago – First telephone call

14. 226 years ago – Death of Mozart

15. 234 years ago – End of the American Revolution

16. ~250 years ago – Industrial Revolution: causes massive extinction of plants and animals

17. 401 years ago – Death of Shakespeare

18. ~500 years ago – Scientific Revolution: humankind admits its ignorance and begins to acquire unprecedented power. Europeans begin to conquer the Americas and the oceans. The rise of capitalism. Lives of Leonardo da Vinci & Michelangelo

19. 664 years ago – End of the Black Plague

20. 790 years ago – Death of Genghis Khan

21. 1,408 years ago – Birth of the Quran and Islam

22. 2,017 years ago – Birth of Christianity

23. ~2,040 years ago – Rise of the Roman Empire

24. ~2,320 years ago – Lives of Socrates, Plato, Aristotle & Alexander the Great

25. ~2,500 years ago – The Persian Empire. Rise of Buddhism in India. The invention of coinage, a universal money

26. ~4,250 years ago – First empire, the Akkadian Empire of Sargon

27. ~5,170 years ago – Dawn of Ancient Egyptian Civilization

28. ~5,520 years ago – Earliest evidence of writing, thus recorded history begins

29. ~11,000 years ago – Agricultural Revolution: humans first cultivate wheat

30. ~13,000 years ago – Extinction of Homo Floresiensis. At least 6 different species of human (Homo) walked the earth concurrently. We modern day humans (Homo sapiens) are now the only surviving species of the genus Homo. Everyone reading this book is presumably a Homo sapiens: the species Sapiens (wise) of the genus Homo (man)

31. ~15,000 years ago – Last ice age glacial period ends

32. ~16,000 years ago – Homo sapiens settle in America

33. ~30,000 years ago – Extinction of Neanderthals (Homo Neanderthalensis)

34. ~42,000 years ago – Earliest known cave paintings

35. ~45,000 years ago – Homo sapiens settle in Australia

36. ~52,000 years ago – Homo sapiens considered to have complex language for the first time. Homo sapiens become the only animal with the ability to transmit information about things that don't exist. We can express ourselves about things we've never seen, touched or smelled before. Legends, myths, gods and religions appear for the first time. These stories give Homo sapiens the unprecedented ability to cooperate flexibly in large groups and with countless numbers of strangers due to the belief in common stories that only exist in people's collective imaginations

37. ~62,000 years ago – Cognitive Revolution. Homo sapiens migrated out of

Africa for the first time. Homo sapiens began to form elaborate structures called cultures. The subsequent development of these human cultures is called history

38. ~100,000 years ago – Homo sapiens rise to the top of the food chain in an extremely short period of time. In comparison to sharks, lions or other predators who evolved into their positions gradually over millions of years, thus giving the ecosystem time to adjust along with them. For example, gazelles evolving to run faster than lions

39. ~200,000 years ago – Homo sapiens existed as we modern humans (also Homo sapiens) look today. But they did not speak as there was no language and they did not write. They also did little migration as they remained mostly in Africa. So present day until our earliest evidence of recorded history (~5,500 years ago) is only 3% of the 200,000 years of our species' existence. What we consider ancient history (Romans, Vikings, Aztecs) is a tiny percentage of our species' time on Earth. This also means the previous 1,408 years ago since Islam was established is less than 1% of our species' 200,000 years on Earth

40. ~300,000 years ago – Daily usage of fire

41. ~2.3 million years ago – Beginning of the Homo genus. First stone tools used. It took around 2 million years to come from the ape-like Homo genus to the human-like Homo sapiens we are today

42. ~4 million years ago – Beginning of the Stone Age

43. ~6 million years ago – Last time chimps and humans shared a living common ancestor as the Hominini Tribe splits into two. One side is the Pan genus which eventually led to modern day chimpanzees, and the other is the Homo genus which eventually led to modern day humans

44. ~66 million years ago – Asteroid extinction event kills all the dinosaurs and wipes out 75% of all species alive at the time. Mammals begin to thrive as they'd spent the previous 134 million years at the bottom of the food chain

45. ~155 million years ago – First birds

46. ~200 million years ago – First mammals. The Supercontinent Pangea begins to break up to form separate continents. Each of the continents move a couple of centimeters a year. This eventually formed the seven-continent model we

Homo sapiens live on today: North America, South America, Europe, Africa, Asia, Australia and Antarctica

47. ~231 million years ago – Reign of the dinosaurs begins lasting for approximately 165 million years. In comparison, our species (Homo sapiens) existence has only been around 200,000 years and counting. This also means a Tyrannosaurus Rex from the Upper Cretaceous Period 65 million years ago is closer in time to us today, than it is to a Stegosaurus from the Late Jurassic period 150 million years ago

48. ~300 million years ago – Supercontinent Pangea forms

49. ~300 million years ago – First reptiles

50. ~400 million years ago – First insects

51. ~475 million years ago – First land plants

52. ~500 million years ago – First fish

53. ~600 million years ago – First animals

54. ~1 billion years ago – First multi-cellular life

55. ~2 billion years ago – First complex cells with a nucleus, called eukaryotes

56. ~3.4 billion years ago – Photosynthesis begins and oxygen first enters the atmosphere as a waste product of the process

57. ~3.5 billion years ago – Last time every current being on Earth today shared a common ancestor

58. ~3.6 billion years ago – Life begins for the first time. Certain molecules combined to form structures called microorganisms. They are simple cells called prokaryotes. This means it took around 3 billion years from the first microorganisms (prokaryotes) to evolve into the first organisms (animals). So all the time life has even been on Earth (3.6 billion years), around 80% of it (3 billion years) has been no more than microorganisms. The story of microorganisms and organisms is called biology

59. ~4.6 billion years ago – Birth of the sun in our solar system. It took around

9.1 billion years after the Big Bang for the birth of our sun. The scientific understanding is that the sun formed from a giant cloud of floating gas (the solar nebula) and planet Earth formed from the excess debris circling around the sun around 4.54 billion years ago. So it took around 60 million years after the sun first formed, for planet Earth to form. Therefore if life first began around 3.6 billion years ago, and the sun was formed around 4.6 billion years ago, this means it took around 1 billion years for Earth to settle from constant asteroid impacts for its atmosphere to be conducive enough to allow simple cells (prokaryotes) to exist

60. ~13.7 billion years ago – The Big Bang and the universe begins. Matter, energy, time and space come into being. The story of these fundamental features of our universe is called physics. Around 380,000 years after matter and energy appear, they start to blend into complex structures called atoms. These atoms then combined to create molecules. The story of atoms, molecules and their interactions is called chemistry

You may need to put this book down for a moment and take a few deep breaths; it's a lot of information to absorb in such a short period of time!

These abridged 60 steps (all backed up by significantly more than words in an ancient book) may have provided us with the knowledge we needed to refocus our version of reality for what it truly is. But, it may also have left many of us overwhelmed, confused or disheartened about our existence on Earth. If latter is the case, you may desire to skip ahead to a later chapter in this book entitled '*Meaning of life*'.

Science and technology provide all this information by creating models which explain the world in the best possible way. It is the best possible way because it uses testable, repeatable and verifiable evidence. As time progresses, further research produces more evidence, and the models for explaining the world revise and update accordingly.

If progressive Muslims believe in this science but they also believe in God, just as I did, then they too may find it difficult to understand why He decided to come to us mammals only a few thousand years ago. A few thousand years ago isn't a long time when we Homo sapiens have been around for 200,000 years, life on this earth began 3.6 billion years ago, and the universe existed around 13.7 billion years ago.

The abilities of God means He already knows everything that has happened, is happening and will happen (but He still has a desire to see how it all works out in the end). During the period of time He did chat to us, He did so only by whispering to a handful of men (his preferred gender to speak to).

God also only chose men from the deserts of Arabia, He had no desire to go to China for example, which had a much more advanced civilization at the time of Islam's birth.[2]

In the 21st century there's nothing to reasonably suggest creationism is an accurate account of how life on Earth began, regardless of how guilty the Quran makes us feel about it.

> Quran 56:57-73 – We created you; therefore why will you not believe? Have you considered the seed you spill? Do you yourselves create it, or are We the Creators? We have decreed among you Death; We shall not be outstripped; that We may exchange the likes of you, and make you to grow again in a fashion you know not. You have known the first growth; so why will you not remember? Have you considered the soil you till? Do you yourselves sow it, or are We the Sowers? Did We will, We would make it broken orts, and you would remain bitterly jesting — 'We are debt-loaded; nay, we have been robbed!' Have you considered the water you drink? Did you send it down from the clouds, or did We send it? Did We will, We would make it bitter; so why are you not thankful? Have you considered the fire you kindle? Did you make its timber to grow, or did We make it? We Ourselves made it for a reminder, and a boon to the desert-dwellers.

> Quran 78:6-16 – Have We not made the earth as a cradle and the mountains as pegs? And We created you in pairs, and We appointed your sleep for a rest; and We appointed night for a garment, and We appointed day for a livelihood. And We have built above you seven strong ones, and We appointed a blazing lamp and have sent down out of the rainclouds water cascading that We may bring forth thereby grain and plants, and gardens luxuriant.

Claims like the universe's creation was in 6 days or eras, and Adam was the first human (see chapters '*Origins of the universe*' and '*Adam*') can't be proven true, but there is verified scientific evidence available which proves it isn't true. So we can choose to ignore the evidence, but it means we're choosing God out of ignorance, fear or faith. Or, we can choose to acknowledge the evidence, and it'll mean we're choosing science out of rationality, probability

2. Lewis, Mark Edward. China's Cosmopolitan Empire: The Tang Dynasty. Cambridge, MA: Belknap Press of Harvard University Press, 2012.

and a coherent argument. Muslims can continue to ask if science is compatible with the Quran and God, but in reality, Muslims ought to ask if the Quran and God are compatible with the proven science.

28

Origins of the universe

"We long for a parent to care for us, to forgive us for our errors, to save us from our childish mistakes. But knowledge is preferable to ignorance. Better by far to embrace the hard truth than a reassuring fable. If we crave some cosmic purpose, then let us find ourselves a worthy goal" – Carl Sagan

Let's begin at the beginning. In this chapter we'll look at what science has to say about the origins of the universe. But first, we'll start with the Quran and what Muslims are told to believe.

In the Quran, God states He created the Heavens and Earth in 6 days.

> Quran 7:54 – Surely your Lord is God, who created the heavens and the earth in six days — then sat Himself upon the Throne, covering the day with the night it pursues urgently — and the sun, and the moon, and the stars subservient, by His command. Verily, His are the creation and the command. Blessed be God, the Lord of all Being.

Earth took 2 of those 6 days to be created.

> Quran 41:9 – Say: 'What, do you disbelieve in Him who created the earth in two days, and do you set up compeers to Him? That is the Lord of all Being.

In the other 4 days God raised up the Heavens, erected mountains, and stretched out the earth. He also put everything we would need for sustenance onto the planet.

> Quran 41:10 – 'And He set therein firm mountains over it, and He blessed it, and He ordained therein its diverse sustenance in four days, equal to those who ask.'

Quran 88:17-20 – What, do they not consider how the camel was created, how heaven was lifted up, how the mountains were hoisted, how the earth was outstretched?

The Heavens and the earth were originally one mass but God split them apart and then created every living thing out of water.

Quran 21:30 – Have not the unbelievers then beheld that the heavens and the earth were a mass all sewn up, and then We unstitched them and of water fashioned every living thing? Will they not believe?

God also took the time to spread the Heavens and the earth out wide for us.

Quran 51:47-48 – And heaven — We built it with might, and We extend it wide. And the earth — We spread it forth; O excellent Smoothers!

The Heavens used to be just smoke (but it's not explicitly stated if this was before or after He split the Heavens from the earth).

Quran 41:11 – Then He lifted Himself to heaven when it was smoke, and said to it and to the earth, "Come willingly, or unwillingly!" They said, "We come willingly."

God then divided the Heavens into seven separate parts, so there are now seven Heavens layered one on top of the other.

Quran 67:1-3 – Blessed be He in whose hand is the Kingdom — He is powerful over everything — who created death and life, that He might try you which of you is fairest in works; and He is the All-mighty, the All-forgiving — who created seven heavens one upon another. Thou seest not in the creation of the All-merciful any imperfection. Return thy gaze; seest thou any fissure?

The concept of seven Heavens isn't unique to Islam, it isn't even unique to Abrahamic religions. It's also found in non-Abrahamic religions like Hinduism. According to some Puranas (ancient Hindu texts) the Brahmanda (a cosmological theory of Hinduism) is divided into fourteen worlds and among these worlds are seven upper worlds.[1]

---

1. Dalal, Roshen. Hinduism: An Alphabetical Guide. New Delhi: Penguin Books, 2010. p.224.

The concept of seven Heavens actually predates Islam as it is found in ancient Mesopotamian religions, some as early as 3000 BCE, 3,500 years before the Quran existed. Today Mesopotamia roughly corresponds to most of Iraq, Kuwait and the eastern parts of Syria. It also included the regions along the Iran-Iraq and Turkish-Syrian borders.[2] So the concept of seven Heavens (or the flood myth, see chapter 'Noah') could have been passed on from generation to generation, and religion to religion throughout Arabia, even up until the birth of Islam. Therefore the seven Islamic (and Jewish) Heavens may have had their origins in Babylonian astronomy.[3] This is an example of syncretism within Islam: blending two or more religious beliefs into a new system.

In Heaven, it's the first level (the lowest one) which contains the stars we see in the night sky.

> Quran 37:6-10 – We have adorned the lower heaven with the adornment of the stars and to preserve against every rebel Satan; they listen not to the High Council, for they are pelted from every side, rejected, and theirs is an everlasting chastisement, except such as snatches a fragment, and he is pursued by a piercing flame.

The stars were set by God in what we now call the Zodiac constellations.

> Quran 15:16-18 – We have set in heaven constellations and decked them out fair to the beholders, and guarded them from every accursed Satan excepting such as listens by stealth — and he is pursued by a manifest flame.

God sent down water from the Heavens so we can eat the fruits of the land, and He also created the seas and the rivers. Finally, God set the sun and the moon and put them on a regular path for us so we'd have night and day.

> Quran 14:32-34 – It is God who created the heavens and the earth, and sent down out of heaven water wherewith He brought forth fruits to be your sustenance. And He subjected to you the ships to run upon the sea at His commandment; and He subjected to you the rivers and He subjected to you the sun and moon constant upon their courses, and He subjected to you the night and day, and gave you

2. Foster, Benjamin R., and Karen Polinger Foster. Civilizations of Ancient Iraq. Princeton: Princeton University Press, 2009. p.6.

3. Hetherington, Norriss S. Encyclopedia of Cosmology. Routledge, 2015.

of all you asked Him. If you count God's blessing, you will never number it; surely man is sinful, unthankful!

So, that's it. That's all the information we have to go on. This is what Muslims are told to believe about how the universe, earth, stars, sun and moon were all created. In 6 days, by God.

Some Muslims scholars have interpreted the 6 days not as 6 literal days, but 6 eras. This is due to an ayah stating a day for God is like a 1,000 years for us mere humans. Therefore perhaps it wasn't 6 days, but 6,000 years in which God created everything.

> Quran 22:47 – And they demand of thee to hasten the chastisement! God will not fail His promise; and surely a day with thy Lord is as a thousand years of your counting.

> Quran 32:5 – He directs the affair from heaven to earth, then it goes up to Him in one day, whose measure is a thousand years of your counting.

It's unclear whether it's 6 days or 6,000 thousand years but nevertheless, neither are particularly long nor persuasive since dinosaur fossils empirically proven to be hundreds of millions of years old are in museums across the world.[4]

So let's now move on to what science has to say about the origins of the universe. To aid with this explanation we'll review an article from space.com, a website chronicling space exploration and astronomy news. The article is titled 'The Universe: Big Bang to Now in 10 Easy Steps'. What follows is a compressed version, but a link to the full article can be found in the footnote.[5]

1. The broadly accepted theory for the origin and evolution of our universe is the Big Bang model. It states the universe began as an incredibly hot, dense point roughly 13.7 billion years ago. However, the Big Bang was not an explosion in space as the theory's name suggests, instead it was the appearance of space everywhere in the universe. Cosmologists are unsure what happened before this moment, but space missions, powerful telescopes and complex

4. Ceurstemont, Sandrine. "This May Be the World's Oldest Jurassic Dinosaur Fossil." New Scientist, January 20, 2016. https://www.newscientist.com/article/2074126-this-may-be-the-worlds-oldest-jurassic-dinosaur-fossil/.

5. Chow, Denise. "The Universe: Big Bang to Now in 10 Easy Steps." Space.com, October 18, 2011. http://www.space.com/13320-big-bang-universe-10-steps-explainer.html.

calculations have helped provide some understanding. A key part of this understanding comes from observations of the cosmic microwave background which contains the afterglow of light and radiation left over from the Big Bang. This relic of the Big Bang pervades the universe and is visible to microwave detectors, allowing scientists to piece together clues of the early universe.

In 2001, NASA launched the Wilkinson Microwave Anisotropy Probe (WMAP). Its mission was to study the conditions as they existed in the early universe by measuring radiation from the cosmic microwave background. Among other discoveries, WMAP was able to determine the age of the universe, around 13.7 billion years old.

2. When the universe was extraordinarily young it underwent an incredible growth spurt. This took place around a hundredth of a billionth of a trillionth of a trillionth of a second. During this burst of expansion the universe grew exponentially, doubling in size at least 90 times. This expansion is known as inflation. After inflation, the universe continued to grow but at a slower rate, and as space expanded, the universe cooled and matter formed.

3. Light chemical elements were created within the first three minutes of the universe's formation, and as the universe's expansion caused temperatures to cool, protons and neutrons collided to make deuterium. Deuterium is an isotope of hydrogen. Isotopes are versions of an atom or an element with the same number of protons but different number of neutrons. Much of this deuterium combined to make helium.

The first 380,000 years of the universe's existence produced intense heat and this made it too hot for light to shine. But eventually atoms began to crash together and it happened with enough force to break up into a dense, opaque plasma of protons, neutrons and electrons. This caused light to scatter like a fog.

4. Around 380,000 years after the Big Bang, matter cooled enough for electrons to combine with nuclei. This formed neutral atoms in a phase called recombination. The absorption of free electrons caused the universe to become transparent and the light unleashed then is detectable today in the form of radiation from the cosmic microwave background. Following the era of recombination was a period of darkness before eventually, stars and other bright objects formed.

5. Roughly 400 million years after the Big Bang, the universe began to come out of its dark ages. This period in the universe's evolution is called the age of re-ionization. During this time, clumps of gas collapsed enough to form the

first stars and galaxies. There was ultraviolet light emitted from these energetic events and this UV light cleared out and destroyed most of the surrounding neutral hydrogen gas. The process of re-ionization and the clearing of foggy hydrogen gas caused the universe to become transparent to UV light for the first time.

6. It's estimated our solar system was born around 9 billion years after the Big Bang. This makes it about 4.6 billion years old today. According to current estimates, our sun is one of more than 100 billion stars in our Milky Way galaxy alone. Our sun orbits roughly 25,000 light-years from the galactic core of the Milky Way galaxy. Many scientists think our solar system formed from a giant, rotating cloud of gas and dust known as the solar nebula. As gravity caused the nebula to collapse, it spun faster and flattened into a disk. During this phase, most of the material was pulled toward the center to form the sun.

7. In the 1960s and 1970s astronomers began to think there might be more mass in the universe than what's visible. Astronomer Vera Rubin began to observe the speeds of stars at various locations in galaxies. Basic Newtonian physics implied stars on the outskirts of a galaxy would orbit slower than stars at the center. But Vera found no difference in the velocities of stars farther out. In fact, she found all stars in a galaxy seem to circle the center at more or less the same speed. This mysterious and invisible mass became known as dark matter. Dark matter is inferred because of the gravitational pull it exerts on regular matter. One hypothesis states dark matter forms from exotic particles that don't interact with light or regular matter. This may be why it has been so difficult to detect. Dark matter is thought to make up 23% of the universe. In comparison, regular matter, what constitutes the stars, planets and us, composes only 4% of the universe.

8. In the 1920s, astronomer Edwin Hubble made a revolutionary discovery about the universe. Using a newly constructed telescope, Hubble observed the universe is not static, but rather, it is expanding. Decades later in 1998 a prolific space telescope was named after the famous astronomer, the Hubble Space Telescope. It studied distant supernovas and it found out a long time ago the universe was expanding slower than it is today. This discovery was surprising because it was long thought the gravity of matter in the universe would slow its expansion or even cause it to contract. Dark energy is thought to be the strange force pulling the cosmos apart at increasing speeds but it remains undetected and shrouded in mystery. The existence of this elusive energy is a hotly debated topic in cosmology. Dark energy is thought to make up 73% of the universe, while dark matter makes up 23% and regular matter 4%.

9. Astronomers are still combing the universe looking for the eldest and most distant galaxies. This is all in the hope that it'll help them understand the properties of the early universe. As previously mentioned, astronomers are also working backwards to understand the universe's formation. They're doing this by studying the cosmic microwave background which contains the afterglow of light and radiation left over from the Big Bang.

10. Much has been discovered about the creation and evolution of the universe but there are enduring questions that still remain unanswered. Two of the biggest ones are dark matter, thought to be responsible for much of the mass in the universe, and dark energy, the force believed to be making the universe larger. Cosmologists continue to probe the universe, all in the hope of better understanding how it all began.

Science's description of the universe's origins differs somewhat from the Quran's description. It may be more complex to follow and understand, but, it's also verified by supporting evidence. To deliver the Big Bang model scientists have used consistent and reliable scientific methods, providing empirical results which can be mathematically replicated by physicists from anywhere in the world. Therefore, the Big Bang model is widely accepted as most likely to be true.[6] Unlike the Quran, which has zero evidence to support its claims, and none of the claims it does have can be independently tested and validated. Therefore, nothing contained in the Quran's account of the universe's origins can be said to be most likely true.

The religious often struggle with the concept of the Big Bang model and some of this is due to the difficulty of understanding how something can be created from nothing (though science has shown something can be created from nothing).[7] But let's follow the line of logic many Muslims, Christians and Jews follow, that the universe had to be created from something or by someone and that someone is God. But, if God created everything, then who or what created God? If we're following the reasoning of the religious (everything has a creator, like the universe) then God must require a creator as well. If religious people claim God doesn't need a creator, then why must everything else?

6. The Editors of Encyclopædia Britannica. "Big-bang Model." Encyclopædia Britannica. December 2, 2015. https://www.britannica.com/topic/big-bang-model.

7. Hawking, Stephen W., and Leonard Mlodinow. The Grand Design. London: Bantam Press, 2010.

Asking these questions may have caused Muhammad problems during his prophethood. But, he is of course supported by the Quran which advises Muslims not to ask the types of questions which they would apparently have no benefit in knowing the answer of.

> Quran 5:101-102 – O believers, question not concerning things which, if they were revealed to you, would vex you; yet if you question concerning them when the Koran is being sent down, they will be revealed to you. God has effaced those things; for God is All-forgiving, All-clement. A people before you questioned concerning them, then disbelieved in them.

Naturally there will be Muslims who don't believe the universe was created in 6 days or 6 eras. But it's difficult to understand where these Muslims draw the line and how they decide what to believe and what not to believe in the Quran. I say that now because these were some of the main dilemmas I wrestled with when I was attempting to overcome the blatant inconsistencies the Quran put forward. Eventually, I had to side with reason.

When we try to consider the enormity of the universe, it's too vast to comprehend, and when we consider how long it took for it to form, our time on it as Homo sapiens has been insignificant in comparison (see chapter 'Evolution'). So it's somewhat narcissistic of our species to think we have an important cosmic role to play, to believe the entire universe and Earth was created just for us. But we are by and large a narcissistic species. After all, we do call our planet Earth because that's the parts we live on, even though two thirds of it is actually water (do we start calling it planet Ocean?).

As we obtain more information about the past, the evidence is increasing (not decreasing) that God doesn't exist. Since we won't be getting more information from God anytime soon, this trend is set to continue. Until one day, it's no longer a trend. Since everything about religion represents a static defence and everything about science represents a dynamic offence, it's not difficult to predict how that's going to end over time.

The universe and Earth didn't need us before we arrived and if all the humans died or disappeared tomorrow, Earth will still continue to rotate without us. In fact, plants and other animals will all start to thrive in our absence. It's unlikely the solar system will stop existing because there are no more humans; it has operated for billions of years without us and there's nothing to indicate it'll stop operating in the same manner if we're gone.

There's also been nothing to suggest humans have a predestination or divine plan in store for them. We can continue to believe otherwise, but it would be based upon faith and sentiment rather than evidence and logic. We can also continue to believe a god created the universe just for us, but it does an extreme disservice to the universe and all its wonders. Condensing its 13.7 billion years into 6 days or eras is an ungrateful thing we, as a narcissistic species, do for it in return.

29

The Quran's science

"The lack of understanding of something is not evidence of God. It is evidence of a lack of understanding" – Lawrence M. Krauss

The Quran comments on a wide range of sciences including astronomy, biology and cosmology. Muslim scholars have often taken the Quran's verses on these topics and claimed them as scientific discoveries and proof of the Quran's divinity.

But in truth, no scientific discoveries have resulted from the Quran verses. This is true because if the Quran contained scientific discoveries, Islamic scholars would have revealed them before any scientists actually discovered them. But instead it's the other way round. It's the scientists who make the scientific discoveries, then, Muslim scholars go back to review what's in the Quran and loosely interpret it in a manner which makes it seem like the Quran foretold it all along. This loose interpretation is used as 'proof' that the Quran wasn't man-made since humans in ancient Arabia couldn't have had this scientific knowledge at the time.

So, let's review some of these most popular 'scientific discoveries of the Quran'. Perhaps the most cited example of a 'scientific discovery' from the Quran is its description of human embryology.

> Quran 23:12-14 – We created man of an extraction of clay, then We set him, a drop, in a receptacle secure, then We created of the drop a clot then We created of the clot a tissue then We created of the tissue bones then We garmented the bones in flesh; thereafter We produced him as another creature. So blessed be God, the fairest of creators!

Around 400 years before the Quran there was an account on embryonic development by Galen of Pergamon.[1] Galen was a prominent Greek physician and surgeon in the Roman Empire. He's now referred to as the 'Father of Greek Medicine'. Galen was well known and influential in Islamic medicine during Prophet Muhammad's time. Prophet Muhammad himself wasn't in Islamic medical schools which taught such Greek inspired medical learning, but he was still a well-traveled merchant, working for decades across all of Arabia. He would have encountered many people throughout his career, so it's reasonable to suggest Prophet Muhammad may have previously encountered this information by speaking to other people, for example, from the Sasanian (Persian) empire or the Byzantine (Roman) empire.

But let's assume Prophet Muhammad didn't come across this information from other people, that he got it from God. Also, let's assume Galen's work on anatomy and physiology 400 years before the Quran's first revelation wasn't known in early Islamic medicine. Even if we take these assumptions as true, the Quran's description is too vague to be of any use and, more importantly, it's inaccurate.

First, the verses in *Quran 23:12-14* state humans are created from clay, which of course we know is false. These verses also state that in an embryo bone and flesh develop sequentially, and in that order. However, bone and flesh develop simultaneously in an embryo. The tissue which bones originate from is called mesoderm. It's this same tissue, the mesoderm, that *'flesh'* develops from as well.[2] So the idea that bones develop first, and then flesh 'garments' them, is scientifically incorrect.

The Quran continues with its account on embryology by stating humans are created from dust (not clay this time although both are incorrect) and referring to a *'sperm-drop'* (Arberry's translation of semen, not the Quran's acknowledgment of sperm's existence) but with no mention of ovaries. A vague *'blood-clot'* is mentioned which could be referring to a fetus.

> Quran 75:36-39 – What, does man reckon he shall be left to roam at will? Was he not a sperm-drop spilled? Then he was a blood-clot, and He created and formed, and He made of him two kinds, male and female.

However this information wasn't revolutionary in 7th century Arabia as

1. Touwaide, Alain. "GALEN, On Semen, Edition, Translation and Commentary by Philippe De Locy, Berlin, Akademie Verlag, 1992, 291 Pp. (= Corpus Medicorum Graecorum, V, 3, 1)." Nuncius 9, no. 1 (1994): 333-35. doi:10.1163/182539184x00171.

2. Dudek, Ronald W. High-yield Embryology. Philadelphia: Wolters Kluwer/Lippincott Williams & Wilkins, 2014.

previous civilizations (and Galen) knew about the significance of semen and fetuses for human reproduction as well.

Next is water, which the Quran claims all living things were created from.

> Quran 21:30 – Have not the unbelievers then beheld that the heavens and the earth were a mass all sewn up, and then We unstitched them and of water fashioned every living thing? Will they not believe?

> Quran 24:45 – God has created every beast of water, and some of them go upon their bellies, and some of them go upon two feet, and some of them go upon four; God creates whatever He will; God is powerful over everything.

Water is certainly important to all plants (agriculture) and animals (hydration) on a biological level, but this was also known by humans before Prophet Muhammad's time. In addition, the Quran is vague when it talks about water, and doesn't provide any new information about its role or function. In addition, it isn't technically accurate when it claims everything was created from water.

Earth is the next substance in a line of materials the Quran claims we're fashioned from.

> Quran 11:61 – And to Thamood their brother Salih; he said, 'O my people, serve God! You have no god other than He. It is He who produced you from the earth and has given you to live therein; so ask forgiveness of Him, then repent to Him; surely my Lord is nigh, and answers prayer.

Somewhat similar to earth and clay is a clay of mud, which humans were also apparently '*moulded*' from.

> Quran 15:26-28 – Surely We created man of a clay of mud moulded, and the jinn created We before of fire flaming. And when thy Lord said to the angels, 'See, I am creating a mortal of a clay of mud moulded.

The Quran's 'science' was sufficient at a time when people relied on religion to provide explanations of the world. But it's counter-intuitive to keep relying on 'science' written 1,400 years ago that has no empirical evidence or calculations in sight. Humanity's knowledge has increased exponentially since the holy scriptures were written, and what was previously attributed to God or gods (volcanoes, earthquakes or solar eclipses) is now accurately explained to us by science. We now know events like these will occur regardless of how much people have sinned in the world, which isn't what people used to believe.

Science doesn't know the answers to everything, and it may never will. Though just because something isn't understood, it doesn't mean God did it. A religious person can claim God caused something because there's no evidence to prove otherwise, but this would be a fallacious argument called *argumentum ad ignorantiam* (argument from ignorance).

It's okay to accept we don't understand how something happened, it doesn't automatically have to mean it has a supernatural origin, it only means more research is required to understand it, or, that we may never understand it in our lifetime. For instance, magicians can do impressive tricks, and we don't understand how they do them. However it doesn't mean magicians have supernatural powers we don't, it just means we don't know how their tricks work.

Not knowing the answer to a magician's trick or the answer to something that happens in our world doesn't give us licence to make something up to explain it. The same logic also applies to science. We call the Big Bang model a theory because it's the prevailing cosmological model for the universe's origins; it hasn't been proven to be 100% true. Nonetheless, the Big Bang model is based upon strong scientific empirical evidence. This means it is a highly probable truth, not a made up truth, and that's why it's the scientific community's most accepted model about our universe's origin (see chapter 'Origins of the universe'). This is unlike the religious community which often inserts God into any explanation that doesn't have an answer, a 'God of the gaps' so to speak. But we can't solve a mystery by using a bigger mystery as the answer.

There's a significant difference between the Quran's 'science' and real science. Science doesn't assume it knows or will know all the answers to life's big questions. This contrasts with religion, which actually uses this attitude as one of its main selling points. Religions like Islam claim to give you everything you'll ever need to know about life and how to live it. Science is more modest than this since science can admit its ignorance. Science knows there's so much still to learn and even with the things we do know, science accepts it could be proven wrong in the future if we gain more knowledge. So unlike religion, in science no theory, concept or idea is sacred and beyond challenge.

The reason for this is because science is continually exploring, updating and self-correcting, while religion is set in ink. Religion only changes when its male leaders decide it should change, and religion rarely admits it is wrong.

Science on the other hand is always happy to try and prove itself wrong in the pursuit of truth. Religion may get a few things correct, and it can provide timeless ancient wisdom, but it doesn't mean we can ignore the tens of things it gets wrong, for every one thing it gets correct. But even in the unlikely chance religion does admit it's wrong, it often tries to force its square beliefs into a science shaped circle, just so it can make sense of what's in its holy books.

In the Quran, one of Prophet Muhammad's titles is 'Seal of the Prophets' because he is the last prophet chosen by God.

> Quran 33:40 – Muhammad is not the father of any one of your men, but the Messenger of God, and the Seal of the Prophets; God has knowledge of everything.

This means there'll be no more knowledge passed on from God to us by any human. But in science, there's no such thing as someone who's the 'Seal of the Scientists'. No one would call Darwin the 'Seal of the Biologists' after his theory of evolution by natural selection. No respectable scientist would ever claim there's nothing more to be discovered or revealed.

There aren't anymore facts to be taken from the holy scriptures which we haven't already uncovered over the past few thousand years; only life philosophies and 'morals' from its stories remain for us. In the fast-changing world we live in, it'll be the learners who shall inherit the Earth, and the 'learned' will find themselves well-equipped to deal with a world that no longer exists. If Muhammad is indeed the last prophet, and we're not going to get any more knowledge from him or God, then it's left to science, not religion, to advance humankind's knowledge from now on.

PART VII

Women

The lives of modern day Muslim women vary throughout the Islamic world due to the geographical and cultural diversity of the global Muslim population. Meaning, there are several factors determining a Muslim woman's position and role in her society. Muslim countries may share similar laws and religious components, but there's a discrepancy on how they're enforced and interpreted. Nonetheless in all Muslim countries, women play a vital role.

Within Islam there's a particular emphasis placed on the feminine and masculine polarity, and this can be seen in the separation of sexes in social functions within Islamic cultures. Commonly in Muslim families a woman's sphere of operation is the home: this is where she's the dominant figure. A man's sphere of operation is outside the home: the rest of the world. Many Muslims believe having such defined gender roles ensures the smooth running of the family.

Islam acknowledges God as having created women and men both physically and psychologically differently. As a result, Islam sees women as having the traditional caregiver role in Muslim families, with children's development entrusted to her. Muslims generally believe God created women to handle the physical tasks of bearing children and God also gave her more empathy and emotional intelligence than men. This is why it's common in Islam for men and women to have unequal responsibilities; Muslims believe it's due to the differing biological makeup God has imparted upon them.

Almost all Muslims celebrate Islam as a religion which has done much to progress women's rights, particularly at a time and location in which they didn't have many. Socially, for example, female infanticide (the pre-Islamic Arabian custom of burying unwanted female infants) was condemned by Islam.[1] In addition, economically, women were allowed to own and inherit property; a right not entitled to many women in the West until as recently as the 19th

---

1. "Female Infanticide." BBC. Accessed January 17, 2017. http://www.bbc.co.uk/ethics/abortion/medical/infanticide_1.shtml.

century.[2] Islam surpassed many cultures in the 7th century when it came to women's rights.[3] But since then, Muslim countries have been caught up and overtaken. Now there are more non-Muslim countries with women's societal and legal rights equal to men, with many Muslim countries' women's rights seen as archaic in comparison.

This part will look at the roles and rights Islam has given women, and the impact cultural influences have played. We'll discuss if Islam and the Quran is beneficial for women, for men, or for Muslim communities as a whole.

2. Lewis, Bernard. What Went Wrong?: Western Impact and Middle Eastern Response. Oxford: Oxford University Press, 2002. pp.82-83.

3. Watt, William Montgomery. "Interview: William Montgomery Watt." Interview by Bashir Mann and Alastair McIntosh. AlastairMcIntosh.com. 1999. http://www.alastairmcintosh.com/articles/ 2000_watt.htm.

30

Women as unequals

"To no form of religion is woman indebted for one impulse of freedom" – Elizabeth
Cady Stanton

The status of women in Islamic societies has changed considerably over the
past few hundreds of years, and it has become increasingly different between
Muslim countries themselves. We now have secular Muslim countries like
Turkey, and conservative Muslim countries like Saudi Arabia.

Historically, in all Muslim countries a woman's role has been at home. This
led to less opportunities for Muslim women than Muslim men to hold positions
of responsibility, thus leading to men dictating the major decisions of women's
lives. But this 'traditional' dynamic has been, and still is, common in many
societies and religions, not just the ones within Islam.

However when reading the Quran, it's clear it was a book written for men.
The same level of detail and guidance given to men in the Quran is not given to
women; there are no complementary instructive suras for the benefit of women.
Since Muslim men have always held the power in Islam, it's as though God
always speaks directly to them.

> Quran 4:23-24 – Forbidden to you are your mothers and daughters,
> your sisters, your aunts paternal and maternal, your brother's
> daughters, your sister's daughters, your mothers who have given
> suck to you, your suckling sisters, your wives' mothers, your
> stepdaughters who are in your care being born of your wives you
> have been in to — but if you have not yet been in to them it is
> no fault in you – and the spouses of your sons who are of your
> loins, and that you should take to you two sisters together, unless it
> be a thing of the past; God is All-forgiving, All-compassionate; and
> wedded women, save what your right hands own. So God prescribes
> for you. Lawful for you, beyond all that, is that you may seek, using

179

your wealth, in wedlock and not in licence. Such wives as you enjoy thereby, give them their wages apportionate; it is no fault in you in your agreeing together, after the due apportionate. God is All-knowing, All-wise.

Quran 64:14 – O believers, among your wives and children there is an enemy to you; so beware of them. But if you pardon, and overlook, and if you forgive, surely God is All-forgiving, All-compassionate.

The Quran only mentions a handful of women in the entire book and most are secondary to the male protagonist; they are the mothers or wives of male leaders and prophets. There's actually only one woman in the entire Quran mentioned by name: Mary, mother of Jesus (Maryam in Arabic). Although interestingly Mary is mentioned more times in the Quran than she is in the New Testament.[1]

It's odd there aren't more women in the Quran since half the Muslims in the world at any one time are female. It's also worth asking why there has never been a single female prophet. Many Muslims would find this question blasphemous, and that in itself says a great deal about the male-dominated mindset Islam has created. Prophethood, and speaking to God, is a man's domain in Islam.

Even when God speaks about Heaven, He makes sure to let men know about the sexual pleasures in store for them (the concept of 72 virgins are only mentioned in 'hasan' (good) Hadith, not the Quran).[2] Although women can go to Heaven too, it sounds more like a Heaven catered to men.

Quran 44:51-57 – Surely the godfearing shall be in a station secure among gardens and fountains, robed in silk and brocade, set face to face. Even so; and We shall espouse them to wide-eyed houris, therein calling for every fruit, secure. They shall not taste therein of death, save the first death, And He shall guard them against the chastisement of Hell — a bounty from thy Lord; that is the mighty triumph.

Quran 55:55-59 – O which of your Lord's bounties will you and you

1. Esposito, John L. What Everyone Needs to Know about Islam. Oxford: Oxford University Press, 2011. p.76.

2. At-Tirmidhi, Abu `Isa Muhammad. "The Book on Virtues of Jihad - Jami` At-Tirmidhi." Sunnah.com. Accessed November 28, 2016. https://sunnah.com/tirmidhi/22/46. Vol. 3, Book 20, Hadith 1663

deny? therein maidens restraining their glances, untouched before them by any man or jinn — O which of your Lord's bounties will you and you deny? lovely as rubies, beautiful as coral — O which of your Lord's bounties will you and you deny?

Quran 56:25-38 – Therein they shall hear no idle talk, no cause of sin, only the saying 'Peace, Peace!' mid thornless lote-trees and serried acacias, and spreading shade and outpoured waters, and fruits abounding unfailing, unforbidden, and upraised couches. Perfectly We formed them, perfect, and We made them spotless virgins, chastely amorous, like of age for the Companions of the Right.

Quran 78:31-34 – Surely for the godfearing awaits a place of security, gardens and vineyards and maidens with swelling breasts, like of age, and a cup overflowing.

So the Quran says Muslim men will be wed to untouched maidens with swelling breasts, wide-eyed houris (fair females), and spotless virgins. Muslim women can be left to wonder if they'll also have their sexual desires satisfied by handsome men in Heaven.

There are also instances in the Quran where the value of two women equals one man. The first example is seen with inheritance: the Quran states a daughter's inheritance is less than a son's.

Quran 4:11 – God charges you, concerning your children: to the male the like of the portion of two females, and if they be women above two, then for them two-thirds of what he leaves, but if she be one then to her a half; and to his parents to each one of the two the sixth of what he leaves, if he has children; but if he has no children, and his heirs are his parents, a third to his mother, or, if he has brothers, to his mother a sixth, after any bequest he may bequeath, or any debt. Your fathers and your sons — you know not which out of them is nearer in profit to you. So God apportions; surely God is All-knowing, All-wise.

At the time of the Quran's revelations this made practical sense. In 7th century Arabia it was the man who had to bear all the expenses for his wife and family. This included housing, clothing, food and other necessities. Women were generally exempt from these expenses as their father or husband would have provided for her and the family. Therefore any inheritance a woman received could be spent entirely on herself; whereas any inheritance a man received would need to be spent on his wife and family. So a woman may be entitled to less inheritance in Islam, but she would actually get to keep most of it, if not all of it, for herself. This is in addition to a dowry a Muslim bride would receive from her husband upon marriage.

But a problem occurs when the Quran asks Muslims to treat it as valid for all time. Around 1,400 years ago women and men didn't have access to the education and technology we have today; raising children and maintaining the home was challenging due to a lack of resources. Therefore for women 1,400 years ago not to be 'burdened' by matters of the outside world may have been advantageous to families at the time. It would have reduced the risk of jeopardizing her primary responsibility as a wife and mother.

But this isn't as applicable today as it was in 7th century Arabia, and it will continue to be even less applicable in the future. Now in the 21st century women are more independent than they have ever been in human history. Broadly speaking, they're no longer reliant upon men to protect and provide for them.

Unfortunately, many Muslim women across the Islamic world still receive less inheritance than men. The Sharia law in those countries are in line with what the Quran said 1,400 years ago, not in line with the century and society we're in now.[3] Regrettably, it took until the 20th century to establish women's rights in western legal systems, and even today, women are still fighting for equal pay and opportunities. But women's rights in Islamic law aren't tied to our century, they're fixed to the Quran and Hadith from the 7th and 9th century, and even then, they're subject to the patriarchal interpretations of male Islamic jurists and male Muslim clerics.

The second example of the value of one man equaling two women in the Quran is regarding women providing legal testimony.

> Quran 2:282 – O believers, when you contract a debt one upon another for a stated term, write it down, and let a writer write it down between you justly, and let not any writer refuse to write it down, as God has taught him; so let him write, and let the debtor dictate, and let him fear God his Lord and not diminish aught of it. And if the debtor be a fool, or weak, or unable to dictate himself, then let his guardian dictate justly. And call in to witness two witnesses, men; or if the two be not men, then one man and

3. Muslim Women's League. "Islamic Inheritance." Muslim Women's League. September 1995. http://www.mwlusa.org/topics/rights/inheritance.html.

two women, such witnesses as you approve of, that if one of the two women errs the other will remind her; and let the witnesses not refuse, whenever they are summoned. And be not loth to write it down, whether it be small or great, with its term; that is more equitable in God's sight, more upright for testimony, and likelier that you will not be in doubt. Unless it be merchandise present that you give and take between you; then it shall be no fault in you if you do not write it down. And take witnesses when you are trafficking one with another. And let not either writer or witness be pressed; or if you do, that is ungodliness in you. And fear God; God teaches you, and God has knowledge of everything.

Quran 2:282 (the single longest verse in the Quran) means the Sharia law in many Muslim countries only values a woman's testimony as half of a man's testimony in a court of law. Regarding the legal systems in the Middle East and North Africa region, a 2011 report from UNICEF has even concluded:

"The legal system in every country in the MENA [Middle East and North Africa] region contains provisions which could be considered discriminatory against women from a human rights perspective, in particular in relation to the personal status codes."[4]

Curiously, outside the Middle East and North Africa region, Muslim women have not only overcome a less liberal legal system and Muslim society, but they've been elected as Prime Ministers or Presidents in Muslim-majority countries. These include countries such as Pakistan, Bangladesh, Turkey, Senegal, Indonesia, Kyrgyzstan and Mali. Particularly noteworthy is Bangladesh, with a population of 146 million Muslims. Since 2017, Bangladesh has been ruled by a female Muslim Prime Minister for 24 of the last 27 years. This contrasts sharply with western democracies like the USA who've never had a female president. This isn't to say women's legal rights or independence in Muslim countries are equal to or better than those in western democracies. But increasing education and opportunities have seen progressive movements for Muslim women to seek more roles in politics, particularly in the last 30 years.[5]

4. UNICEF. Regional Overview for the Middle East and North Africa MENA - Gender Equality Profile - Status of Girls and Women in the Middle East and North Africa. Report. October 2011. https://www.unicef.org/gender/files/REGIONAL-Gender-Eqaulity-Profile-2011.pdf.

5. Bhutto, Benazir. "Politics and the Muslim Woman." In Liberal Islam, edited by Charles Kurzman. New York: Oxford Univ. Press, 2011.

Yet due to centuries of patriarchal interpretations of the Quran and Hadith, many Muslim men still see women predominantly as wives and mothers. This has led to some Muslims discouraging women directly and indirectly from taking up leadership positions outside the household. But since we've seen female Muslim leaders outside of the Middle East and North African region, it could be a cultural influence rather than a fault of Islam. However it's also clear Islam doesn't make it easy for women to hold positions of power. A particular ayah which highlights this point, and always attracts criticism, is in sura 4 al-Nisa (The Women).

> Quran 4:34 – Men are the managers of the affairs of women for that God has preferred in bounty one of them over another, and for that they have expended of their property. Righteous women are therefore obedient, guarding the secret for God's guarding. And those you fear may be rebellious admonish; banish them to their couches, and beat them. If they then obey you, look not for any way against them; God is All-high, All-great.

In this verse, God says he sees men as the dominant protective authority over women, and He encourages women to be obedient to this position. It also says that if women are rebellious, men are within their rights to punish them.

Some Muslim scholars claim the '*beat them*' part is not supposed to be done aggressively by men; they claim there are various derivations and definitions of that particular Classical Arabic word.[6] However, it's this verse which has resulted in some Muslim courts refusing to prosecute cases of domestic abuse. Naturally, the Sharia law of those Muslim states are criticized by women's rights groups.[7]

Staying within the family dynamic, whom a Muslim woman is able to marry also reflects her subservient standing in Islam. Muslim men have the freedom to marry whoever they wish as long as she believes in the Abrahamic God (Muslims, Christians, Jews), but Muslim women are only allowed to marry Muslim men. This is for two reasons. First, any children Muslims have must be raised Muslim too. Within Islam, children always take the father's religion and the father's name (traditionally in Islam the wife doesn't take her husband's name in marriage).[8] Second, Islam forbids Muslim women (who have a superior

---

6. Kabbani, Muhammad Hisham., and Homayra Ziad. The Prohibition of Domestic Violence in Islam. Washington, D.C.: World Organization for Resource Development and Education, 2011. pp.6-12.

7. Ennaji, Moha, and Fatima Sadiqi. Gender and Violence in the Middle East. New York, NY: Routledge, 2011. pp.162-247.

religion) to marry a non-Muslim man (who has an inferior religion) so to avoid her placing herself in a subservient position to someone with an inferior religion.

It's not all one-sided though, there are examples within early Islam of Muslim women taking on leadership positions. Prophet Muhammad trusted his wife Aisha greatly, and after his death she continued to spread his message and serve the Muslim community for another 44 years.[9] She is looked upon favorably in Sunni tradition as a model example of a Muslim woman; though unfavorably in Shia tradition as they accuse her of hating Ali ibn Abi Talib, and defying him during his caliphate in the Battle of the Camel, when she fought men from Ali's army.[10] The Quran also mentions one female leader who held political power outside the traditional gender role of women in Islamic society, the Queen of Sheba.

> Quran 27:22-23 – But he tarried not long, and said, 'I have comprehended that which thou hast not comprehended, and I have come from Sheba to thee with a sure tiding. I found a woman ruling over them, and she has been given of everything, and she possesses a mighty throne.

After Prophet Muhammad's death, the role of women in Islamic communities changed. It became dictated by interpretations of Islamic texts from a patriarchal Muslim polity, a framework which still exists 1,400 years later. So when some opportunities arose for a woman to undertake a 'man's role', it became suppressed as it conflicts with Islam's male elite.

This isn't true for all Muslim countries, there are now numerous women in business, media and politics compared to previous generations. Many Muslim states call to attention women's rights and role in society, and open discussions are now being held by Muslim youth thanks to the advent of the internet and social media. The voices of Muslim women are becoming heard, not just within their families, but in their Muslim community and on a national and global scale.

Muslim women like 49 year old Egyptian/American journalist Mona

---

8. Jawad, Haifaa A. The Rights of Women in Islam: An Authentic Approach. IX, 150 S.: Palgrave, 2002.

9. Aleem, Shamim. Prophet Muhammad(s) and His Family: A Sociological Perspective. Bloomington, IN: AuthorHouse, 2007. p.130.

10. Goodwin, Jan. Price of Honor: Muslim Women Lift the Veil of Silence on the Islamic World. New York: Plume, 2003.

Eltahawy who speaks out on behalf of women's rights in the Arab world, and in 2015 published her book, 'Headscarves and Hymens: Why the Middle East Needs a Sexual Revolution' (a delightful book title).[11]

Or stand-up comedian Sakdiyah Ma'ruf, a 34 year old Indonesian Muslim woman, who in her comedic routines, addresses the rise of Islamic fundamentalism in her country which she fears is leading to increased violence, censorship and suppression. One of her jokes includes, "My motto in life is don't judge a man by his penis – they have enough problems already."[12]

How about women's rights activist and social media figure Loujain al-Hathloul? She's a 27 year old Saudi woman who in 2014 was arrested and detained for 73 days after attempting to cross the border from the UAE to Saudi Arabia in her car, thus breaking the Saudi Arabian ban on women driving. Ms al-Hathloul recorded and live-streamed her efforts on Facebook, Twitter and YouTube (which had large followings), gaining her global attention and widespread recognition.[13] She was no doubt inspired by many brave Saudi women before her like 37 year old Mana al-Sharif, a women's rights activist who helped start a women's right to drive campaign in Saudi Arabia in 2011. She was also arrested for driving in the Kingdom and posting a video of herself driving on Facebook and YouTube.[14]

Artist Atena Farghadani, an Iranian 30 year old political activist, was imprisoned for 18 months from 2015 for protesting her government's measure to curb birth control. Her crime was drawing a caricature of her government as apes, cows and other animals and posting it on Facebook. Amnesty International called her a "prisoner of conscience" and said that the "detention for her artistic work is a flagrant assault on freedom of expression."[15]

11. Eltahawy, Mona. Headscarves and Hymens: Why the Middle East Needs a Sexual Revolution. London: Weidenfeld & Nicolson, 2016.

12. Clarke, Lisa. "Sakdiyah Ma'ruf: The Muslim Comedian Using Punchlines for a Purpose."Australia Plus, November 15, 2016. http://www.australiaplus.com/international/in-person/the-fearless-muslim-comedian-pushing-the-boundaries/8026696.

13. Mackey, Robert. "Saudi Women Free After 73 Days in Jail for Driving." The New York Times, February 12, 2015. http://www.nytimes.com/2015/02/13/world/middleeast/saudi-women-free-after-73-days-in-jail-for-driving.html.

14. Galliot, Lorena, and Wajeha Al-Huwaider. "The Saudi Woman Who Took to the Driver's Seat." The Observers - France 24, May 23, 2011. http://observers.france24.com/en/20110523-saudi-woman-arrested-defying-driving-ban-manal-al-sharif-khobar.

15. "Iran: Serious Health Fears for Artist on Prison Hunger Strike." Amnesty International, March 2, 2015. https://www.amnesty.org/en/latest/news/2015/03/imprisoned-iranian-artist-atena-farghadani-on-hunger-strike/. See also Cavna, Michael. "Cartoonist Atena Farghadani, Sentenced for Satirizing Government as Animals, Is Freed in Iran." The Washington Post, May 4, 2016.

Journalist, politician and human rights activist Tawakkol Karman, a 38 year old Yemeni Muslim woman, became the first Yemeni, the first Arab woman, the second Muslim woman, the third female journalist, and at the time, at the age of 32, the youngest recipient of the Nobel Peace Prize in 2011. The Nobel Committee said of Mrs Karman, "In the most trying circumstances, both before and during the 'Arab spring', Tawakkul Karman has played a leading part in the struggle for women's rights and for democracy and peace in Yemen." Since 2005, Mrs Karman has been jailed several times for her activism, condemned in the official state media, and physically attacked. A prominent activist and advocate of human rights and freedom of expression, Tawakkul Karman has led regular protests and sit-ins calling for the release of political prisoners. She has also campaigned to raise the minimum age at which women are married in Yemen, a country with a high rate of child marriages (see chapter 'Prophet Muhammad as a role model').[16]

The title of the youngest-ever Nobel Prize laureate at the age of 17 is the irrepressible Malala Yousafzai. Born to a Sunni-Muslim family of Pashtun ethnicity in Pakistan, Malala, now living in the UK, is an activist standing up for the right of female education and freedom across the world. Malala knew how important education was to her and to all young girls from an early age. In early 2009 at the age of only 11, Malala began blogging about living under the Taliban's threats to deny her and other girls an education. She did so under the pseudonym of 'Gul Makai' for BBC Urdu. She was revealed to be the blogger later that year and as a result she and her family received many death threats for a number of years. On October 9, 2012, a Taliban gunman boarded her school bus as she was travelling home and fired three shots at her, with one of the bullets entering and exiting her head and lodging itself in her shoulder. Seriously wounded, Malala was airlifted to a Pakistani military hospital in Peshawar, and then four days later, to an intensive care unit in Birmingham, England. Once in the UK, Malala was taken out of a medically induced coma. She required multiple surgeries, including the repair of a facial nerve to fix the paralysed left side of her face, but she suffered no major brain

https://www.washingtonpost.com/news/comic-riffs/wp/2016/05/04/cartoonist-atena-farghadani-sentenced-for-satirizing-government-as-animals-is-freed-in-iran/.

16. The Norwegian Nobel Committee. Nobel Media AB. "The Nobel Peace Prize for 2011 to Ellen Johnson Sirleaf, Leymah Gbowee and Tawakkul Karman - Press Release." News release, October 7, 2011. Nobelprize.org. http://www.nobelprize.org/nobel_prizes/peace/laureates/2011/press.html. See also Karman, Tawakkul. "Yemeni Activist Tawakkul Karman, First Female Arab Nobel Peace Laureate: A Nod for Arab Spring." Interview by Amy Goodman. Democracy Now! October 7, 2011. https://www.democracynow.org/2011/10/7/yemeni_activist_tawakkul_karman_first_female.

damage. After weeks of treatment and therapy, in March 2013, Malala was able to attend school again only 5 months after she was attacked, this time in Birmingham. She survived, and her incredible story and recovery resulted in a global outpouring of support for her. She has since continued to speak out on the importance of education for all children. Her bravery and human rights activism earned her a nomination for the Nobel Peace Prize in 2013, and then another nomination in 2014 which she won, becoming its youngest ever recipient.[17]

Hopefully Islamic laws and mindsets across the Muslim world will continue updating to reflect contemporary society and not just 7th century Arabian society. It would lead to more Muslim women being treated as equals; encouraged to take public leadership positions, receiving the equal value of inheritance due to her, receiving an equal voice in an Islamic court of law, receiving more protection from domestic abuse, receiving education, receiving healthcare, and finally, receiving equality.

Muslims can try and operate within the constraints of the Quran and Hadith, but there's only so much Islam can do if we wish to provide women with real equality. If we truly wish to advance women's rights further, it has to be done outside of Islam's limitations.

17. Peer, Basharat. "The girl who wanted to go to school." The New Yorker, October 10, 2012. http://www.newyorker.com/news/news-desk/the-girl-who-wanted-to-go-to-school?currentPage=all See also Associated Press. "Malala Yousafzai Becomes Youngest-Ever Nobel Prize Winner." People.com, October 10, 2014. http://www.people.com/article/malala-yousafzai-wins-nobel-prize.

31

Women's clothing

Muslim women's clothing is a hot topic getting hotter as multiculturalism spreads across the world. Unlike Muslim men, most Muslim women have their religion displayed publicly for everyone to see due to their clothing. This may be insignificant for Muslim women living in Muslim countries, but in non-Muslim countries making your religious beliefs public is often disadvantageous. Rasmieyh Abdelnabi, a 27 year old Muslim woman living in America, says:

> "When you wear hijab and you walk into a room, everyone notices you; everyone stares at you; everyone makes assumptions about you. When you put the scarf on, you have to understand that you are representing a community. And that is huge. That's a huge responsibility. And I don't know if it's for everyone."[1]

We'll begin by distinguishing between the three most commonly worn items of Islamic female clothing:

> 1. **Burqa** – an outer garment worn which covers the entire female body. It has a transparent grille over the face so that a woman can see through it, but no one else can see her.
> 2. **Niqab** – like a burqa in that it covers the body, but it has a place cut out for the eyes to see through. Therefore you can see a Muslim woman's eyes when she wears a niqab, but no other parts of her body.
> 3. **Hijab** – the most common form of garment worn by Muslim

---

1. Khalid, Asma. "Lifting The Veil: Muslim Women Explain Their Choice." NPR, April 21, 2011. http://www.npr.org/2011/04/21/135523680/lifting-the-veil-muslim-women-explain-their-choice.

women. It's a scarf or veil which can be worn loose or tight-fitting. It covers the head and can go as far down as the chest. You can see all of a woman's face when she wears a hijab. The rest of her body is not covered by a hijab, but it's customary in Muslim societies for women not to wear anything revealing too much skin or anything which may highlight her body's figure.

Religious clothing like the burqa and niqab are cultural adoptions, not religious obligations from Islam. Veiled dresses like the burqa and niqab actually precede Islam, Christianity and Judaism.[2] Today there are still some enduring examples of veiling women in contemporary society, for example, a wedding veil worn over a bride's face and head to symbolize her virginity or modesty. So in this chapter we'll only focus only on the hijab as it's the most worn garment globally worn by Muslim women, and the concept of hijab is referenced in the Quran (though not explicitly).

There are differing views regarding the hijab among Muslim women. Many enjoy wearing it as a sign of modesty, privacy or to connect them closer to Islam. Other women don't enjoy wearing a hijab as it's too constraining, literally and figuratively, but they have no issue with other women wearing them. However some Muslim women are against themselves and others wearing a hijab, believing it strips them of their individuality and carries oppressive connotations. This oppression has even lead to women policing other Muslim women on their clothing.[3]

Islamic belief suggests women shouldn't diminish their value with clothes and aesthetics. Doing so will only lead to a never-ending competition between women regarding their bodies' sexuality, all the while stirring up the physical and carnal desires of men around them. This would ultimately culminate in a destructive social environment for the Muslim community. Islamic belief also states any forms of physical pleasures (by sight and hearing as well as touch) must remain in heterosexual (but not necessarily monogamous) marriages. Anything other than this will also lead to the pollution and impurity of values in Muslim societies.

Liberal Muslims and non-Muslims oppose these kinds of restrictions and believe societies must not control and regulate a woman's appearance. They

2. Ahmed, Leila. *Women and Gender in Islam: Historical Roots of a Modern Debate.* Philadelphia: University of Pennsylvania Pr., 2011.

3. *(un)veiled: Muslim Women Talk About Hijab.* Directed by Ines Hofmann Kanna. Produced by Ines Hofmann Kanna. Documentary Educational Resources. 2007. http://www.der.org/films/unveiled.html.

contest women must be free to express themselves and their own individuality, just as society allows men to do.[4]

Many young Muslim women in the 21st century promote these progressive approaches to Islam, having been told from a young age that they should be kept pure and special in the eyes of God why is why it's important for them to dress modestly. Many young women have also critiqued the conservative interpretations of Islam and how it made them feel growing up as a Muslim, including Nasreen (not her real name) who at the time was 29 years old and living in London:

> "I've had bouts of clinical depression. The thing is, Islam teaches you to grow up with low self-esteem and lack of self-identity. Without the collective, you're lost. You've been taught to feel guilty and people-pleasing as a woman, and you do that from a very young age. I kept thinking, 'Why do I want to wear short skirts? That's so disgusting!' No, it's not disgusting. It took me a long time to appreciate my sexuality and my femininity. There was a lot of stress. I lost my friends. You're very lonely and you're ostracised."[5]

The various interpretations of women's dress in Islam are due to cultural influences and the ambiguity of the Quran's verses. The following is the clearest ayah available in the Quran regarding women's dress code.

> Quran 24:31 – And say to the believing women, that they cast down their eyes' and guard their private parts, and reveal not their adornment save such as is outward; and let them cast their veils over their bosoms, and not reveal their adornment save to their husbands, or their fathers, or their husbands' fathers, or their sons, or their husbands' sons, or their brothers, or their brothers' sons, or their sisters' sons, or their women, or what their right hands own, or such men as attend them, not having sexual desire, or children who have not yet attained knowledge of women's private parts; nor let them stamp their feet, so that their hidden ornament may be known. And turn all together to God, O you believers; haply so you will prosper.

4. Khalid, Asma. "Lifting The Veil: Muslim Women Explain Their Choice." NPR, April 21, 2011. http://www.npr.org/2011/04/21/135523680/lifting-the-veil-muslim-women-explain-their-choice.

5. Anthony, Andrew. "Losing Their Religion: The Hidden Crisis of Faith among Britain's Young Muslims." The Guardian, May 17, 2015. https://www.theguardian.com/global/2015/may/17/losing-their-religion-british-ex-muslims-non-believers-hidden-crisis-faith.

In this verse Muslim women are asked to cover their private parts and bosoms. In addition, they must not show any part of their body to anyone except their husband, or to select family members, other women, doctors and children. But the extent to which Sharia law and Muslim women chose to enforce this and *'reveal not their adornment save such as is outward'* has been open to interpretation. It's dependent upon many variables such as the believer's particular time in human history, the culture they find themselves in, and where in the world they live. This is why some Muslim countries demand their women cover from head to toe, some only require the hijab, and others leave the decision with the women themselves.

Some Muslims claim God intentionally made it vague so it's flexible for women throughout history. They argue if God wanted to, He could have listed all the acceptable body parts in detail.[6] But if this is indeed what God intended then it can also be argued that He would have said it explicitly, and not left it up for debate and potential distortion by Muslims throughout history. To claim God left it deliberately vague is to look back and retroactively assign omissions He made as deliberate (but only if doing so makes Him appear more favorable).

The Sharia law of most Muslim countries leans towards keeping their women more modest in appearance, just in case. This is because God instructed Prophet Muhammad's wives, daughters and female followers to conduct themselves modestly.

> Quran 33:59 – O Prophet, say to thy wives and daughters and the believing women, that they draw their veils close to them; so it is likelier they will be known, and not hurt. God is All-forgiving, All-compassionate.

The Quran holds the wives of Prophet Muhammad in high esteem, referring to them as 'Mothers of the Believers'. So, for Muslim women to imitate Prophet Muhammad's wives is seen as an admirable goal. But the Quran also states the Prophet's wives aren't like other women, which is why some Muslims interpret God's rules as only applicable to them alone.[7]

> Quran 33:32 – Wives of the Prophet, you are not as other women. If

---

6. "Islam: Hijab." BBC. September 3, 2009. http://www.bbc.co.uk/religion/religions/islam/beliefs/hijab_1.shtml.

7. Wadud, Amina. Qur'an and Woman: Rereading the Sacred Text from a Woman's Perspective. Oxford University Press, 1999. p.34.

you are godfearing, be not abject in your speech, so that he in whose heart is sickness may be lustful; but speak honourable words.

One way in which Muslim women differed from the Prophet's wives is that if Muslim men wished to speak to his wives, they could only do so behind a curtain or veil as God said it would be better for Muslim men, and for the Prophet's wives.

> Quran 33:53 – O believers, enter not the houses of the Prophet, except leave is given you for a meal, without watching for its hour. But when you are invited, then enter; and when you have had the meal, disperse, neither lingering for idle talk; that is hurtful to the Prophet, and he is ashamed before you; but God is not ashamed before the truth. And when you ask his wives for any object, ask them from behind a curtain; that is cleaner for your hearts and theirs. It is not for you to hurt God's Messenger, neither to marry his wives after him, ever; surely that would be, in God's sight, a monstrous thing.

So since many Islamic jurists believe the Prophet's wives are ideal examples for Muslim women, they also believe women should be spoken to behind their own curtain or veil. Like a burqa or niqab.

But other Islamic jurists interpret it much differently, stressing the Quran only instructs women to dress modestly, guard their private parts, cover their bosoms and even then, only in the presence of certain people. They point out that the Quran doesn't actually say anything about covering a woman's head, hair, or face at all.

Critics of Islam will stand by their assessment of burqas, niqabs and hijabs as a sign of oppression or a security threat, but the contemporary practice of Muslim women wearing these clothes may just be a result of tradition and custom, rather than Islam itself. Many Muslim women embrace their Islamic clothing as it's a way of emulating Prophet Muhammad's wives, who are so revered by God in the Quran. It's also a sign of them celebrating their religion, enabling them to feel more intellectually powerful, rather than being objectified as a sex object by some men. Many Muslim women also continue to wear these clothes because their mother and other women in their family wear them as well, thus connecting her to her family as well as Islam.[8]

---

8. (un)veiled: Muslim Women Talk About Hijab. Directed by Ines Hofmann Kanna. Produced by Ines Hofmann Kanna. Documentary Educational Resources. 2007. http://www.der.org/films/unveiled.html.

Women's clothing in Islam is a complex and layered issue. There's no definitive answer on what Muslim women must and must not wear. But this is why women's clothing in Islam is so important to discuss. As each year passes, the world changes considerably, and if we're to live peacefully together we must find a way of respecting our neighbor's customs.

We've already begun to see issues with Muslim women's clothing occur in the 21st century. In April 2011, France became the first European nation to ban face covering in public spaces based on principles of security. This means no burqas and niqabs, but France does permit the hijab in public spaces as it doesn't hide the face. Since then, Belgium, Chad and Congo-Brazzaville have also enforced a national ban on face covering, and Cameroon, Italy, the Netherlands, Niger, Spain, Switzerland and Turkey have enforced partial (not national) bans.[9]

There's no personal conclusion to be drawn here as there has been with previous chapters. This writer is a man, so I'll never understand nor appreciate what it's like to be a Muslim woman in any country. But I do have empathy for the Muslim women who don't have a choice of what they wear, everyday. Many Muslim women are happy with their situation with regards to clothing, but so many others aren't as fortunate. They have no say in the matter due to the vast number of interpretations possible from the Quran.

It's disappointing Muslim women can't wear what they want in Muslim countries; but it can also be argued it's disappointing when Muslim women can't wear what they want in non-Muslim countries. A compromise must be met, and I believe Muslim women need to be the ones leading the discussion – not Muslim men and the patriarchal dominance pervasive throughout the Islamic world. Muslim men in Iran and other parts of the Persian world have already begun to speak up about ending the enforced requirement of wearing a hijab outdoors and giving the choice back to women. In a small movement called Men In Hijab, Muslim men are wearing the hijab as a sign of solidarity with their wives or female family members.[10]

It's the 21st century. It's their bodies. We can place our faith in women to make the right decisions for themselves, whichever path they choose to take.

9. Sanghani, Radhika. "Burka Bans: The Countries Where Muslim Women Can't Wear Veils." The Telegraph, July 8, 2016. http://www.telegraph.co.uk/women/life/burka-bans-the-countries-where-muslim-women-cant-wear-veils/.

10. Saul, Heather. "Men in Hijab: Two Men Explain Why They Are Covering Their Heads to Support Their Wives and Family in Iran." Independent, July 31, 2016. http://www.independent.co.uk/news/people/men-in-hijab-iran-solidarity-wives-family-veil-islam-muslim-womens-rights-a7164876.html.

32

Women and polygyny

"I encourage all of us, whatever our beliefs, to question the basic narratives of our world, to connect past developments with present concerns, and not to be afraid of controversial issues" – Yuval Noah Harari

We'll begin by defining some terms. Monogamy is marriage with only one person at a time; worldwide it's the most common form of marriage practiced regardless of religion, race or nationality. Polygamy is the practice of having more than one wife or husband at the same time; this is less common than monogamy but it is still prevalent in some cultures.

Polyandry is when a woman has more than one husband; Islam forbids this. One of the reasons is the uncertainty as to who the father of any child would be. Although this is not an issue now with DNA tests, it was at the time of the Quran's revelations. In addition, it was also seen as unbecoming of a righteous and honorable woman to have multiple male partners.

Polygyny is when a man has more than one wife; Islam permits this. Men who practice polygyny can still be seen as righteous and honorable. Polygyny was practiced by Prophet Muhammad himself: he had a total of 11 wives.[1]

The requirement from Muslim men who take more than one wife is to treat them all equally and fairly. A Muslim man must also never do anything to hurt one wife in order to please another. If a Muslim man cannot meet these requirements, then he can only marry one woman. The majority of Muslims and Muslims scholars agree the Quran permits a Muslim man to have up to four wives.

Quran 4:2-3 – Give the orphans their property, and do not exchange the corrupt for the good; and devour not their property with your

---

1. "Marriages of the Holy Prophet." Al-Islam.org. Accessed January 25, 2017. https://www.al-islam.org/life-muhammad-prophet-sayyid-saeed-akhtar-rizvi/marriages-holy-prophet.

property; surely that is a great crime. If you fear that you will not act justly towards the orphans, marry such women as seem good to you, two, three, four; but if you fear you will not be equitable, then only one, or what your right hands own; so it is likelier you will not be partial.

Quran 4:2-3 was most likely revealed after the Battle of Uhud in 625 CE. Many Muslim men died in this battle which is why there's a reference to orphans. This reference has been interpreted to mean God requests Muslim men not to marry orphan girls in order to take their property (a pre–Islamic practice in ancient Arabia).[2] It has also been interpreted to mean don't marry the mothers of 'orphans' just to gain access to the wealth the orphans would have inherited from their deceased fathers.[3] Instead, Muslim men are better marrying other women who seem good to them; two, three, four of them (or more depending on your interpretation of this phrase).

There are many reasons why Islam permits Muslim men to have multiple wives, most of which are more relevant to 7th century Arabia than the 21st century world.

1. To support underprivileged women and care for them. For example, widows who've lost their husbands from war.
2. To ensure the safety of clan–less women who have no male relatives as it was particularly dangerous for them in 7th century tribalist Arabian cultures.
3. To increase the spread of Islam and its followers through the number of children a man can produce, since in Islam children always take the religion of the father.
4. To spread the message of Islam by marrying women from various Arab tribes.
5. To provide a man with a wife who can bear children in case one of his wives can not. In particular, a boy, so that the man can pass on his assets and the family name can continue.
6. Finally, to actually *decrease* the number of wives men were allowed to have. Many powerful male leaders wanted to convert to Islam, but they didn't want to forgo their harem of wives. Having a harem of women was custom at the time in some Arab cultures and not all

2. A., Abdel Haleem M. The Qur'an: English Translation and Parallel Arabic Text. Oxford: Oxford University Press, 2016.

3. "Dealing Justly with Wives and Orphans (Qur'an 4:3)." WikiIslam. July 9, 2015. https://wikiislam.net/wiki/Dealing_Justly_with_Wives_and_Orphans_(Qur%27an_4:3).

men treated these women with respect. But getting these powerful and influential men to convert to Islam was important. So to be accommodating to local Arab customs at the time, Islam allowed men to have multiple wives. However, it was limited to 'only' four wives, and they must all be treated equally. If a Muslim man already has the maximum number of four wives, then he must divorce an existing wife if he wishes to marry another woman.[4]

Muslim countries approach polygyny in various ways. In some countries it's quite common, while in others it's rare or non-existent. Muslims all follow the same holy book, but since it's interpreted differently, Muslims approach and apply its guidance differently.

In the Muslim countries Algeria, Bangladesh, Iran, Iraq, Jordan, Kuwait, Lebanon, and Morocco women are allowed to put a clause in marriage contracts that prohibits polygyny. In addition, in Iran and Pakistan men are required to get permission from their first wife in order to take a second wife; they must also show a court of law the proof of the first wife's consent.[5] This may seem logical, but it is significant as the Quran doesn't state Muslim men need approval from their wife or wives for additional marriages, therefore many Muslim men don't seek it.

Turkey was the first Muslim country to ban polygyny legally in 1926 but it wasn't based on religious reasons, it was a secular ban.[6] Tunisia was the next country to ban polygyny through legislation passed in 1956, this time it was on religious grounds. Tunisian jurists interpreted the Quran as limiting the practice of polygyny. They claimed that the Quran doesn't actually support polygyny and it had always intended for it to be eliminated over time. Their justification for this was the Quran's obligation of equal treatment of all the wives in a polygynous marriage. Tunisian jurists deemed this impossible, so consequently this makes the practice of polygyny against the word of God and illegal.[7]

Muslims critical of polygynous marriages also point to another ayah in the Quran which supports the argument men can't be equal to all their wives.

Quran 4:129 – You will not be able to be equitable between your wives, be you ever so eager; yet do not be altogether partial so that

4. Ahmed, Leila. Women and Gender in Islam: Historical Roots of a Modern Debate. Philadelphia: University of Pennsylvania Pr., 2011.

5. Ali-Karamali, Sumbul. The Muslim Next Door: The Qur'an, the Media, and That Veil Thing. Ashland, Oregon: White Cloud Press, 2008. p.145.

6. Ibid., p.142.

7. Ibid., p.145.

you leave her as it were suspended. If you set things right, and are godfearing, God is All-forgiving, All-compassionate.

This makes the matter more confusing as the Quran has both permitted this practice and not permitted it. Prophet Muhammad himself had at least 11 wives in his lifetime, even he must have struggled to treat all of them equally (after all, he performed no miracles in his prophethood).

There are feminist Muslim scholars who view the issue of polygyny as a societal problem, rather than a problem with Islam itself. They claim Prophet Muhammad set rules which treated women progressively for that era, and he respected his wives a great deal.[8] They also claim the Quran permits polygyny so fatherless children of widowed women could be cared for. Therefore, polygyny is permissible since it can be a charitable and honorable act.[9]

So if Prophet Muhammad is held as the role model for Muslims to emulate and the Quran is a book valid for all time, then there's nothing to suggest the practice of polygyny was to be fazed out over time. If an argument is put forward that no one can have more than one wife and treat them all equally, if Prophet Muhammad could do it (with even more than four wives), shouldn't Muslim men try, since they aspire to emulate him?

It's clear polygyny served a purpose in 7th century Arabia and it served specific purposes for Prophet Muhammad himself (see chapter 'Prophet Muhammad's self-serving rules'). God Himself may have permitted it in the Quran, but there is a reason why so many Muslim countries have put restrictions on it; Algeria, Bangladesh, Egypt, Iran, Iraq, Jordan, Kuwait, Lebanon, Morocco, Sudan and Syria, and there's a reason why Turkey and Tunisia have made it illegal.[10] These Muslim governments decided this particular practice doesn't serve the same purpose in their modern world as it used to in the 7th century. Since a precedence has been set in the 20th and 21st century of limiting a practice approved of by God in the Quran and practiced by Prophet Muhammad, perhaps it's only a matter of time before Muslims

8. Ahmed, Leila. Women and Gender in Islam: Historical Roots of a Modern Debate. Philadelphia: University of Pennsylvania Pr., 2011.

9. Wadud, Amina. Qur'an and Woman: Rereading the Sacred Text from a Woman's Perspective. Oxford University Press, 1999. p.83.

10. Ali-Karamali, Sumbul. The Muslim Next Door: The Qur'an, the Media, and That Veil Thing. Ashland, Oregon: White Cloud Press, 2008. p.145. See also Kusha, Hamid R. "Polygyny." In The Oxford Encyclopedia of the Islamic World, edited by John L. Esposito. Oxford: Oxford Univ. Press, 2009.

realize there are other customs they disagree with too. We may be unable to modernize Islam, but, thankfully, Muslims can modernize themselves.

PART VIII

The Modern World

Islam's development from its humble beginnings in the 7th century Arabian desert to the 21st century is remarkable. Islam has become the second most practiced religion in the world after Christianity, with 1.7 billion Muslims globally.[1] It is also the fastest growing religion in the world due to its high birth rate.[2] Perhaps even Prophet Muhammad would have been surprised at how far his message has spread.

A lot has happened in the last 1,400 years. There has been the rise and fall of civilizations, the world has become deeply connected through the internet, people live longer due to the advancement of medicine, humans have reached other planets in our solar system, and old laws have been updated.

In Prophet Muhammad's time, if someone had gone back or forward 50 years life would only be a little bit different. It wouldn't have changed so much that they wouldn't understand how it all worked. Today, if someone went back in time only 50 years ago, they'd have to adjust to how things were, but they'd find their feet quickly enough. But, if a woman or man went forward in time 50 years from the 1960s to the 2010s, they'd be amazed by how much life has changed. Everyone carries tiny telephones which can seemingly do everything, people live and work their entire lives in front of computer screens, they travel on planes across the world as if it's as easy as catching a local bus, and in some countries two women or two women can even marry each other.

It goes to show how fast the world is evolving and how rapidly society is developing in recent times. It can be hard to keep up. In the last 50 years we've made breakthroughs in infant mortality rates, life expectancies, renewable

---

1. Johnson, Todd M., Gina A. Zurlo, Albert W. Hickman, and Peter F. Crossing. Christianity 2015: Religious Diversity and Personal Contact. Report. Vol. 39. Series 1. South Hamilton: International Bulletin of Missionary Research, 2015. Accessed October 18, 2016. http://www.gordonconwell.edu/ockenga/research/documents/2IBMR2015.pdf.

2. The Future of World Religions: Population Growth Projections, 2010-2050. Report. April 2, 2015. http://www.pewforum.org/2015/04/02/religious-projections-2010-2050/.

energies, trade networks, economic growth and space travel. Our cultures have changed dramatically in such a short period of time and it won't be slowing down. In fact, judging by the recent advancements made, it'll only be accelerating in speed. With all these changes, it's exciting to see what's in store for us in the next 50 years.

But, while we're moving forward, Muslims must simultaneously adhere to static and antiquated laws from the past. Since the Quran claims itself as a book for all time, Muslims have no choice but to stick by it, even if they don't agree with everything in it.

So, this part will be looking at examples of conflicting opinions between modern society in the 21st century, and Islam.

33

Sharia law

"Religion is dangerous because it allows human beings who don't have all the answers to think that they do" – Bill Maher

Sharia law is a term which has become familiar to non-Muslims since Western media mentions it often. Sharia law covers all aspects of a Muslim's life: public issues such as trade, crime and economics, and personal issues such as sex, diet and fasting. Sharia in Arabic means 'way' or 'path' and its aim is to promote human welfare within Muslim communities.

The laws derived from Sharia are from a combination of sources. These include the Quran, the Hadith (sayings, actions and practices of Prophet Muhammad) and fatwas (rulings of Islamic scholars). Sharia is required for any issues not directly addressed in the Quran or Hadith, but, the derivation of Sharia law differs between countries and sects of Muslims.

There's a general disagreement between Muslims and non-Muslims regarding what Sharia law symbolizes. Some non-Muslims associate it with barbaric punishments like stonings and lashings and therefore view it as non-progressive and draconian. Muslims on the other hand view Sharia law as something which protects and nurtures humanity, it helps women and men realize their full potential. Muslims don't see it as something primitive just because it is based on texts from as far back as the 7th century, but rather they see it as laws which were divinely revealed.

How Muslims perceive Sharia law can depend on which sect of Islam they follow (Sunni or Shia) and which country they live in. This is because much of Sharia law is the human interpretation of Islamic texts by (male-dominated) Islamic jurists, clerics and governments. If something is unclear in the Quran or Hadith, these Muslim men interpret the texts and determine what God or Prophet Muhammad would have wanted. This is why even Islamic scholars have suggested Sharia law has become a product of human interpretation, and is not the purely divine law it's supposed to be. This human element is also why there are different rulings of Sharia law between Muslim countries, leading to various degrees of legislation enforced upon citizens' actions, freedom of speech and freedom of religion throughout the Islamic world.[1] Though the Quran claims it has made everything clear for us, the only thing that is clear is that it hasn't, since there's no consensus among Muslims with Sharia law (see chapters 'Ambiguity of the Quran' and 'Inadequacy of the Quran').

> Quran 16:89 – And the day We shall raise up from every nation a witness against them from amongst them, and We shall bring thee as a witness against those. And We have sent down on thee the Book making clear everything, and as a guidance and a mercy, and as good tidings to those who surrender.

This matter is burdened further when we take into account the 'law of abrogation' within the Quran (Naskh in Arabic). To abrogate means to revoke or cancel something officially or formally. The majority of Islamic jurists accept the principle of the law of abrogation within the Quran and the Quran itself introduces it in two ayahs.

> Quran 2:106 – And for whatever verse We abrogate or cast into oblivion, We bring a better or the like of it; knowest thou not that God is powerful over everything?

> Quran 16:101 – And when We exchange a verse in the place of another verse and God knows very well what He is sending down — they say, 'Thou art a mere forger!' Nay, but the most of them have no knowledge.

The law of abrogation is God's way of saying that something He recently said may contradict something He previously said. If this happens, then we're to take what God said most recently as valid, and neglect what He said previously. It's the Quran's 'get out of jail free' card. The 'perfect' Quran gives itself the ability to change what it told us with something else it prefers at a later date.

> Quran 4:82 – What, do they not ponder the Koran? If it had been from other than God surely they would have found in it much inconsistency.

1. Uddin, Asma, Religious Freedom Implications of Sharia Implementation in Aceh, Indonesia (March 7, 2011). University of St. Thomas Law Journal, Vol. 7, No. 3, 2010. https://ssrn.com/abstract=1885776.

It's no surprise this has raised problems for Muslims. Muslim scholars have to chronologically analyze all the verses of the Quran of which there's no definitive consensus (even the ayahs in the same sura weren't revealed at the same time). Then, they have to determine which revelations will overrule the older revelations (of which there is also no consensus among Muslims). All this contradicts the Quran's claim that it is perfect, easy to follow, and there is no need to change its words.

> Quran 10:63-64 – Those who believe, and are godfearing — for them is good tidings in the present life and in the world to come. There is no changing the words of God; that is the mighty triumph.

There are verses in the Quran which try to be as clear as possible about what God desires from Muslims. For example, the Quran discusses inheritance law and the verses covering it are used to establish Sharia law. Unfortunately, this is also has its own problems.

> Quran 4:11 – God charges you, concerning your children: to the male the like of the portion of two females, and if they be women above two, then for them two-thirds of what he leaves, but if she be one then to her a half; and to his parents to each one of the two the sixth of what he leaves, if he has children; but if he has no children, and his heirs are his parents, a third to his mother, or, if he has brothers, to his mother a sixth, after any bequest he may bequeath, or any debt. Your fathers and your sons — you know not which out of them is nearer in profit to you. So God apportions; surely God is All-knowing, All-wise.

> Quran 4:12 – And for you a half of what your wives leave, if they have no children; but if they have children, then for you of what they leave a fourth, after any bequest they may bequeath, or any debt. And for them a fourth of what you leave, if you have no children; but if you have children, then for them of what you leave an eighth, after any bequest you may bequeath, or any debt. If a man or a woman have no heir direct, but have a brother or a sister, to each of the two a sixth; but if they are more numerous than that, they share equally a third, after any bequest he may bequeath, or any debt not prejudicial; a charge from God. God is All-knowing, All-clement.

> Quran 4:176 – They will ask thee for a pronouncement. Say: 'God

pronounces to you concerning the indirect heirs. If a man perishes having no children, but he has a sister, she shall receive a half of what he leaves, and he is her heir if she has no children. If there be two sisters, they shall receive two-thirds of what he leaves; if there be brothers and sisters, the male shall receive the portion of two females. God makes clear to you, lest you go astray; God has knowledge of everything.

There's a lot of information contained in these three verses so it can be difficult to follow who gets what when it comes to inheritance. But using these three verses, let's present some simple examples to see if God's mathematics adds up.

For the first example, let's say a man dies and leaves behind 3 daughters, his 2 parents, and his wife.

- The 3 daughters will receive ⅔ equally shared between the three of them (*Quran 4:11*).

- The parents will receive *1/6* each, so ⅓ in total between them (*Quran 4:11*).

- the wife will receive ⅛ (*Quran 4:12*).

We can now see that the ⅔ for the daughters, the ⅓ for the parents and the ⅛ for the wife is more than what's available to inherit by ⅛. God's numbers don't add up.

But let's try another example. A man dies and leaves behind his mother, his wife, and his 2 sisters.

- The mother will receive ⅓ (*Quran 4:11*).

- The wife will receive ¼ (*Quran 4:12*).

- The 2 sisters will either receive:

    - ⅓ combined together, so *1/6* each (*Quran 4:12*).

    - or, ⅔ shared equally between them, so ⅓ each (*Quran 4:176*).

If the sisters receive the former, then this adds up to $^{11}/_{12}$ (⅓ + ¼ + ⅓) of the available inheritance which is satisfactory. But if it's the latter, this adds up to $^{15}/_{12}$ ($\frac{1}{3}$ +$\frac{1}{4}$ + $\frac{2}{3}$) of the available inheritance, which is more than is available.

What fraction of the inheritance for the 2 sisters do we use, the $\frac{1}{3}$ from *Quran 4:12* or the $\frac{2}{3}$ from *Quran 4:176*? Perhaps it is the $\frac{1}{3}$ (*Quran 4:12*) since it would allow $^{11}/_{12}$ of the inheritance to be distributed fairly. But if the $\frac{2}{3}$ (*Quran 4:176*) came in a later ayah, does this not abrogate the earlier ayah? But remember, the ayahs in the same suras may not even be in chronological order. Quite a messy situation. So either God didn't do us any favors by having a law of abrogation in His book, or, the Quran as it is has not been compiled in a manner worthy of its self-declared status (see chapter '*Inaccuracy of the Quran*').

These problems may not trouble most people or keep them up at night, but when Muslims are told to take the Quran literally as the word of God, there are more troubling concerns which do arise. Because when it comes to implementing Sharia law, nowhere does it concern people most than with its strict and inhuman punishments. For example, amputation of hands as the punishment for theft.

> Quran 5:38-39 – And the thief, male and female: cut off the hands of both, as a recompense for what they have earned, and a punishment exemplary from God; God is All-mighty, All-wise. But whoso repents, after his evildoing, and makes amends, God will turn towards him; God is All-forgiving, All-compassionate.

This excessive and cruel punishment can be avoided if the thief repents and it is accepted by the Islamic jurist. However they're not always this fortunate. It may be an uncommon punishment administered in the Islamic world today, but Iran, Saudi Arabia and Northern Nigeria have all delivered on this ruling in recent years. Some for as little as stealing chocolate.[2]

Another excessively cruel punishment is 100 lashes for fornicators, delivered in public to shame them and to discourage others.

---

2. "Iranian Chocolate Thief Faces Hand Amputation." BBC News, October 17, 2010. http://www.bbc.com/news/world-middle-east-11559750. See also Abdorrahman Boroumand Foundation. "Cruel, Inhuman and Degrading Punishments." Human Rights & Democracy for Iran. Accessed November 27, 2016. https://www.iranrights.org/library/collection/142/amputation-and-eye-gouging. See also The Associated Press. "Saudi Arabia Cuts Off Thief's Hand as Punishment." Haaretz, December 15, 2014. http://www.haaretz.com/middle-east-news/1.631994. See also Bello, Ademola. "Who Will Save Amputees of Sharia Law in Nigeria?" The Huffington Post, May 25, 2011. http://www.huffingtonpost.com/ademola-bello/who-will-save-amputees-of_b_532949.html.

Quran 24:2 – The fornicatress and the fornicator — scourge each one of them a hundred stripes, and in the matter of God's religion let no tenderness for them seize you if you believe in God and the Last Day; and let a party of the believers witness their chastisement.

Interpretations of Hadith has also seen Sharia law in some Muslim countries serve 80 lashes for drinking alcohol.[3] Additionally, in some countries if any Muslim tries to leave Islam (apostasy), they're given the death penalty.[4] Therefore it's worth asking, are people more compelled to worship God out of love and because they believe in His guidance for us? Or, are they compelled to out of fear, in this life and the next?

It becomes more and more difficult to defend the 'timeless' Quran (and the Sharia law which comes from it) when it asks such worrying things of us. It has led to laws incompatible with the most basic of modern day human rights: freedom of speech (see chapter 'Censorship'), freedom of religion (see chapter 'Apostasy'), right of privacy (see chapter 'Sex'), women's rights (see part 'Women'), LGBT rights (see chapter 'Homosexuality'), and even aspects of democracy (see chapter 'Islamization'). Muslims may believe people have free will but it also seems Sharia law always does its best to stop people from implementing it. There are risks involved with believing in God.

Muslims can claim they've nothing to lose if they spend their lives worshiping something which may not be real in the end. But, there is a high price to be paid. Powerful Islamic countries around the world make significant political decisions based on a belief in God. God's words create the rights of individuals and societies in those countries. Armed conflicts across the world are still fought in His name everyday. The lives of billions of people, believers *and* non-believers, are affected by religious beliefs. Religious people can claim there's no harm in believing in God, but the actions of governments and heads of states suggest the contrary.

The problem with Islam is that it's a religion which creates submissiveness, conformity and dependency among its followers. This coupled with Sharia law can create a stifling, manipulative and archaic environment. It results in a nanny

3. Mansfield, Katie. "Christians Sentenced to 80 Lashes by Sharia Court for Drinking Communion Wine." Express Newspapers, November 16, 2016. http://www.express.co.uk/news/world/733081/ christians-sentenced-80-lashes-Sharia-court-drinking-communion-wine.

4. Spencer, Richard. "Saudi Arabia Court Gives Death Penalty to Man Who Renounced His Muslim Faith." Telegraph, February 24, 2015. http://www.telegraph.co.uk/news/worldnews/middleeast/ saudiarabia/11431509/Saudi-Arabia-court-gives-death-penalty-to-man-who-renounced-his-Muslim-faith.html.

state controlled by outdated rules and medieval punishments where people live in the past, and many of them, in fear. There will always be powerful Muslim men who want to remain in power; they'll want to maintain the status quo and keep Sharia law as it is. But the Islamic world can no longer ignore the modern world it finds itself in, that's one thing that can't be abrogated.

34

Homosexuality

"Atheists' anger doesn't prove that we're selfish, or joyless, or miserable. It shows that we have compassion, and a sense of justice. We're angry because we see terrible harm all around us, and we feel desperately motivated to stop it" – Greta Christina

The subject of homosexuality has begun to polarize the global Muslim community. Older and traditionally conservative Muslims maintain homosexuality is a sin and a punishable crime. They believe it's unnatural, immoral and condemned by God.

> Quran 26:165-166 – What, do you come to male beings, leaving your wives that your Lord created for you? Nay, but you are a people of transgressors.

They also fear homosexuality may become accepted by Muslim cultures with homosexuals granted the same rights as heterosexuals, leading to homosexual marriages and homosexual parents raising children. The belief is that this would harm the foundations of a Muslim community, though there's no evidence to support this belief. Nor is there any evidence to suggest their fear that homosexual parents will raise children to become homosexuals is true (the homosexual parents most likely came from heterosexual parents anyway). In addition, despite numerous attempts, there is also no science to conclusively prove that a 'gay gene' exists and homosexuality is hereditary, should they wish to have children via donor insemination or surrogacy.

In contrast, younger and progressively liberal Muslims don't view homosexuality in this negative light. They believe people don't choose to be LGBT (Lesbian, Gay, Bisexual, Transgender), it's just something you are or are not. They recognize it as natural among humans so it shouldn't be punished as a crime.

There are also Muslims who are somewhat down the middle: they believe

212 Atheism For Muslims

if someone is gay then they can't be 'reversed', but it is still haram (forbidden) to act upon any homosexual inclinations. If those gay Muslims do commit homosexual acts, then they're often encouraged to repent rather than confess their sins publicly as it's shameful for Muslims to be gay. Muslim cultures don't approve of same-sex acts but some tolerate it as long as it doesn't happen in public, and if it doesn't challenge any existing family or social order. It's similar to turning a blind eye, avoiding the issue and adopting a 'don't ask, don't tell' approach.[1]

In 2016, the International Lesbian, Gay, Bisexual, Trans and Intersex Association (ILGA) released its annual State Sponsored Homophobia Report. It concluded that there are 12 countries worldwide which punishes homosexuality with the death penalty. They are Afghanistan, Iran, Iraq, Mauritania, Nigeria (provincially), Pakistan, Qatar, Saudi Arabia, Somalia (provincially), Sudan, United Arab Emirates and Yemen. The only countries in the world which punish homosexuality with death are all Muslim countries.

The report found there are 19 Muslim majority countries which don't carry the death penalty, but where homosexual acts are still illegal. They are Algeria, Bangladesh, Brunei, Gambia, Guinea, Indonesia (provincially), Kuwait, Lebanon, Libya, Malaysia, Maldives, Morocco, Oman, Senegal, Sierra Leone, Syria, Tunisia, Turkmenistan and Uzbekistan.

Thankfully, the report also found same-sex acts are legal in 16 Muslim majority countries. They are Albania, Azerbaijan, Bahrain, Bosnia and Herzegovina, Burkina Faso, Chad, Djibouti, Egypt, Guinea-Bissau, Jordan, Kazakhstan, Kyrgyzstan, Mali, Niger, Tajikistan and Turkey.[2] Albania and Turkey have even seen the subject of same sex marriage raised in their governments. Although it hasn't amounted to anything yet, it's still encouraging to see anti-discrimination laws like these proposed.[3] It's clear Muslim attitudes towards the LGBT community range from outright disgust and hostility, to tolerance and complete acceptance.

The social and legal Islamic prejudice against LGBT people are due to

1. Ali, Kecia. Sexual Ethics and Islam: Feminist Reflections on Qur'an, Hadith, and Jurisprudence. Oxford: Oneworld, 2012.

2. Carroll, Aengus. State Sponsored Homophobia 2016: A World Survey of Sexual Orientation Laws: Criminalisation, Protection and Recognition. Report. 11th ed. Geneva: International Lesbian, Gay, Bisexual, Trans and Intersex Association, May, 2016. http://ilga.org/downloads/ 02_ILGA_State_Sponsored_Homophobia_2016_ENG_WEB_150516.pdf.

3. "No Gay Marriage for Albania." Pink News, February 5, 2010. http://www.pinknews.co.uk/2010/ 02/05/no-gay-marriage-for-albania. See also "The BDP's Debate on Gay Marriage (Turkish Language)." Timeturk, May 15, 2012. http://www.timeturk.com/tr/2012/05/15/bdp-nin-escinsel-evlilik-istegi-tartisiliyor.html.

what the Quran says about homosexuality. Like the Bible, the argument against homosexuality centers on the Prophet Lot (Lut in Arabic) and the destruction of Sodom. The Islamic version is similar to the Christian version of Sodom and Gomorrah, and its interpretation as opposing homosexuality is commonly accepted by Islamic scholars. This story is the reason homosexuals have been persecuted by Muslims throughout human history.

In the Quran, Lot is the nephew of Abraham and a prophet God sent to save the people of Sodom. It follows a familiar story found in the Quran about a prophet sent by God to save his community, who don't heed the prophet's warnings, and so God kills them all.

> Quran 7:80-84 – And Lot, when he said to his people, 'What, do you commit such indecency as never any being in all the world committed before you? See, you approach men lustfully instead of women; no, you are a people that do exceed.' And the only answer of his people was that they said, 'Expel them from your city; surely they are folk that keep themselves clean!' So We delivered him and his family, except his wife; she was one of those that tarried. And We rained down upon them a rain; so behold thou, how was the end of the sinners!

Though God is all-knowing and all-powerful, He makes the same mistake again and again; using the same method with almost every prophet until eventually He gets fed up and just decides to kill everyone.

In addition, there's also a disturbing account of obedience to God by Prophet Lot. In the Quran, God sent two angels disguised as handsome young boys to speak to Lot. The people of Sodom see them and are overjoyed new young boys have come to their city, so they try to take the boys from Lot to have their way with them. In what was apparently an admirable act, Lot offers his own daughters instead in return for the angels, however the people of Sodom refuse this offer.

> Quran 11:77-79 – And when Our messengers came to Lot, he was troubled on their account and distressed for them, and he said, 'This is a fierce day.' And his people came to him, running towards him; and erstwhile they had been doing evil deeds. He said, 'O my people, these are my daughters; they are cleaner for you. So fear God, and do not degrade me in my guests. What, is there not one man among you of a right mind?' They said, 'Thou knowest we have no right to thy daughters, and thou well knowest what we desire.'

God had previously commended Lot's uncle Abraham for his willingness to sacrifice his son (see chapter 'Abraham'). God had also approved Khidr killing a young boy because he wasn't devout like his parents (see chapter 'Moses'). So, it's no surprise offering one's daughters for rape is also commended by God, even if it is to save angels He sent into danger and could have saved Himself.

Lot was powerless to protect the angels disguised as boys, so the angels tell Lot to leave and escape during the night. They also tell Lot to leave behind his wife as she has become sinful like the people of Sodom. The morning came and God turns the city of Sodom upside down and rains upon it 'stones of baked clay'.

> Quran 11:81-83 – They said, 'Lot, we are messengers of thy Lord. They shall not reach thee; so set forth, thou with thy family, in a watch of the night, and let not any one of you turn round, excepting thy wife; surely she shall be smitten by that which smites them. Their promised time is the morning; is the morning not nigh?' So when Our command came, We turned it uppermost nethermost, and rained on it stones of baked clay, one on another, marked with thy Lord, and never far from the evildoers.

There's a lot of hostility in the Quran toward homosexuals even though homosexuality wasn't uncommon during the Prophet's time, and in his part of Arabia.[4] However, God doesn't prescribe a punishment for it (we're currently unable to turn cities upside down and rain down stones of baked clay). Many Muslim jurists interpret God's actions to mean the death penalty is the correct punishment for same-sex acts (though one can argue God killed the people of Sodom for attempted rape of his angels, not same-sex acts).

As mentioned, not all Muslims or Muslim countries agree with this punishment. In fact most modern day punishments for same-sex acts come from Hadith (not from the Quran) just as they come from Hadith for apostasy (see chapter 'Apostasy') and blasphemy (see chapter 'Censorship'). Though as we've discussed, Hadith are an even less credible source of authority than the Quran (see part 'Hadith'). So since there is no consensus regarding the punishment for same-sex acts, it's left to the interpretation and discretion of local and national Muslim authorities.

This is one of many examples in Islam where the rights of humans are in disagreement with the supposed 'laws of God'. The theological principle behind

---

4. Kugle, Scott Siraj Al-Haqq. "Sexuality, Diversity, and Ethics in the Agenda of Progressive Muslims." In Progressive Muslims: On Justice, Gender and Pluralism, edited by Omid Safi, p.222. Oxford: Oneworld, 2010.

the immorality of homosexuality is that it challenges God's creation, it's a revolt against God Himself and his law of natural order. Critics and homophobes can argue homosexual tendencies are against God's laws, but they would be mistaken if they argued they're unnatural and against nature's laws. We already know humans can be homosexual, but homosexual behavior is also common across the entire animal kingdom. It occurs in other mammals like us, as well as birds, fish, reptiles and even insects.[5]

The attitude of many Muslim countries towards people in the LGBT community has seen human rights groups like Amnesty International condemn such 'laws of God', that is, Islamic laws which make homosexual relations between consenting adults a crime.[6] In addition, the United Nations Human Rights Committee ruled in 1994 that such laws also violate the right to privacy guaranteed in the International Covenant on Civil and Political Rights and the Universal Declaration of Human Rights.[7]

The scientific community would also support these anti-discrimination laws to be upheld against Islamic law. There's a scientific consensus that being LGBT is compatible with normal mental health and social adjustment.[8] Mental health groups have actively discouraged people who try to change anyone's sexual orientation, as attempting to do so can be harmful to the mental health of the individual. People who've tried such conversion therapy face 8.9 times the rates of suicide ideation, and depression at 5.9 times the rate of their peers in comparison to those who didn't go through such conversion therapy.[9]

It's not only a situation gay people find themselves in, but gay Muslims as well. Muslim parents have been known to 'exorcise' the sin out of their children and even force them into marriages in the hope that it'll change their ways. The latter is what happened to 26 year old British Muslim Naman Parvaiz who recounts his experience of coming out:

5. Sommer, Volker, and Paul L. Vasey. Homosexual Behaviour in Animals: An Evolutionary Perspective. Cambridge: Cambridge University Press, 2006.

6. AI International Secretariat. Love, Hate and the Law: Decriminalizing Homosexuality. Report. July 4, 2008. https://www.amnesty.org/en/documents/POL30/003/2008/en/.

7. United Nations. General Assembly. "UN: General Assembly Statement Affirms Rights for All." News release, December 18, 2008. Human Rights Watch. https://www.hrw.org/news/2008/12/18/un-general-assembly-statement-affirms-rights-all.

8. "Submission to the Church of England's Listening Exercise on Human Sexuality." Royal College of Psychiatrists. Accessed November 26, 2016. http://www.rcpsych.ac.uk/workinpsychiatry/specialinterestgroups/gaylesbian/submissiontothecofe.aspx.

9. American Psychological Association. Report of the American Psychological Association Task Force on Appropriate Therapeutic Responses to Sexual Orientation. Report. August 2009. http://www.apa.org/pi/lgbt/resources/sexual-orientation.aspx.

"It's crushing to realise that your parents don't accept who you really are. Coming to terms with your own sexual identity is difficult enough but being rejected for something which is a part of you and that you have no control over is devastating."[10]

LGBT Muslims arguably have an even more difficult personal life than LGBT people from other religions due to the low tolerance Muslim families generally adopt. Also, most Muslims have been raised with some level of pressure regarding marriage; this pressure is often much greater in Muslim countries than it is in western countries. To be single (particularly for women) can be equated to a social disaster for Muslim parents and families. Once academic studies have been completed and a job secured, it's common for the next priority for a young Muslim to be marriage. This can put LGBT Muslims under an extreme amount of stress if they have to ignore, avoid or delay questions and pressure from family members their whole lives about starting their own family. As for those who have family members who take it upon themselves to arrange their marriages, they really are the unfortunate ones.

To be heterosexual, lesbian, gay, bisexual or transgender is something you are or are not. For many people they know who they are, while some people are uncertain and still on their journey to figuring it out, and others may change their sexual orientation as they develop throughout their lives. This is natural; these behaviors have existed for thousands of years. As time passes we'll become less surprised when more and more Muslims announce they're not heterosexual; whether they're our leaders, teachers, friends, or family members. If there are 1.7 billion Muslims in the world, the odds are we have LGBT Muslims all around us who don't have the freedom to be their authentic self.

Hopefully the negative attitudes and stereotypes about the entire LGBT community will be broken down in Muslim communities, just as they have been across the world in the 20th and 21st century. Over time, all people will hopefully agree that everyone deserves the same human rights and liberties regardless of their sexual orientation.

It's unfair and harmful to tell anyone in the LGBT community there's something mentally or spiritually wrong with them; even if the Quran disapproves of their sexual orientation. We must learn to use our own intelligence and heart. To judge for ourselves if people deserve to be

10. Archer, Elizabeth. "Young Gay Muslim on Cost of Coming Out: "It's Crushing That My Parents Don't Accept Me"." Mirror Online, March 31, 2016. http://www.mirror.co.uk/news/real-life-stories/ young-gay-muslim-what-comin-7659452.

condemned for life. To be persecuted and punished with the full force of the law such as death. All because they love another human being.

35

Drugs

"A reliable way to make people believe in falsehoods is frequent repetition, because familiarity is not easily distinguishable from truth" – Daniel Kahneman

Islam has strict conditions to follow on the prohibition of drugs, stemming from two main concerns. First, the effects from their intoxication, which causes *'enmity and hatred'* among Muslims.

> Quran 5:90-91 – O believers, wine and arrow-shuffling, idols and divining-arrows are an abomination, some of Satan's work; so avoid it; haply So you will prosper. Satan only desires to precipitate enmity and hatred between you in regard to wine and arrow-shuffling, and to bar you from the remembrance of God, and from prayer. Will you then desist?

In *Quran 5:90-91*, Islamic scholars signify *'wine'* as all alcohol, and *'arrow-shuffling'* as gambling (arrow-shuffling is a game of chance in which lots are drawn by arrows).[1]

Second, the effects from their intoxication causes harm to the human body. In the Quran, God asks Muslims not to do anything which harms themselves.

> Quran 2:195 – And expend in the way of God; and cast not yourselves by your own hands into destruction, but be good-doers; God loves the good-doers.

Muslim belief follows that the drugs which are halal (permitted) for Muslims to take are anything medicinal, non-addictive and non-toxic. Muslims believe all

---

1. "Islamic Finance | What Is the Difference Between Qimar and Maisir?" Investment and Finance. November 23, 2013. http://investment-and-finance.net/islamic-finance/questions/what-is-the-difference-between-qimar-and-maisir.html.

other non-prescribed drugs are the works of Satan, and he designed them to lead people away from God. This is the prevailing thought because addictive and intoxicating drugs enable people to 'escape' reality, making Muslims incapable of consciously serving God.

It's commonly known alcohol is haram (forbidden) for Muslims as the Quran makes several references to its negative effects. Therefore alcohol is illegal in Muslim countries, but there are a few which allow consumption in specially designated areas such as hotels for non-Muslims. Despite this ban there are still several Muslim countries where home-brew alcoholic drinks are made illegally. For example, raki in Iran and Turkey, boukha in Tunisia and wine in Algeria and Morocco.

Tobacco is not mentioned explicitly in the Quran like alcohol, and tobacco smoking is not considered haram by Muslims in the same way alcohol is. But smoking cigarettes is toxic due to the inhalation of poisonous chemicals found in the tobacco smoke. Carbon monoxide, cyanide and carcinogens are all contained in tobacco smoke and they're all proven to cause heart disease, lung disease and cancer. According to the World Health Organization (WHO) tobacco smoking is the single greatest cause of preventable death globally.[2] It is the cause of 6 million deaths annually (about 10% of all deaths) with 600,000 of those deaths occurring in non-smokers due to secondhand smoke.[3]

Smoking is also addictive due to the drug nicotine, a stimulant contained in tobacco, causing smokers of cigarettes to develop a tolerance and dependence to them. But even though tobacco is toxic and addictive, smoking is still practiced by Muslims and it is accepted socially throughout the Islamic world which appears inconsistent with what the Quran requests of Muslims.

Tobacco smoking in the form of cigarettes is practiced by around 1 billion people in the world, even though all smokers now know the toxic and fatal implications of smoking.[4] This is a staggeringly high number when there are around 7.4 billion people in the world.[5] What's interesting is about 80% of all smokers worldwide, around 800 million people, are men.[6] A report from

2. WHO Report on the Global Tobacco Epidemic, 2008: The MPOWER Package. Geneva: World Health Organization, 2008. p.14. http://www.who.int/tobacco/mpower/mpower_report_full_2008.pdf

3. "Tobacco." World Health Organization. June 2016. http://www.who.int/mediacentre/factsheets/fs339/en/.

4. "Tobacco." World Health Organization. June 2016. http://www.who.int/mediacentre/factsheets/fs339/en/.

5. "U.S. and World Population Clock." United States Census Bureau. Accessed March 01, 2017. http://www.census.gov/popclock.

6. "2.1 The Global Tobacco Epidemic." In World Cancer Report 2014, edited by Christopher P. Wild and Bernard W. Stewart. Lyon: International Agency for Research on Cancer, 2014.

the British Medical Journal in 2006 also highlighted the smoking prevalence of men in some Muslim countries as reaching as high as 62% of all men in Tunisia (7.5% of women), 69% of men in Indonesia (3% of women) and 77% of men in Yemen (29% of women). This is considerably higher than many Western countries, for example the United Kingdom which has a 28% smoking prevalence in men (26% in women).[7]

These are meaningful numbers considering it's Muslim men who enforce Sharia law and direct the Islamic world. So arguably Muslim men may carry a conflict of interest as they're the ones mostly addicted to tobacco. Muslim women are less likely to smoke due to social pressures in Islamic cultures. It's seen as inappropriate for a Muslim woman to smoke due to the image it portrays, and there aren't many public spaces where Muslim women can smoke freely without feeling judged by her community.

Tobacco smoking is not only popular with Muslims in the form of cigarettes, but through hookahs as well. In the Islamic world, people smoke hookah waterpipes as part of their culture. A hookah (also known as shisha, nargile, argilah or goza) is an instrument for vaporizing and smoking flavoured tobacco. Its smoke passes through the water basin at the bottom before it's inhaled through a pipe by the user. Smoking hookahs is a social activity common in Arab cafes: these are some of the main gathering places for Muslims, similar to bars in the USA and pubs in the UK. Many Muslim countries have previously tried to impose smoking and hookah limitations but this has varied in implementation from country to country.

It's curious how so many Muslims are happy to smoke tobacco in the form of cigarettes and hookah, yet disregard what the Quran says about not throwing '*your own hands into destruction*'. What's more surprising is that there's evidence to suggest hookah may even be more harmful and addictive than cigarettes. Therefore the hookah culture prevalent in Muslim countries would theoretically be disobeying God even further.

The tobacco found in hookah smoking is no less toxic than that found in a cigarette: hookah smoke can contain high levels of toxic compounds including tar, heavy metals and carcinogens. It's a common misconception that the water in the hookah filters out toxic ingredients from the tobacco smoke. In fact, hookah smokers may actually inhale more toxic smoke, like carbon monoxide, than cigarette smokers do. This is due to the large volume of smoke inhaled in hookah smoking sessions, which can last as long as 60 minutes.[8] Typical hookah

http://publications.iarc.fr/Non-Series-Publications/World-Cancer-Reports/World-Cancer-Report-2014

7. Ghouri, Nazim. "Influence of Islam on Smoking among Muslims." BMJ 332, no. 7536 (2006): 291-94. doi:10.1136/bmj.332.7536.291.

sessions can actually deliver 1.7 times the nicotine dose of a cigarette, and the nicotine absorption rate can be the equivalent of smoking 10 cigarettes a day.[9]

This all leads to hookah smokers having urges to smoke regularly, experience withdrawal symptoms, and show an increasing desire to smoke hookah alone; the same signs and symptoms of dependence and addiction associated with cigarettes. Hookah smoking is also linked with all the same diseases as cigarette smoking such as lung cancer and oral cancer, and it poses the same dangers identified with secondhand smoke. Hookah is addictive not only because smokers inhale nicotine, but because it's a social activity shared among friends. In addition, the pipes used in hookahs may not be hygienically cleaned by cafes, so this increases the risk of obtaining and spreading infectious diseases, even if disposable mouthpieces are used.

Perhaps it's no surprise there's an inconsistency among Muslims regarding tobacco. The Quran itself is inconsistent about whether alcohol is a good or bad drug. It's clear that God denounces alcohol in the Quran, claiming it does more harm than good.

> Quran 2:219-220 – They will question thee concerning wine, and arrow-shuffling. Say: 'In both is heinous sin; and uses for men, but the sin in them is more heinous than the usefulness.' They will question thee concerning what they should expend. Say: 'The abundance.' So God makes clear His signs to you; haply you will reflect; in this world, and the world to come. They will question thee concerning the orphans. Say: 'To set their affairs aright is good. And if you intermix with them, they are your brothers. God knows well him who works corruption from him who sets aright; and had He willed He would have harassed you. Surely God is All-mighty, All-wise.'

What's interesting is at no point is alcohol explicitly forbidden in the Quran. God either advises Muslims to avoid it (*Quran 50:90-91* earlier in this chapter), or He says it does more harm than good (*Quran 2:219*). Tobacco smoking is not

8. Hays, J. Taylor, MD. "Hookah Smoking: Is It Safer than Cigarette Smoking?" Mayo Clinic. June 17, 2015. http://www.mayoclinic.org/healthy-lifestyle/quit-smoking/expert-answers/hookah/faq-20057920.

9. Eissenberg, Thomas, and Alan Shihadeh. "Waterpipe Tobacco and Cigarette Smoking." American Journal of Preventive Medicine 37, no. 6 (2009): 518-23. doi:10.1016/j.amepre.2009.07.014. See also Neergaard, James, Pramil Singh, Jayakaran Job, and Susanne Montgomery. "Waterpipe Smoking and Nicotine Exposure: A Review of the Current Evidence." Nicotine & Tobacco Research 9, no. 10 (2007): 987-94. doi:10.1080/14622200701591591.

mentioned in the Quran, only the expression not to throw '*your own hands into destruction*', which most Islamic scholars agree reference any harmful practices to the body and mind. So, the word haram (forbidden) is never used explicitly in the Quran to refer to either alcohol or tobacco. This is in contrast to pig meat for example, which God clearly forbids several times over.

> Quran 2:173 – These things only has He forbidden you: carrion, blood, the flesh of swine, what has been hollowed to other than God. Yet who so is constrained, not desiring nor transgressing, no sin shall be on him; God is All-forgiving, All-compassionate.

> Quran 5:3 – Forbidden to you are carrion, blood, the flesh of swine, what has been hallowed to other than God, the beast strangled; the beast beaten down, the beast fallen to death, the beast gored, and that devoured by beasts of prey – excepting that you have sacrificed duly — as also things sacrificed to idols, and partition by the divining arrows; that is ungodliness. Today the unbelievers have despaired of your religion; therefore fear them not, but fear you Me. Today I have perfected your religion for you, and I have completed My blessing upon you, and I have approved Islam for your religion. But whosoever is constrained in emptiness and not inclining purposely to sin — God is All-forgiving, All-compassionate.

> Quran 6:145 – Say: 'I do not find, in what is revealed to me, aught forbidden to him who eats thereof except it be carrion, or blood outpoured, or the flesh of swine — that is an abomination — or an ungodly thing that has been hallowed to other than God; yet whoso is constrained, not desiring nor transgressing, surely thy Lord is All-forgiving, All-compassionate.'

God hasn't made this clear distinction for any drugs in the Quran, but it's clear pig meat is forbidden, even though it isn't toxic nor addictive, it's just considered 'unclean'. It's a ruling in Islam that Muslims accept and adhere to strictly, but it's worth asking why God forbids something harmless, while He does not explicitly forbid toxic items.

With regards to alcohol, it may be because God doesn't actually hate it, nor does He hate the idea of Muslims consuming it. We know this because one of the rewards God says devout Muslims will receive in Paradise is delicious wine. God tells us there will be so much wine for Muslims after they die, entire rivers of it will be flowing through Heaven.

> Quran 47:15 – This is the similitude of Paradise which the godfearing have been promised: therein are rivers of water unstaling, rivers of milk unchanging in flavour, and rivers of wine — a delight to the drinkers, rivers, too, of honey purified; and therein for them is every fruit, and forgiveness from their Lord — Are they as he who dwells forever in the Fire, such as are given to drink boiling water, that tears their bowels asunder?

That God thinks a river of wine is a good way to incentivize Muslims who have been abstinent from alcohol their entire lives is peculiar. Also, for God to allow what he calls 'Satan's work' (Quran 5:90-91) in Heaven is puzzling.

God's inconsistency with alcohol seems to match many Muslims' inconsistency with tobacco. Perhaps we can safely assume man has created God in his own image when it turns out He loves all the same drugs they do.

36

Children

"The great trouble is that the preachers get the children from six to seven years of age and then it is almost impossible to do anything with them" – *Thomas Edison*

Children from religious families are likely to follow the same religion as their parents; they raise their children to believe what they believe about the world and our place in it. It's rare for Muslim parents to allow their children to find their own meaning to life. This means children from Muslim families have less opportunities to explore the world in an alternative or contemporary way if they wish to do so. Instead, children are indoctrinated with the attitudes and bias of their religious families. However well, or ill-advised, these perceptions may be, they're the beliefs our future generations will carry with them as they grow up to become adults.

The problem is discouraging children from the freedom to consider anything else can stifle their ability to objectively analyze the world they live in, and this capacity to critically problem solve is crucial for the advancement of humanity's future. But many children raised in religious families often don't have the opportunity to develop this skill. Instead they're told they *must* believe in a God and He created the world in a few days and all of us from one man. They're told fantastical stories about prophets as though they're all historically accurate. Children are essentially threatened with eternal pain and torture if they don't believe what they're told to believe: they're told if they don't obey the rules and submit, when they die they'll go to a place of pain and burn there forever.

If we'd received this 'insight' for the first time as adults, we'd explore the credibility of these claims. But since most of us are told these stories as children, it's harder to question them. Then they become ingrained into our minds, almost irreversibly. It's difficult for children to break free from this indoctrination since they're told by all the adults in their lives that the stories are unquestionably true.

Growing up we're all impressionable: we believe what we're told by those who care for us. We're reliant upon our families who feed us, clothe us, bathe us and love us. There's no reason or incentive to question such caring and affectionate people, they clearly only have the best of intentions in mind for us.

But drilling into children's minds biased guidance can inhibit their means to wisely evaluate the world, and how they'll choose to spend their time on it. Spreading religious stories, and the consequences of denying them, as absolute truths never to be questioned is to mislead future generations. Religious critics like evolutionary biologist Richard Dawkins even goes as far as to say it's intellectual and emotional abuse of children. He's angered by labels such as 'Muslim child' or 'Catholic child'. Dawkins questions how a child can be intellectually mature enough to have developed their views on the cosmos and humanity's place within it. He asks if we're to follow such a line of logic, why not have a 'Communist child', 'Marxist child' or 'Republican child' as well?[1]

Children who are raised with Islam are raised to conform. If they don't, they're told they'll be punished by their parents, and if they're deceiving their parents, then God will know. Children are raised to believe an invisible entity is watching them all the time and it can even tell what they're thinking. With the fear and threat of punishment in this lifetime or the next, Islam's intimidating behavior towards children keeps them submissive. Does this count as intellectual and emotional child abuse?

It's one thing to teach a child religion exists; to tell them this is the religion the family believes in, to encourage them to learn about this religion, and to talk to them about why the family believe what they believe. But it's another to tell a child everyone else is wrong, this is the only religion which makes sense, and they'll face the ultimate punishment if they don't do as they're told. If Islam is indeed true, you'd think its followers wouldn't have to use fear and intimidation so much to get children to practice it devoutly.

Children must have guidance in their lives and parents are entitled to teach their children what they believe is true about the world and raise them how they were raised too. But the dialogue that takes place in religious homes and schools needs to be open-minded and reasoned. If I'm to speak (and paraphrase) from experience, it can't always be:

> "Here's the way it is. Everyone else is wrong. They'll likely burn in Hell for not following the rules, regardless of how good a person you think they are. This is how it's always been. So you should be fearful

1. Dawkins, Richard. "The Future Looks Bright." The Guardian. June 21, 2003. https://www.theguardian.com/books/2003/jun/21/society.richarddawkins.

if you don't believe it too. Otherwise God will punish you and you'll burn in Hell forever."

Our parents believe this rhetoric so strongly because their parents told them the same thing when they were young. Muslim parents are particularly fearful about what could happen to them if they don't pass on their religion and traditions to their children, the same ones they received from their parents, our grandparents. Our parents deeply worry an almighty God will punish them and send them to burn in Hell forever if they don't raise devout Muslim children, who then go on to give them devout Muslim grandchildren. If the concerns of my parents are anything to go by, I'd go as far as to say that this is a concern all Muslims have had to face from their parents.

Muslim youth can't be indoctrinated with speculative ancient stories about how the world was if we wish them to discover how it will be. Muslim children must be encouraged and educated to think critically for themselves: to learn how to evaluate evidence and challenge authority figures respectfully. Not to be shut down or censored when they have honest, practical questions about why they must pray, or why people deserve to be punished for leaving Islam. Rather than react with shock, anger or fear, Muslim parents ought to encourage intelligent and thoughtful questions and respond in kind. The 'believe this or else' approach does a disservice to children, and it's at the expense of everyone's future.

37

Sex

"People are told that they are inherently bad or sinful and that the only way to become good is by giving over control of their lives to faith. As there is no evidence that any of that is true, religion, in effect, is creating an imaginary problem simply so that it can sell you an imaginary solution" – Armin Navabi

Islam advocates modesty with regards to any relationships between women and men. The Quran also has strict rules on remaining chaste outside and loyal inside of marriage, meaning strict prohibitions on premarital sex and extramarital sex. But sex isn't discouraged in Islam if it's between a wife and husband, and it's not only reserved for procreation so contraceptive use is permitted. However there are some limitations.

For example, oral sex, while not haram, is considered highly undesirable. This is due to issues of modesty, cleanliness, and using the mouth and tongue on genitals when it's also used to recite the Quran. Something similar can be said for masturbation. While not haram, it's also considered undesirable due to issues of modesty, but it is also considered to be the lesser of two evils if it removes the desire to engage in premarital sex.

Anal sex is generally considered haram. Islamic jurists point to a word in the Quran (*'tillage'* in Arberry's translation) which refers to cultivation or agriculture. The semen in the womb is likened to seeds planted in the ground, both of which produce life. Therefore only vaginal sex is permissible as this is the place where offspring are produced.

> Quran 2:223 – Your women are a tillage for you; so come unto your tillage as you wish, and forward for your souls; and fear God, and know that you shall meet Him. Give thou good tidings to the believers.

A Muslim man must also not have sex with his wife recently after she has given birth and during the daylight hours of Ramadan (fasting). Nor is he to do so during her menstruation, as God states in the Quran.

> Quran 2:222 – They will question thee concerning the monthly course. Say: 'It is hurt; so go apart from women during the monthly course, and do not approach them till they are clean. When they have cleansed themselves, then come unto them as God has commanded you.' Truly, God loves those who repent, and He loves those who cleanse themselves.

Many Muslims aren't surprised to see fornication and adultery so prevalent in the West. The Islamic view is that it's a consequence of the sexual freedoms permitted, since western societies place a large emphasis on fulfilling one's sexual desires. Muslim societies place much less of an emphasis on sex because it's seen as a weakness: premarital sex may lead to trouble within families and the community. To Muslims, family and community are of the utmost importance, so the idea of premarital sex leading to women as single mothers or having abortions is abhorrent. Such issues are what Muslims seek to avoid, which is why the western tolerance of premarital sex is seen as a dangerous influence on Muslim communities: it disrespects the customary practices and codes central to Islam.

> Quran 17:32 – And approach not fornication; surely it is an indecency, and evil as a way.

The subject of sex didn't use to be as taboo in Islamic societies as it has become in contemporary Islam. The Islamic world used to produce significant works of erotic literature (much like Indian, Chinese or Japanese civilizations of the past) and centuries before such attitudes were culturally accepted in the western world. An example is *The Perfumed Garden of Sensual Delight* by Muhammad ibn Muhammad al-Nafzawi. It's a 15th century Arabic sex manual presenting advice on sexual techniques and sexual health. It also narrates erotic stories for context and amusement.[1]

Muslims originally had a much less 'guilty' approach to sex but this openness and dialogue has been lost in many Muslim societies over time. However, this may be a result of cultural influences rather than religious influences. The Quran emphasizes the importance of sex, and the bond between

---

1. Al-Nafzawi, Muhammad. The Perfumed Garden of Sensual Delight. Translated by Jim Colville. London: Kegan Paul International, 1999.

two people. So much so that it admonishes celibacy and monasticism in Islam. The monastic life of monks and nuns may be common in a lot of religions but it is discouraged for Muslims.

> Quran 57:27 – Then We sent, following in their footsteps, Our Messengers; and We sent, following, Jesus son of Mary, and gave unto him the Gospel. And We set in the hearts of those who followed him tenderness and mercy. And monasticism they invented — We did not prescribe it for them — only seeking the good pleasure of God; but they observed it not as it should be observed. So We gave those of them who believed their wage; and many of them are ungodly.

While the Quran understands the importance of sex between a wife and husband, it also draws distinct lines on how much it disapproves of premarital sex. God encourages Muslims to be publicly violent and to show no mercy when two unmarried adults do something as natural and healthy as have consensual sex with each other.

> Quran 24:2 – The fornicatress and the fornicator — scourge each one of them a hundred stripes, and in the matter of God's religion let no tenderness for them seize you if you believe in God and the Last Day; and let a party of the believers witness their chastisement.

Those 'guilty' are given an opportunity to avoid the harsh punishment if they repent. But acceptance of their repentance is dependent on their Islamic jurists.

> Quran 4:16 – And when two of you commit indecency, punish them both; but if they repent and make amends, then suffer them to be; God turns, and is All-compassionate.

With regards to infidelity, there's an unusual request from God in the Quran: if anyone accuses a married woman of infidelity, they need to produce four eyewitnesses to support their accusation.

> Quran 24:4-5 – And those who cast it up on women in wedlock, and then bring not four witnesses, scourge them with eighty stripes, and do not accept any testimony of theirs ever; those — they are the ungodly, save such as repent thereafter and make amends; surely God is All-forgiving, All-compassionate.

How such an event could ever occur is perplexing. Realistically, the probability of four people catching a married woman in the middle of an extramarital act is extremely low. This isn't to say infidelity and breaking one's vows isn't unethical, but the existence of such strange requests ought to raise questions about how seriously we must take all the verses in the Quran.

However, in the unlikely event it does occur, God deems death by house arrest as a potentially suitable punishment for the woman involved in the act.

> Quran 4:15 – Such of your women as commit indecency, call four of you to witness against them; and if they witness, then detain them in their houses until death takes them or God appoints for them a way.

Not only is this excessive, but there's also no mention of the man's punishment for committing the same sin. Only the woman is singled out in the Quran.

The Quran also states a fornicator can only marry another fornicator.

> Quran 24:3 – The fornicator shall marry none but a fornicatress or an idolatress, and the fornicatress — none shall marry her but a fornicator or an idolator; that is forbidden to the believers.

Muslim women can only marry Muslim men, so marrying a fornicator isn't an issue as Muslim men are required to remain celibate until marriage. However Muslim men can marry any women they want, as long as she is a follower of an Abrahamic religion (Islam, Christianity, Judaism) and they raise their children Muslim. There are likely tens of millions of Muslim men worldwide who have married a non-Muslim woman. One can safely assume many of these non-Muslim women will have had sex before marriage and are, in the words of God, '*a fornicatress*'. It appears to be a rule which Muslim men turn a blind eye to, even though God clearly states it is forbidden.

Another example of an inconsistency between men and sex within Islam is the rule that Muslim men can have sex with their female slaves, '*what your right hand owns*' (see chapter '*Slavery*').[2]

> Quran 23:1-9 – Prosperous are the believers who in their prayers are humble and from idle talk turn away and at almsgiving are active and guard their private parts save from their wives and what their right hands own then being not blameworthy (but whosoever seeks after

2. Suad, Joseph, and Najmabadi Afsaneh. Encyclopedia of Women & Islamic Cultures. Leiden: Brill, 2007.

more than that, those are the transgressors) and who preserve their trusts and their covenant and who observe their prayers.

Is this a way around the sin of premarital sex, afforded only to Muslim men? Sex between a male Muslim slaveholder and his unmarried female slave is legal by Sharia law. Slavery is not as widely practiced now since it has been abolished in every country worldwide, but this ruling in the Quran would have fostered sexual slavery in the Islamic world.[3]

There is one thing taken away from all Muslim men though: the foreskin on their penis. Muslims are the single largest religious group to circumcise boys (khitan in Arabic). This practice isn't mentioned in the Quran, its origins are based on traditions and the Hadith. There's also no mention of female circumcision, or any female genital mutilation, in the Quran or the Hadith. Female circumcision and female genital mutilation is based upon cultural traditions, not any religious reasons from Islam. This is why it is correctly condemned throughout the Islamic world.[4]

The main reason young Muslim boys are circumcised is due to cleanliness: Muslims believe removing the foreskin reduces the risks against infection and diseases. There have been studies to support this but it hasn't reached a consensus in the international medical community.[5] Even so, there are those who question the right to permanently and non-consensually change a boy's body. It's controversial because the procedure is non-diagnostic, non-therapeutic, and can be performed when the boy is older and able to provide consent. This is why critics of circumcision interpret it as a lifelong irreversible injury and a violation of the human rights of the child.[6]

It's strange why a tradition of removing a part of the body God Himself created is so prevalent among Muslims; it's as if they are questioning His design choices.

Quran 40:64 – It is God who made for you the earth a fixed place and

3. Brunschvig, R., "'Abd", in: Encyclopaedia of Islam, Second Edition, Edited by: P. Bearman, Th. Bianquis, C.E. Bosworth, E. van Donzel, W.P. Heinrichs. Accessed 01 March 2017. http://dx.doi.org/10.1163/1573-3912_islam_COM_0003

4. "Islam: Circumcision of Boys." BBC. August 13, 2009. http://www.bbc.co.uk/religion/religions/islam/islamethics/malecircumcision.shtml.

5. WHO and UNAIDS. "WHO and UNAIDS Announce Recommendations from Expert Consultation on Male Circumcision for HIV Prevention." News release, March 28, 2007. World Health Organization. http://www.who.int/hiv/mediacentre/news68/en/.

6. "Home." Doctors Opposing Circumcision. Accessed January 28, 2017. http://www.doctorsopposingcircumcision.org/.

heaven for an edifice; And He shaped you, and shaped you well, and provided you with the good things. That then is God, your Lord, so blessed be God, the Lord of all Being.

According to some Islamic traditions Prophet Muhammad was born without a foreskin (aposthetic).[7] So a reason for Muslim men to get circumcised is to be more like Prophet Muhammad. This can be refuted though, for if Prophet Muhammad was born without a foreskin then he was not circumcised, therefore to be like him is to not be circumcised as well.

In the Quran, Satan himself threatens God and says he'll lead people astray and they'll alter His creation. Does circumcision not count as altering God's creation?

> Quran 4:118-119 – He said, 'Assuredly I will take unto myself a portion appointed of Thy servants, and I will lead them astray, and fill them with fancies and I will command them and they will cut off the cattle's ears; I will command them and they will alter God's creation.' Whoso takes Satan to him for a friend, instead of God, has surely suffered a manifest loss.

If Muslims are to believe God is perfect and infallible, then it means God created us the way He wanted to. To remove something on our bodies is to imply God didn't make us perfectly, so humans need to fix the mistake He made.

> Quran 95:1-6 – By the fig and the olive and the Mount Sinai and this land secure! We indeed created Man in the fairest stature then We restored him the lowest of the low — save those who believe, and do righteous deeds; they shall have a wage unfailing.

It's therefore illogical a foreskin is a birth defect God added. God makes no mention of removing it in the Quran, rather the contrary, He takes great pride in what He has created. Male circumcision is a good example of cultural (not religious) practices which have become absorbed into everyday Muslim life. Cultural practices can become blind spots to us since we stop approaching them from first principles, and stop asking why they exist in the first place. But it doesn't have to stop there; why not question the religious practices we adopt too? Like the idea that two unmarried adults loving each other is reprehensible,

---

7. "Islam: Circumcision of Boys." BBC. August 13, 2009. http://www.bbc.co.uk/religion/religions/islam/islamethics/malecircumcision.shtml.

but publicly torturing and shaming what consenting adults do in the privacy of their homes is not.

The punishments God enforces in the Quran are excessively cruel for the corresponding act committed. The punishments described may have fit the accepted morals of the time and culture it was written in, but it doesn't automatically make them acceptable today, or in the future. For example, someone today could kill someone else over extramarital acts but they wouldn't be lauded for their moral behavior as they may have been in the past; a judge and jury would prosecute them as a murderer. Over time our views of what's acceptable in society changes and adapts as we develop. This is why sticking to societal rules from the past are problematic in the present day: they've expired. So as humanity progresses globally, Muslims are in danger of being left behind.

Forcing biological creatures like us to repress healthy and normal sexual desires is incongruent with the laws of nature. Premarital sex doesn't automatically lead to families and communities falling apart. We know this is true because around the world there are healthy societies of adults meeting their sexual desires, and doing so with decency and temperance. Pre-marital sex and healthy societies are not mutually exclusive.

Liberal advocates have also expressed a concern about the effects of systematically keeping sexual desires in check and the repercussions potential gender segregation can create. There are fears it fosters a pent-up sexually frustrated environment among women and men, especially with the youth. These suppressed and manipulated environments can lead to negative reactions from Muslims, manifesting themselves in ways even unhealthier than what the Islamic world perceive western societies to be like. For example, it's not unknown for predatory behavior to occur in young Muslim boys since they grow up to see the opposite gender only as sex objects, instead of learning how to interact with Muslim girls at a young age in a healthy and respectful way. This behavior obviously isn't exclusive to Muslim societies, but there are concerns Islam promotes censored environments through gender segregation which can foster this negative behavior.[8]

It's not a question of western nations imposing their rights and beliefs upon the Islamic world. It's a matter of giving people the freedom to live their lives without fear and to adopt ethical principles. Principles that say everyone is entitled to basic human rights because she or he is a human being too.

But it only works if people are educated and given the opportunity to understand. If Muslims are advised well from a young age about sex,

8. Husain, Ed. The Islamist: Why I Joined Radical Islam in Britain, What I Saw inside and Why I Left. London: Penguin Books, 2007. p.244.

relationships and respecting one's body, then repressed and constricting societies are less likely to occur. If they have good role models they can trust and speak to, then they'll be advised well and hopefully lead an enjoyable and healthy lifestyle.

Muslim adults don't have to endure a stifled and censored sexual experience just because their parents went through the same thing (when we can be safely sure they didn't want to either at the time). But instead of two consenting adults loving each other in the privacy of their homes, Muslims are commanded by a 'merciful and compassionate' God to cruelly torture people in public as a punishment for such an act. We ought to ask ourselves from the heart, is this what love is from God?

38

Slavery

"Sooner or later, false thinking brings wrong conduct" – Julian Huxley

The concept of slavery has existed throughout the world for almost 4,000 years.[1] It was once institutionally recognized by most societies throughout human history, but it's now abolished in all countries. The last country to abolish slavery was the Muslim country Mauritania in 1981, however no criminal laws were passed to enforce the ban at the time. The Mauritanian government only passed a law to make slavery illegal and prosecute slaveholders in 2007, under international pressure.[2]

Unfortunately slavery still exists in various forms, for example domestic servants kept in captivity, child soldiers, human trafficking, and forced marriages. The growth of the global human population in recent centuries means there are now more slaves today than anytime in human history, with an estimated 46 million slaves worldwide.[3]

Muslim societies were no exception, they too practiced slavery; slavery isn't unique to any one religion, ethnicity or nationality. Sharia law accepted (and in theory still accepts) slavery just as other ancient legal systems did like Hebrew law, Byzantine Christian law, Hindu Law, Roman law and African customary law.[4]

Though Sharia law permits slavery under certain conditions, such conditions are rare in today's modern world. Therefore slavery is effectively

---

1. Hellie, Richard. "Slavery." Encyclopædia Britannica. March 24, 2016. https://www.britannica.com/topic/slavery-sociology.

2. Okeowo, Alexis. "Freedom Fighter." The New Yorker, September 8, 2014. http://www.newyorker.com/magazine/2014/09/08/freedom-fighter?currentPage=all.

3. "45.8 Million People Are Enslaved in the World Today." Global Slavery Index. October 18, 2016. http://www.globalslaveryindex.org/.

4. "Islam: Slavery in Islam." BBC. July 7, 2009. http://www.bbc.co.uk/religion/religions/islam/history/slavery_1.shtml.

illegal in contemporary Islam. Many Muslim countries have even gone a step further and used secular law to prohibit slavery even though the Quran permits it and Prophet Muhammad himself practiced it.

In addition to owning slaves, Muslims can also gain slaves. If two slaves belonging to the same Muslim give birth to a child, then that child is also under the ownership of the Muslim slaveholder. The Quran also allows Muslim men to marry their slaves if they wish to. Muslim men can even marry the women they've captured legally (by Sharia law) as spoils of war.

> Quran 24:32 – Marry the spouseless among you, and your slaves and handmaidens that are righteous; if they are poor, God will enrich them of His bounty; God is All-embracing, All-knowing.

The Quran often refers to slaves as 'what your right hand owns'.

> Quran 4:3 – If you fear that you will not act justly towards the orphans, marry such women as seem good to you, two, three, four; but if you fear you will not be equitable, then only one, or what your right hands own; so it is likelier you will not be partial.

The expression 'what your right hand owns' appears regularly in the Quran and depending on the preferred interpretation it can be seen in two ways. First, as the women that you own and use for your personal needs (slaves), or second, the women that you've saved from destitution (widows or orphan girls).

With the latter, the argument put forward is that Muslim and non-Muslim men killed in wars left behind widows and orphan girls who had no financial support since men (their husbands and fathers) were the common breadwinners at the time of the Quran's revelations. Therefore it's suggested that 'what your right hand owns' is more about compassion towards women, rather than men and their egos or lust.

The Quran does continually stress the importance of treating slaves with compassion and kindness.

> Quran 4:36 – Serve God, and associate naught with Him. Be kind to parents, and the near kinsman, and to orphans, and to the needy, and to the neighbour who is of kin, and to the neighbour who is a stranger, and to the companion at your side, and to the traveller, and to that your right hands own. Surely God loves not the proud and boastful

The Quran even encourages Muslims to free slaves (but slaves must convert to Islam first).[5]

> Quran 90:13-20 – The freeing of a slave, or giving food upon a day of hunger to an orphan near of kin or a needy man in misery; then that he become of those who believe and counsel each other to be steadfast, and counsel each other to be merciful. Those are the Companions of the Right Hand. And those who disbelieve in Our signs, they are the Companions of the Left Hand; over them is a Fire covered down.

However, the Quran also permits Muslim men who've enslaved women legally by Sharia law to have sex with them (Muslim women are not permitted to have sex with their male slaves).[6]

> Quran 23:1-11 – Prosperous are the believers who in their prayers are humble and from idle talk turn away and at almsgiving are active and guard their private parts save from their wives and what their right hands own then being not blameworthy (but whosoever seeks after more than that, those are the transgressors) and who preserve their trusts and their covenant and who observe their prayers. Those are the inheritors who shall inherit Paradise therein dwelling forever.

But Islam does not permit prostitution: male masters can have sex with their female slaves, but they cannot force female slaves to have sex with other men.

> Quran 24:33 – And let those who find not the means to marry be abstinent till God enriches them of His bounty. Those your right hands own who seek emancipation, contract with them accordingly, if you know some good in them; and give them of the wealth of God that He has given you. And constrain not your slave-girls to prostitution, if they desire to live in chastity, that you may seek the chance goods of the present life. Whosoever constrains them, surely God, after their being constrained, is All-forgiving, All-compassionate.

5. Lovejoy, Paul E. Transformation in Slavery: A History of Slavery in Africa. New York: Cambridge University Press, 2009.

6. Lewis, Bernard. Race and Slavery in the Middle East: An Historical Enquiry. New York: Oxford University Press, 1992.

This means Muslim men are permitted to have concubines: women who are sexually available to their master and live with him, but are not married to him. In addition, male Muslim masters are not limited by the number of concubines they may have.[7] Like slavery, concubinage was not unique to Islam and was prevalent in other cultures throughout ancient history.

There's no doubt sexual slavery in Islam is detestable but a fortunate few may have actually gained some benefits; such as increased social status, or a greater opportunity for freedom as they could become the mother of the master's child. If a female slave's male owner dies, she is free, and her child will also be free since the child's father was a free man.[8]

Nonetheless, under Islam it's legal for Muslim men to have non-consensual sex with their female slave, and although there is no universal definition of rape or sexual assault, having non-consensual sex is still an act globally recognized as reprehensible.[9] Also under Islam, it's still legal to buy and sell human beings. As mentioned before, this isn't unique to the religion of Islam or Muslim cultures, but the difference is in Islam Sharia law provides a religious foundation to legally enslave non-Muslims.

In hindsight, it's easy to look back on history and say all forms of slavery are disgraceful since they infringe on basic human rights. But it's important to note that the slavery which existed in Muslim cultures was dissimilar to the slavery which occurred in the West: the Atlantic slave trade.

The Atlantic slave trade took place across the 15th to 19th centuries and enslaved and transported millions of Africans to the Americas; most of which were actually sold by other Africans to European slave traders from Britain, France, the Netherlands, Portugal and Spain.[10]

It would be inappropriate to call the Islamic practice of slavery the Islamic slave trade since the Atlantic slave trade is not called the Christian slave trade, even though most of those responsible for it were Christians. In addition, slavery in the Atlantic slave trade was highly racist whereas in Islam there was much less institutionalized racism. Masters and slaves were of a wide range of backgrounds and colors in the Islamic world. Slaves came from the Balkans,

7. Lovejoy, Paul E. Transformation in Slavery: A History of Slavery in Africa. New York: Cambridge University Press, 2009.

8. Ali, Kecia. "Slavery and Sexual Ethics in Islam." In Beyond Slavery: Overcoming Its Religious and Sexual Legacies, edited by Bernadette Joan. Brooten, by Jacqueline L. Hazelton. New York: Palgrave Macmillan, 2010.

9. "Crime and Clarity." The Economist, September 1, 2012. http://www.economist.com/node/21561883.

10. Klein, Herbert S. The Atlantic Slave Trade. Cambridge: Cambridge University Press, 2010.

central Asia, Mediterranean Europe, as well as Africa. There was not the same level of segregation and separation within the Islamic world among slaves and masters as there was in the Atlantic slave trade.[11]

The result is that under the Atlantic slave trade, former African slaves remained a discriminated-against underclass. It's difficult to believe the American civil rights movement only began as recently as the 1950s. So the survival of racism seen today in the USA for example is different from the type seen in Muslim countries. This may also be because the Atlantic slave trade was solely motivated by economics: Africans were enslaved as a cheap and disposable workforce, imported for plantations, mines, field work and servitude. Generally speaking, slaves in the Atlantic slave trade were just units of productive labor, they had no protections or rights.[12]

Muslims scholars point to Islam's progressive approach to slavery in comparison to other cultures as a testament to Prophet Muhammad. Islam provides limitations on enslaving people, it commends freeing slaves, and it regulates the way slaves are treated.

Though slavery in Islam wasn't entirely based on economics, it did have other motives. Slavery was already fundamental to the structure of Arabian society before Prophet Muhammad's time, so it wouldn't have been realistic to abolish it. Doing so would have estranged many Arab tribes the Prophet wanted to bring into Islam.

Additionally, slavery contributes to the control of people, and it's better for Islam if the people in control are Muslims: Muslim slave owners can then assimilate their slaves into the Islamic way of life and consequently increase the Muslim population of a region. If the slaves wanted to be freed (which the Quran encourages) and the owner was willing, then the slave also had to convert to Islam first.[13]

It's curious how Muslims can abide by Sharia law, but most detest the idea of slavery (it's abolished throughout the entire Islamic world). Yet slavery is still a part of Sharia law because slavery is in the Quran, in the Hadith, and Prophet Muhammad himself practiced owning slaves. To remove it entirely from Sharia law would be to admit a fault in any of those three. Although Muslims cannot do this, they have technically already done so by banning slavery, thus bringing 7th century Islam into the 21st century. It's as though Muslims have taken an

11. Lewis, Bernard. Race and Color in Islam. New York: Harper & Row, 1971. p.38.

12. "Islam: Slavery in Islam." BBC. July 7, 2009. http://www.bbc.co.uk/religion/religions/islam/history/slavery_1.shtml.

13. Lovejoy, Paul E. Transformation in Slavery: A History of Slavery in Africa. New York: Cambridge University Press, 2009.

archaic wrong which God decreed in the Quran, and turned it into a modern day right.

Some Muslims maintain Prophet Muhammad intended for slavery to come to a gradual end by limiting opportunities to acquire slaves and encouraging existing slaves to be set free. However this intention doesn't appear in the Quran, or even in any authentic Hadith. In contrast, other Muslims maintain slavery is an acceptable practice and by regulating slavery the Prophet gave his blessing for its continued existence; that Prophet Muhammad had slaves himself and Muslims are to model his behavior is the indication of his approval. Therefore as Islam grew, it may have actually done more to protect and expand slavery, rather than the reverse.[14]

In the Quran God even accepts the inequality between a free human and a slave as part of His natural order. God uses this as an example of His grace: the inequality between humans (free people and slaves) is under His divinely established order of things.

> Quran 16:71 – And God has preferred some of you over others in provision;, but those that were preferred shall not give over their provision to that their right hands possess, so that they may be equal therein. What, and do they deny God's blessing?

At the end of the day, a slave is still a slave: a human held against their will by another human as their property. The Quran may have been progressive in the 7th century with its approach to slavery, but since it claims it's a book for all time, it's now a religion which has laid down legal regulations for buying, owning, and selling slaves for all time.

So how are Muslims to approach the issue of slavery in Islam? Most don't have to since it's now abolished worldwide and it doesn't affect their daily lives. But it's only illegal in the Islamic world because Muslims made it illegal, not because God, Prophet Muhammad or Sharia law made it illegal. For all intents and purposes if Muslim men acquired female slaves legally by Sharia law, they're entitled to have sex with them and then sell them. Courts of law may punish them but according to the Quran, God will not. In fact, since the Quran is open to interpretation, some Muslims will feel that questioning slavery is questioning Islam and the natural order God has set.[15]

14. Manning, Patrick. Slavery and African Life: Occidental, Oriental and African Slave Trades. Cambridge: Cambridge Univ. Press, 2006.

15. Okeowo, Alexis. "Freedom Fighter." The New Yorker, September 8, 2014. http://www.newyorker.com/magazine/2014/09/08/freedom-fighter?currentPage=all.

This is the ongoing issue with using laws and customs from a book thousands of years old in the present day. To most of us, it's common sense slavery is banned and basic human rights are upheld. So much so that slavery has been abolished globally, even throughout the Islamic world.

There's no consensus on what defines a good or bad Muslim. But since most Muslims disagree with the practice of slavery in the modern world, hopefully they'll start to disagree with other outdated practices from the Quran. But if they do, what does this say about Muslims already beginning to overrule God's divine book and laws?

PART IX

A Religion of Peace

The Arabic word 'Islam' means 'to surrender' or 'to submit'; in this case, to God. The consonantal root of the Arabic word 'Islam' is 'S-L-M'. The word 'Muslim' is also drawn from the same verb form, so it too has the consonantal root 'S-L-M'. Muslim is the active participle of the verb, so the Arabic word Muslim means 'one who surrenders' or 'one who submits'.[1]

The root 'S-L-M' forms a large class of Semitic language family words (which Arabic originates from). This root meaning translates to concepts of not only submission, but wholeness, safety and peace. This can be seen in the Arabic greeting 'as-salaamu alaykum' which means 'peace be upon you'. The consonantal root of the word 'salaam' in the Arabic greeting, is also 'S-L-M', and 'salaam' translates to peace. It's also contained in the Hebrew greeting 'shalom' (Hebrew is from the same Semitic language family as Arabic) and it too carries the 'S-L-M' root meaning peace, harmony and completeness.[2]

Islam is a religion with a focus on submission to God: worshiping Him and surrendering to His will. Within the name of the religion (Islam), its adherents (Muslims), and even its greeting (salaam) is the concept of peace and tranquility. So in the 21st century, how has Islam become a religion feared, and its followers looked at with suspicion? Why are Muslims perceived to be intolerant of other people's cultures and customs?

Terrorism, censorship and Islamization are a few matters clouding the West's perception of Muslims. But it's important to differentiate. The overwhelming majority of Muslims are kind, peaceful, and tolerant people. There are only a minority of Muslims who are dangerous, oppressive and prejudiced. Just in the

---

1. Pickett, Joseph P. "Entry for šlm." In The American Heritage Dictionary of the English Language. Boston: Houghton Mifflin, 2006.

2. Jewish Dictionary. Accessed January 30, 2017. http://www.jewishdictionary.org/hebrew-words/shalom.html.

same way the overwhelming majority of Christians are kind-hearted, and the minority are bigoted.

But terrorism, censorship and Islamization can't be ignored. Extremist Islamic groups continue to carry out violent attacks on Muslims and non-Muslims, mass media worldwide are fearful to criticize or even comment on Islam, and strict rules with harsh punishments discourage foreigners from visiting Muslim countries. Therefore people in the West and the East are unsure if Islam is the religion of peace many claim it to be.

This part will be analyzing if Islam does indeed encourage violence and intolerance, or, harmony and understanding. We can then try to understand if Islam is a religion of peace, and if there's anything in the Quran non-Muslims ought to be concerned about.

39

Terrorism

"Certainly anyone who has the power to make you believe absurdities has the power to make you commit injustices" – Voltaire

Throughout history religions have been known to encourage war and violence to achieve their goals, and religious men have often exploited the devotion of followers to promote their causes. So to see religious zealots use violence and exploitation in modern times sadly isn't unusual. Unfortunately the Taliban, al-Qaeda, Boko Haram and ISIS are all household names. But are there any other religions which produces as many global terrorist groups as Islam does in modern times? Are there any other holy scriptures which present as many inflammatory statements as the Quran does?

Terrorists are those who carry out acts with the threatened or actual use of violence to achieve their religious, ideological or political aim. So Islamic terrorists are Muslims who use Islam and their interpretation of the Quran to carry out violent actions in order to achieve their aims.

When non-Muslims hear the word 'Jihad' they often think 'holy war'. But Jihad means more than this. The literal meaning of the Arabic word Jihad is struggle or effort. This struggle or effort can be used to describe three different things for Muslims. First, the internal struggle to live the Muslim faith as best as possible; second, the struggle to build a good Muslim society; and third the struggle to defend Islam, by force if necessary (holy war).[1]

Generally speaking, Islamic terrorists wish to return to the basic Islamic values and laws from the Quran and Hadith (as they've interpreted them). This is why Islamic terrorists have also been called Islamic fundamentalists. In addition, Islamic terrorists seek to eliminate anything perceived to be

---

1. "Islam: Jihad." BBC. August 3, 2009. http://www.bbc.co.uk/religion/religions/islam/beliefs/jihad_1.shtml.

corrupting Islam by any means necessary. This is why they're also called Islamic extremists.

The result of Islamic terrorists' interpretation of the Quran and Hadith has lead to acts of war and terror against anyone (Muslims as well as non-Muslims) they perceive to be committing crimes against Islam or the Muslim community.

A 2013 Pew Research Center Poll found the majority of Muslims globally (72%) consider violence towards civilians as unjustifiable. 10% of Muslims say they are rarely justified, and 8% of Muslims say violence against civilian targets are sometimes justified. Only 3% of Muslims worldwide say suicide bombings and other violence against civilians are often justified.[2]

Several factors can influence a Muslim's opinion on civilian casualties, but one of the main ones is their subjective interpretation of the Quran. As the Pew Poll suggests, there are Muslims who feel all means are often justified for the benefit of Islam; whether it's to defend Islam, or to reach their desired ambition of a global and universal Islam. This is their interpretation of what God asks of Muslims. Muslim critics of Islamic terrorists argue they've misinterpreted the Quran, but Islamic terrorists would say the same back to them.

> Quran 9:33 – It is He who has sent His Messenger with the guidance
> and the religion of truth, that He may uplift it above every religion,
> though the unbelievers be averse.

For some Muslims, particularly Islamic terrorists, the Quran doesn't acknowledge differences between militaries and civilians, only between Muslims and non-believers. Therefore they believe spilling civilian blood to achieve their aim is acceptable to God.

In addition, a study analyzing 300 cases of people charged with Islamic terrorist activities in the USA since September 11 2001 found that terrorists were also influenced by more than just a militant Islamic ideology. They were also motivated by factors such as a:

> "dislike of American foreign policy in the Muslim world; a need to
> attach themselves to an ideology or organization that gave them a
> sense of purpose"; and a "cognitive opening" to militant Islam that
> often was "precipitated by personal disappointment, like the death of

2. Pew Research Center. The World's Muslims: Religion, Politics and Society. Report. April 30, 2013. http://www.pewforum.org/2013/04/30/the-worlds-muslims-religion-politics-society-app-a/. Appendix A: U.S. Muslims — Views on Religion and Society in a Global Context

a parent. For many, joining a jihadist group or carrying out an attack allowed them to become heroes of their own story."[3]

Paradoxically, Prophet Muhammad is a role model for both pacifist and militant Muslims, which tells us a great deal about how differently Islam can be interpreted and practiced. Muslims who condone the use of violence use Prophet Muhammad's example as an army general to justify their means of armed conflict: they're merely emulating their role model for the glory of God. During his prophethood Muhammad sanctioned battles and wars, and often did so by claiming God asked Muslims to battle with His enemies.[4]

Arab tribes had indulged in violence and fierce fighting long before the advent of Islam, so any aggressive verses revealed in the Quran wouldn't have appeared out of place in Arabia 1,400 years ago, even though they do today. Furthermore, Prophet Muhammad's use of warfare wasn't alien to Arab customs at the time either. Therefore Muslims have argued Muhammad needed to be more than just a prophet, but a wartime general as well. Prophet Muhammad's struggle to grow and defend Islam using force was essential to Muslims at the time and if he didn't do so Islam wouldn't be where it is today.[5] So the idea of Islam thriving using pacifistic resistance wouldn't have worked in that environment at that time.

For military conduct, the Quran outlines how Muslims must engage with enemies of Islam, and critics of Islam often use these type of 'Jihad' verses to indicate how violent and aggressive the Quran asks Muslims to be. But, there are three things to keep in mind with these 'Jihad' verses. First, they require historical context which both non-Muslims and Muslims may not be aware of. Second, with or without the historical context, they're still open to subjective interpretation. Third, there's no consensus even among Islamic scholars as to which 'Jihad' verses are abrogated and which are not (see chapter 'Sharia law' for law of abrogation). All of this means there are multiple ways to interpret these 'Jihad' verses and there's no way to definitively say which is correct.

Nonetheless we'll review some of the controversial verses to give you an opportunity to create your own opinion, and as usual, an analysis will be given to provide another perspective. This will also be done without even using the most widely distributed English translation of the Quran, the Hilali-

3. Bergen, Peter. "Why Do Terrorists Commit Terrorism?" The New York Times, June 14, 2016. http://www.nytimes.com/2016/06/15/opinion/why-do-terrorists-commit-terrorism.html?_r=0.

4. Esposito, John L. Islam: The Straight Path. New York, NY: Oxford University Press, 2016.

5. Kumar, Arvind. Encyclopaedia of Human Rights, Violence and Non-violence. Lucknow: Institute for Sustainable Development, 1998. p.187.

Khan, which is considered to contain supremacist and militant interpretations; and without using the Hadith collections respected by Sunnis, and the Hadith collections respected by Shia Muslims, both of which also contain some aggressive messages.[6]

> Quran 2:190-194 – And fight in the way of God with those; who fight with you, but aggress not: God loves not the aggressors. And slay them wherever you come upon them, and expel them from where they expelled you; persecution is more grievous than slaying. But fight them not by the Holy Mosque until they should fight you there; then, if they fight you, slay them — such is the recompense of unbelievers — but if they give over, surely God is All-forgiving, All-compassionate. Fight them, till there is no persecution and the religion is God's; then if they give over, there shall be no enmity save for evildoers. The holy month for the holy month; holy things demand retaliation. Whoso commits aggression against you, do you commit aggression against him like as he has committed against you, and fear you God, and know that God is with the godfearing.

In these verses (*Quran 2:190-194*) God asks Muslims to fight in self-defense (*And fight in the way of God with those; who fight with you*). He asks Muslims to show mercy to those who don't wish to fight (*but aggress not: God loves not the aggressors…but if they give over, surely God is All-forgiving, All-compassionate*). These verses were revealed at a time when Muslims were fighting with established Arab tribes who tried to remove them (*And slay them wherever you come upon them, and expel them from where they expelled you*).[7] So God encourages Muslims to keep fighting them on behalf of the religion of Islam until it prevails, and if the enemy surrenders or repents then not to harm them (*Fight them, till there is no persecution and the religion is God's; then if they give over, there shall be no enmity save for evildoers*). God also asks Muslims not to fight in the holy month of Ramadan, but if they're attacked, then to respond in equal measure (*The holy month for the holy month; holy things demand retaliation. Whoso commits aggression against you, do you commit aggression against him like as he has committed against you*).

---

6. Mohammed, Khaleel. "Assessing English Translations of the Qur'an." Middle East Quarterly 12, no. 2 (2005): 58-71. http://www.meforum.org/717/assessing-english-translations-of-the-quran.

7. Hathout, Maher, and Samer Hathout. Jihad vs. Terrorism. Los Angeles, CA: Multimedia Vera International, 2002. p.49.

The Quran also permits fighting to protect Muslims who have been oppressed.

> Quran 22:39-40 – Leave is given to those who fight because they were wronged — surely God is able to help them — who were expelled from their habitations without right, except that they say 'Our Lord is God.' Had God not driven back the people, some by the means of others, there had been destroyed cloisters and churches, oratories and mosques, wherein God's Name is much mentioned. Assuredly God will help him who helps Him — surely God is All-strong, All-mighty

Muslims can also fight to protect innocent people.

> Quran 4:75-76 – How is it with you, that you do not fight in the way of God, and for the men, women, and children who, being abased, say, 'Our Lord, bring us forth from this city whose people are evildoers, and appoint t us a protector from Thee, and appoint to us from Thee a helper'? The believers fight in the way of God, and the unbelievers fight in the idols' way. Fight you therefore against the friends of Satan; surely the guile of Satan is ever feeble.

Within *Quran 2:190-194*, *Quran 22:39-40* and *Quran 4:75-76* we can begin to see how the same verses can be construed differently among Muslims (due to historical context, subjective interpretation, and the law of abrogation). Some Muslims will read these verses and think it's obvious the Quran doesn't allow fighting except in self-defense: if someone is directly attacking them or their Muslim community. But other Muslims may read these verses and consider themselves and their Muslim communities as being attacked: they are being attacked and oppressed by western ideals, western 'immorality' and western foreign intervention. Therefore they may feel they are constantly under attack, and are within their God given right to attack the West back to defend themselves. There's no definitive answer here, as mentioned, it's up for interpretation.

The Islamic fundamentalists who desire the return of the basic laws and values of Islam may view the West as a decadent and corrupt place. They see people in the West as worshiping all the wrong things: sex, celebrities and money to name a few. Therefore they may interpret this 'misguided focus' as a form of idolatry: they're devoting themselves to something other than God. But once again, it depends how Muslims wish to interpret idolatry.

God discusses idolatry several times in the Quran and gives His instructions on how to deal with a particular set of idolaters.

> Quran 9:5-6 – Then, when the sacred months are drawn away, slay the idolaters wherever you find them, and take them, and confine them, and lie in wait for them at every place of ambush. But if they repent, and perform the prayer, and pay the alms, then let them go their way; God is All-forgiving, All-compassionate. And if any of the idolaters seeks of thee protection, grant him protection till he hears the words of God; then do thou convey him to his place of security — that, because they are a people who do not know.

Quran 9:5-6 is often taken out of context by critics of Islam by isolating the first part as if to indicate God has told Muslims to kill all idolaters and pagans. But these verses are actually referring to a specific event and a specific group of idolaters in Islamic history: it refers to a peace agreement Muslims had with Meccan pagans at the time. So God's permission to ambush, fight and kill is specific to these Arab tribes (already at war with the Muslims) who've breached their peace agreements; whereas the pagans who repented would be spared.[8]

But even with the knowledge of the historical context, Muslims could still portray these verses as God's preferred method of dealing with idolaters: that they should be given a grace period to repent, convert to Islam and worship as a Muslim, but if they don't then God has given permission to kill them. Therefore there's nothing to stop Muslims from interpreting these verses as a precedent set by God for offensive aggression against idolaters if they attempt to exercise their freedom of religion and remain non-Muslim.

Another controversial ayah used by Islam's critics (and likely used by Islamic terrorists too) regards the directive God gave to Muslims about Christians and Jews (people of the book).

> Quran 9:29 – Fight those who believe not in God and the Last Day and do not forbid what God and His Messenger have forbidden — such men as practise not the religion of truth, being of those who have been given the Book — until they pay the tribute out of hand and have been humbled.

8. Ali, Maulana Muhammad. "When Shall War Cease." In The Religion of Islam: A Comprehensive Discussion of the Sources, Principles and Practices of Islam. Lahore, USA: Ahmadiyya Anjuman Ishaat Islam, 1992.

Out of context this ayah reads as an inflammatory command from God for Muslims. But it too has historical context and refers to Muslims fighting the Christians and Jews at the time (*such men as practise not the religion of truth, being of those who have been given the Book*) until they converted to Islam or paid the 'jizya' (*until they pay the tribute out of hand*).

Jizya was a per capita yearly tax collected by Islamic states on certain non-Muslims (known as Dhimmis) who permanently resided in lands under Islamic law.[9] Jizya is mentioned in both the Quran and the Hadith but not its rate or amount. It wasn't an Islamic invention, but a form of taxation adapted from existing systems already established under previous rulers, like those from the Byzantine and Sasanian empires.[10] Its main purpose was to be used as a fee for the protection Muslim rulers provided non-Muslims, to provide exemption from military service for non-Muslims, and as material proof of the non-Muslims' submission to the Muslim state and its laws (*and have been humbled*). The jizya funds were distributed to the Muslim armies, charities and officials.[11]

So without all this historical context, it's easy to see how using this single ayah could provoke animosity among Muslims and non-Muslims, and how it can also provide Islamic fundamentalists with a justification for subjugating non-Muslims.

God also gave Muslims permission to stop anyone who causes '*corruption*' in Islam. This was a law originally directed at Jews.

> Quran 5:32 – Therefore We prescribed for the Children of Israel that whoso slays a soul not to retaliate for a soul slain, nor for corruption done in the land, shall be as if he had slain mankind altogether; and whoso gives life to a soul, shall be as if he ha given life to mankind altogether. Our Messengers have already come to them with the clear signs; then many of them thereafter commit excesses in the earth.

This ayah states if someone kills, and it isn't in retaliation or as a punishment for '*corruption*', it'll be as if that person had killed all humankind. This is a popular ayah also used out of context. Except this time it's used by the apologists of Islam, not the critics, as proof that Islam is a non-violent religion. It's often

9. Fadl, Khaled Abou El, Joshua Cohen, and Ian Lague. The Place of Tolerance in Islam. Boston: Beacon Press, 2002. p.21.

10. Shah, Niaz A. Self-defense in Islamic and International Law: Assessing Al-Qaeda and the Invasion of Iraq. New York: Palgrave MacMillan, 2008. p.20.

11. Esposito, John L. Islam: The Straight Path. New York, NY: Oxford University Press, 2016.

presented out of context along the lines of 'whoever kills an innocent person would be as if they killed all of mankind, and whoever saves a person would be as if they've saved all of mankind'. This variation of the verse is so popular even former US President Barack Obama said it in his 2009 address in Cairo, Egypt.[12]

However reading the entire ayah we can see God is referring to a decree he gave to the Jews (*the Children of Israel*) who'd previously received a set of scriptures from God. God also says whoever kills someone who hasn't caused '*corruption*' in the land, will have sinned. It's this '*corruption*' which is vague and open to interpretation by Muslims dependent on their time period and environment since '*corruption done in the land*' could be murder for some Muslims, or it can be much less for other Muslims. For example, criticizing Islam could be '*corruption done in the land*'. In the Islamic world people who criticize Islam are harassed, imprisoned and even executed, and it will be because of the '*corruption*' they caused in the land (see chapter '*Censorship*'). Corruption could also be interpreted simply as someone who refuses to convert to Islam, thus giving Islamic extremists justification to carry out their acts.

But, although *Quran 5:32* is a popular verse used to showcase Islam's non-violent ideals, the verses immediately following in *Quran 5:33-34* are contrastingly violent. They describe the punishments for the '*corruption*' referred to previously.

> Quran 5:33-34 – This is the recompense of those who fight against God and His Messenger, and hasten about the earth, to do corruption there: they shall be slaughtered, or crucified, or their hands and feet shall alternately be struck off; or they shall be banished from the land. That is a degradation for them in this world; and in the world to come awaits them a mighty chastisement, except for such as repent, before you have power over them. So know you that God is All-forgiving, All-compassionate.

So what at first appeared to be a peaceful message, is in fact a warning to non-believers, and depending on what extent '*corruption*' means to each Muslim (especially for Islamic terrorists) the punishment for the corruptors can always be justified.

---

12. Obama, Barack. "Remarks by the President on a New Beginning." Speech, Remarks by the President at Cairo University, Cairo University, Cairo, Egypt, June 4, 2009. https://obamawhitehouse.archives.gov/the-press-office/remarks-president-cairo-university-6-04-09.

Apologists of Islam (Muslim and non-Muslim) can claim it's because of an individual's mindset or circumstance that they've interpreted the Quran in a negative and hostile way. Muslims in particular will claim it's not the Quran's fault because the Quran is the flawless word of God; it's our fault as imperfect humans for misunderstanding God's words. But there's a reason why many Muslims read the Quran and prefer to be safe rather than sorry on a number of issues it raises (see chapter '*Women's clothing*'); God has made it clear how He feels about those who don't fight for Him in the way of Islam.

> Quran 2:216 – Prescribed for you is fighting, though it be hateful to you. Yet it may happen that you will hate a thing which is better for you; and it may happen that you will love a thing which is worse for you; God knows, and you know not.

Again, reading a verse like *Quran 2:216* in isolation has prompted non-Muslims (and Muslims) to say this is Islam's call to Jihad. This verse is often presented just as it is but looking at the historical context, and the next verse, we get a better understanding as to what it refers to.

> Quran 2:217 – They will question thee concerning the holy month, and fighting in it. Say: 'Fighting in it is a heinous thing, but to bar from God's way, and disbelief in Him, and the Holy Mosque, and to expel its people from it — that is more heinous in God's sight; and persecution is more heinous than slaying.' They will not cease to fight with you, till they turn you from your religion, if they are able; and whosoever of you turns from his religion, and dies disbelieving — their works have failed in this world and the next; those are the inhabitants of the Fire; therein they shall dwell forever.

Muslims weren't accustomed to fighting during the holy month of Ramadan. So when *Quran 2:216* says '*Prescribed for you is fighting, though it be hateful to you. Yet it may happen that you will hate a thing which is better for you*' it's referring to Muslims fighting during the holy month. However, there will also be other times when Muslims won't like fighting or won't be accustomed to doing it, therefore *Quran 2:216* could still be used a rallying cry by Islamic extremists to recruit, motivate or shame those who don't want to fight for them and God.

This is compounded further by more verses which express God's desire for Muslims to fight in times of need.

> Quran 4:95-96 – Such believers as sit at home — unless they have

an injury — are not the equals of those who struggle in the path of God with their possessions and their selves. God has preferred in rank those who struggle with their possessions and their selves over the ones who sit at home; yet to each God has promised the reward most fair; and God has preferred those who struggle over the ones who sit at home for the bounty of a mighty wage, in ranks standing before Him, forgiveness and mercy; surely God is All-forgiving, All-compassionate.

So Muslims are told to believe God has no sympathy for those who don't fight and struggle in His name, and they won't get the rewards from Him in the afterlife either. These revelations were revealed at a time when Muslims needed more fighters, and Muslims needed to take more responsibility, like they did in the Battles of Badr, Uhud and Tabuk against the Meccan forces.[13] But it's easy to see how this could also be used in propaganda to recruit for terrorist groups: it's better to be safe than sorry when it comes to incurring God's wrath, even if Muslims dislike it.

If Muslims do decide to engage in battles and wars for the glory of God and Islam, then they'd better not change their mind or retreat, otherwise God will be most displeased and they will incur His wrath.

> Quran 8:15-17 – O believers, when you encounter the unbelievers marching to battle, turn not your backs to them. Whoso turns his back that day to them, unless withdrawing to fight again or removing to join another host, he is laden with the burden of God's anger, and his refuge is Gehenna — an evil homecoming! You did not slay them, but God slew them; and when thou threwest, it was not thyself that threw, but God threw, and that He might confer on the believers a fair benefit; surely God is All-hearing, All-knowing.

So according to God, it's better for Muslims to persevere against the odds, even if the odds are greatly against them, than it is to back down. This could also apply to any modern day Muslim who had a change in heart and wanted to defect from an Islamic terrorist group: they may believe they'll have to suffer God's punishment in the next life as well as punishment from other terrorists in this life who may kill them for abandoning God and their cause. When *Quran 8:15-17* was revealed it was referring to the Battle of Badr 624 CE, a key battle

---

13. Ghamdi, Javed Ahmad. "The Islamic Law of Jihad." Translated by Shehzad Saleem. In Mīzā n. Lahore: Dar Ul-Ishraq, 2001. http://www.studying-islam.org/articletext.aspx?id=771.

in the early days of Islam between the Muslims of Medina and the Quraish of Mecca.[14]

In *Quran 8:15-17* God even says it wasn't the Muslims who killed the enemy, it was His divine intervention which killed them (*You did not slay them, but God slew them*). So Muslims (terrorists or otherwise) who fight in the name of God may always believe they'll overcome any obstacle because God is on their side. Even if they were to find themselves outnumbered, they shouldn't worry, they should persevere because God will help them.

> Quran 8:65-66 – O Prophet, urge on the believers to fight. If there be twenty of you, patient men, they will overcome two hundred; if there be a hundred of you, they will overcome a thousand unbelievers, for they are a people who understand not. Now God has lightened it for you, knowing that there is weakness in you. If there be a hundred of you, patient men, they will overcome two hundred; if there be of you a thousand, they will overcome two thousand by the leave of God; God is with the patient.

In addition, if any struggle in the name of Islam ends up taking a Muslim's life, they're not likely to be worried as they believe God will reward them for their sacrifice. Islamic terrorists are more willing to die because, like all Muslims, they don't believe dying on earth is the end of their existence; it is in fact the beginning of a wonderful and eternal afterlife in Paradise because they died for God.

> Quran 3:169-171 – Count not those who were slain in God's way as dead, but rather living with their Lord, by Him provided, rejoicing in the bounty that God has given them, and joyful in those who remain behind and have not joined them, because no fear shall be on them, neither shall they sorrow, joyful in blessing and bounty from God, and that God leaves not to waste the wage of the believers.

> Quran 4:74 – So let them fight in the way of God who sell the present life for the world to come; and whosoever fights in the way of God and is slain, or conquers, We shall bring him a mighty wage.

Islam has had this martyrdom influence on its followers more than any other

---

14. The Editors of Encyclopædia Britannica. "Battle of Badr." Encyclopædia Britannica. May 13, 2009. https://www.britannica.com/event/Battle-of-Badr.

religion in recent times. It's one of the reasons why so many Islamic terrorist attacks involve suicide by the perpetrators. It's because of verses like these that critics of Islam are so skeptical that moderate Islam is possible; they argue the presence of Islamic extremism is merely a consequence of taking the Quran literally which is what Muslims are asked to do.[15]

Prophet Muhammad's conquests to spread Islam was one of the main reasons for its growth, so Muslims and apologists can argue Prophet Muhammad did what he did to ensure the survival and growth of Islam. This may well be true, but it doesn't lessen the reality that Prophet Muhammad's actions, and the Quran, influence Islamic terrorists. So even if the Prophet did what he had to do 1,400 years ago, his actions are still being emulated today, both in positive and negative ways by all Muslims.

In Islam's early years Prophet Muhammad was a pacifist, and this may only be because he didn't have any influence. But as his power grew, so did his and the Quran's ruthlessness towards non-believers (see chapter 'Non-Muslims'). He began to live a prophethood which contrasted with most other prophets of God who were peaceful men living simple lives. However, if individuals like Gandhi, Martin Luther King, and Nelson Mandela were all leaders who achieved their goals through non-violence, surely someone like God would have been able to help Prophet Muhammad accomplish his goals without the violent and aggressive verses in the Quran?

Still, it's too simplistic and inaccurate to jump to conclusions about Muslims and who they are as people just because of the Quran's words. As previously stated, the overwhelming majority of Muslims globally lead peaceful and tolerant lives. For example, Iraq was ranked 1st in the world for helping strangers by the Charities Aid Foundation's annual World Giving Index in 2016. This is remarkable considering Iraq is a war torn state which has been blighted with decades of conflict. This recognition of the Iraqi people is all the more noteworthy as it's for the second year running, since they were also ranked first in 2015.[16] Hopefully it goes to show to the rest of the world the kindness and generosity prevalent in Muslims, even when the odds are stacked against them.

Muslims like these don't identify with the terrorist acts of Islamic militants, and they do not identify with how Islamic militants practice Islam. It's unreasonable to tar almost 2 billion people in the world with the same brush

15. Harris, Sam. The End of Faith: Religion, Terror, and the Future of Reason. New York: W.W. Norton & Company, 2005. p.31, p.149.

16. Charities Aid Foundation. CAF World Giving Index 2016. Report. October 2016. https://www.cafonline.org/about-us/publications/2016-publications/caf-world-giving-index-2016.

as the thousands who kill innocent people. Most Muslims are kind, generous and friendly people who have the best interests of their family and community at heart. Muslims share the same universal desire to see less suffering and more peace, just like other people around the world.

Unfortunately, it still shouldn't take away from what's contained in the Quran. Muslims need to at least acknowledge the existence of hostile verses in the Quran by putting themselves in the shoes of non-Muslims and reading them again. Then, Muslims can finally begin to understand why non-Muslims become so fearful when they hear verses from the Quran, even if they're in isolation and out of context. As for the rest of the non-Muslim world, they need to let Muslims know they're not the enemy of anyone; it's Islamic terrorist groups who are the enemy of everyone.

40

Non-Muslims

"The position of the Muslim community in the face of all provocations seems to be: Islam is a religion of peace, and if you say that it isn't, we will kill you" – Sam Harris

The Quran has a lot to say about anyone who's a non-Muslim, but when we review what the Quran says about non-believers we have to make allowances for context. Taking individual verses out of context is an unfair reflection of what the Quran is saying on that particular subject (see chapter *'Terrorism'*). However, when Muslims read the Quran they're looking to it for guidance. So when God refers to non-believers from a particular incident and period of time, Muslims look to this as a source of teaching. It can be seen as God's words and God's example of how they must approach the same type of people.

So Muslims can either decide to see it as an isolated incident with a particular group of Jews, Christians and idolaters. Or, they can decide to see it as God's attitude towards those non-Muslims, and a precedent set on how to behave with them going forward.

This distinction in interpretation is important because when we read what the Quran says about non-believers, it isn't reflective of a religion of peace. Many times throughout the Quran there are aggressive and violent passages, and they all refer to the people who disobey God and choose not to follow Islam. If there was a religious book which spoke about Muslims in the same way that the Quran regularly spoke about non-Muslims, it would cause an outrage in the Islamic world. The Quran fosters an us-versus-them mentality and it continuously promotes Islam's superiority over the ungodly who don't believe in it, and don't convert to Islam.

> Quran 3:110 – You are the best nation ever brought forth to men, bidding to honour, and forbidding dishonour, and believing in God.

Had the People of the Book believed, it were better for them; some
of them are believers, but the most of them are ungodly.

The following list of examples from the Quran about non-Muslims is not
intended to be taken out of context to shock and provoke. They're listed to give
some examples of what the Quran said about non-Muslims 1,400 years ago,
and consequently how Muslims can choose to approach them going forward.
It's up to each Muslim's interpretation of the Quran to decide if they'll still
hold resentment to the non-Muslims who challenged Prophet Muhammad and
Islam 1,400 years ago. Though even if they don't, the Quran certainly had some
choice words to say about them at the time.

The Quran classifies non-believers as people who don't follow Islam even
though God gave them '*clear signs*'.

Quran 2:99 – And We have sent down unto thee signs, clear signs,
and none disbelieves in them except the ungodly.

The Quran compares the ignorance of non-believers to those who are deaf,
dumb and blind.

Quran 2:170-171 – And when it is said to them, 'Follow what
God has sent down,' they say, 'No; but we will follow such things
as we found our fathers doing.' What? And if their fathers had
no understanding of anything, and if they were not guided? The
likeness of those who disbelieve is as the likeness of one who shouts
to that which hears nothing, save a call and a cry; deaf, dumb, blind
— they do not understand.

God advises Muslims not to take non-believers as friends instead of believers,
unless Muslims need to be nice to them out of fear of other consequences.

Quran 3:28 – Let not the believers take the unbelievers for friends,
rather than the believers — for whoso does that belongs not to God
in anything — unless you have a fear of them. God warns you that
You beware of Him, and unto God is the homecoming.

In addition to these non-believers, the people of the book (Jews and Christians)
who don't believe in Islam should not be taken as friends. They are all people
who don't understand.

Quran 5:51 – O believers, take not Jews and Christians as friends; they are friends of each other. Whoso of you makes them his friends is one of them. God guides not the people of the evildoers.

Quran 5:55-58 – Your friend is only God, and His Messenger, and the believers who perform the prayer and pay the alms, and bow them down. Whoso makes God his friend, and His Messenger, and the believers — the party of God, they are the victors. O believers, take not as your friends those of them, who were given the Book before you, and the unbelievers, who take your religion in mockery and as a sport — and fear God, if you are believers — and when you call to prayer, take it in mockery and as a sport; that is because they are a people who have no understanding.

If Muslims do decide to take unbelievers as friends then they'd be adding evil to their '*account*'.

Quran 5:80-81 – Thou seest many of them making unbelievers their friends. Evil is that they have forwarded to their account, that God is angered against them, and in the chastisement they shall dwell forever. Yet had they believed in God and the Prophet and what has been sent down to him, they would not have taken them as friends; but many of them are ungodly.

God tells Muslims not to take as friends '*those who have fought you in religion's cause, and expelled you from your habitations, and have supported in your expulsion*' or they'll be viewed as '*evildoers*' in His eyes.

Quran 60:8-9 – God forbids you not, as regards those who have not fought you in religion's cause, nor expelled you from your habitations, that you should be kindly to them, and act justly towards them; surely God loves the just. God only forbids you as to those who have fought you in religion's cause, and expelled you from your habitations, and have supported in your expulsion, that you should take them for friends. And whosoever takes them for friends, those — they are the evildoers.

But the expression '*those who have fought you in religion's cause*' can be subjectively interpreted by each Muslim. It could mean not befriending nationalities with 'immoral' cultural and religious influences on Muslim communities. Or, it could mean not befriending nationalities whose government interferes with Muslim states. The extent to which people may 'fight' Muslims in *'religion's cause'* is open to interpretation.

God asks Muslims to judge Christians by what the Christians choose to believe in the Quran He sent down. If the Christians do not believe in it, then they are ungodly.

> Quran 5:46-48 – And We sent, following in their footsteps, Jesus son of Mary, confirming the Torah before him and We gave to him the Gospel, wherein is guidance and light, and confirming the Torah before it, as a guidance and an admonition unto the godfearing. So let the People of the Gospel judge according to what God has sent down therein. Whosoever judges not according to what God has sent down — they are the ungodly. And We have sent down to thee the Book with the truth, confirming the Book that was before it, and assuring it. So judge between them according to what God has sent down, and do not follow their caprices, to forsake the truth that has come to thee. To every one of you We have appointed a right way and an open road. If God had willed, He would have made you one nation; but that He may try you in what has come to you. So be you forward in good works; unto God shall you return, all together; and He will tell you of that whereon you were at variance.

The Quran also criticizes Christians for calling Jesus the Son of God, and criticizes Jews for calling Ezra the Son of God. However, Jews do not identify with the statement that Ezra was revered by them as the Son of God, only pious.[1]

> Quran 9:30 – The Jews say, 'Ezra is the Son of God'; the Christians say, 'The Messiah is the Son of God.' That is the utterance of their mouths, conforming with the unbelievers before them. God assail them! How they are perverted!

Idolaters (however a Muslim chooses to perceive idolatry in the modern age) are also to be kept at a distance. Their uncleanliness (morals, deeds, ignorance) is undesirable.

---

1. Kohler, Kaufmann, and Ignatz Goldziher. "Islam." Jewish Encyclopedia. Accessed March 1, 2017. http://www.jewishencyclopedia.com/articles/8263-islam#anchor15.

Quran 9:28 – O believers, the idolaters are indeed unclean; so let them not come near the Holy Mosque after this year of theirs. If you fear poverty, God shall surely enrich you of His bounty, if He will; God is All-knowing; All-wise.

Jews in particular are singled out as being as bad as the idolaters and causing '*corruption*' on Earth; whereas humble Christians (like '*priests and monks*') who have tears in their eyes after hearing the Quran's words are those who are closest to the Muslims.

Quran 5:64 – The Jews have said, 'God's hand is fettered.' Fettered are their hands, and they are cursed for what they have said. Nay, but His hands are outspread; He expends how He will. And what has been sent down to thee from thy Lord will surely increase many of them in insolence and unbelief; and We have cast between them enmity and hatred, till the Day of Resurrection. As often as they light a fire for war, God will extinguish it. They hasten about the earth, to do corruption there; and God loves not the workers of corruption.

Quran 5:82-83 – Thou wilt surely find the most hostile of men to the believers are the Jews and the idolaters; and thou wilt surely find the nearest of them in love to the believers are those who say 'We are Christians'; that, because some of them are priests and monks, and they wax not proud; and when they hear what has been sent down to the Messenger, thou seest their eyes overflow with tears because of the truth they recognize. They say, 'Our Lord, we believe; so do Thou write us down among the witnesses.

Nonetheless, the non-believers (people of the book, idolaters) God curses are '*apes and swine*' to Him.

Quran 5:59-60 – Say: 'People of the Book, do you blame us for any other cause than that we believe in God, and what has been sent down to us, and what was sent down before, and that most of you are ungodly?' Say: 'Shall I tell you of a recompense with God, worse than that? Whomsoever God has cursed, and with whom He is wroth, and made some of them apes and swine, and worshippers of idols — they are worse situated, and have gone further astray from the right way.

Muslims may be tempted to be merciful with non-believers, but God prefers that they're hard against them, and are only merciful to other Muslims.

> Quran 48:29 – Muhammad is the Messenger of God, and those who are with him are hard against the unbelievers, merciful one to another. Thou seest them bowing, prostrating, seeking bounty from God and good pleasure. Their mark is on their faces, the trace of prostration. That is their likeness in the Torah, and their likeness in the Gospel: as a seed that puts forth its shoot, and strengthens it, and it grows stout and rises straight upon its stalk, pleasing the sowers, that through them He may enrage the unbelievers. God has promised those of them who believe and do deeds of righteousness forgiveness and a mighty wage.

God also advises Prophet Muhammad to no longer show leniency to the non-believers and the hypocrites who claim to be Muslim but are not; God will punish both of these people by sending them to Hell.

> Quran 9:72-73 – God has promised the believers, men and women, gardens underneath which rivers flow, forever therein to dwell, and goodly dwelling-places in the Gardens of Eden; and greater, God's good pleasure; that is the mighty triumph. O Prophet, struggle with the unbelievers and hypocrites, and be thou harsh with them; their refuge is Gehenna — an evil homecoming!

For God, the non-believers and idolaters are the worst of all the creatures on Earth. Unlike those who do believe and are devout: they're the best of creatures on Earth.

> Quran 98:6-8 – The unbelievers of the People of the Book and the idolaters shall be in the Fire of Gehenna, therein dwelling forever; those are the worst of creatures. But those who believe, and do righteous deeds, those are the best of creatures; their recompense is with their Lord-Gardens of Eden, underneath which rivers flow, therein dwelling for ever and ever. God is well-pleased with them, and they are well-pleased with Him; that is for him who fears his Lord.

Reflecting on all the verses referenced in this chapter, let's now take a moment to understand some of the historical context they were revealed under.

As previously mentioned in chapter '*Prophet Muhammad as a role model*', suras from the Quran were either revealed in Mecca or Medina depending on where Muhammad was during his Prophethood. The suras which were revealed in Medina were during a time when the Muslim community was more established; it was much larger and more developed in Medina, compared to its initial years as a religion in Mecca. When Islam was young in Mecca, Muslims were a persecuted minority and didn't carry much authority or power. Consequently, during Islam's early years in Mecca the suras revealed in the Quran were pacifistic: they spoke of good morals such as kindness and truthfulness. They also retold stories of prophets from previous Abrahamic holy scriptures and the punishments which came to a prophet's people when they rejected the message of God.

Muhammad was an accomplished statesman and diplomat throughout his prophethood, and particularly so when his following of Muslims was small in Mecca during Islam's early years. He was able to keep good relations with communities, and this served his purposes well at the time since he had little influence.

But when Prophet Muhammad moved to Medina, his authority and following grew stronger over time. Prophet Muhammad became an established leader with a literal army of followers behind him. When people in Medina didn't convert to Islam or caused problems, they became a hindrance to his and Islam's cause. With his rise to power, Prophet Muhammad's attitude and treatment towards non-Muslims changed dramatically and this is reflected in the Medinan suras in the Quran. This is why it's no surprise all the discriminatory verses quoted in this chapter are all Medinan suras from the Quran. Muhammad used his power and his growing supporters to his advantage against the people he once had to be accommodating and amicable towards.

God has many positive names in the Quran (which He gives Himself). He's the compassionate one, the wise one, and the merciful one. But what is it that makes God as merciful as He claims to be in His book, particularly after reading such aggressive verses in the Quran? If someone insults us and threatens us with cruel torture, then says they won't do it if we become their servant and obey their rules, does that make them compassionate? Or is it some form of religious Stockholm Syndrome?

The Quran is not only an aggressive and violent book in many parts, it's an arrogant one as well. It's a book which belittles anyone who doesn't believe in its message, and threatens them with everlasting torture if they don't conform to what it says. Muslims are constantly told how favored and special they are in the eyes of God, and how beneath them non-believers are. It's this group solidarity and mentality which can foster discrimination, especially when one group is regularly demonized in the eyes of another. Since we're also told by God that the Quran is perfect and applies forever, we're left with prejudiced messages about non-Muslims which Muslims will read, recite five times a day in prayer, and internalize for generations. It's reassuring (and somewhat surprising) that the overwhelming majority of Muslims in the world have been able to live tolerant and egalitarian lives, *in spite* of the discriminatory verses in their holy book.

Islam, like all religions, is supposed to be the ultimate guidance process to give people morals and society peace. If that's still true, then there's still some kinks to be worked out. But after several thousand years, how much longer are we going to wait? Even when a theocratic country only has people from the same religion, there's still no guarantee of a utopia. For example, following Islam is meant to be the most accessible way of having a civil society, and Sharia law is supposed to be the perfect legal system since it is based on God's and Prophet Muhammad's instructions. By this logic, Islamic countries ought to be some of the most prosperous and desirable places in the world to live in. But this isn't true. The early 21st century has seen revolutions and uprisings across the entire Arab world because of how uninhabitable and corrupt Islamic countries had become for its citizens. These political, economical and social problems all came to a head in late 2010 with the dawn of the Arab Spring.

One would imagine if a land only had religious people in it then it would be a land of tolerance, understanding and civil peace. After all, the religious all subscribe to the Golden Rule in one form or another: treat others as you'd want to be treated. Unfortunately this isn't the reality. What we've seen in the 'Holy Land' for over 1,000 years now (in particular with the Crusades in the Middle Ages) has been the opposite and it doesn't look like there's an end in sight. If people are unable to determine right from wrong it's not from a lack of religion, it's from a lack of compassion for our fellow human being.

In the end, it's each person's moral compass which guides them. Which is why most Muslims thankfully don't follow such prejudiced verses about non-believers to the letter. However, since it's in the Quran and open to interpretation, it still gives permission to a minority of Muslims to act with animosity towards non-believers

Thankfully for Muslims, the Quran speaks highly of them since they do what it says. So if you're a Muslim, Islam may indeed be a religion of peace from your perspective. But Muslims must understand it doesn't always appear that way to everyone else, and if they're in doubt as to why, then there are plenty of reasons in this chapter alone.

41

Hell

"Fear is the mother of all gods" – Lucretius

According to the Quran there is one fate which will befall all those who don't accept Islam: Hell.

> Quran 3:85 – Whoso desires another religion than Islam, it shall not be accepted of him; in the next world he shall be among the losers.

Muslims believe there will be a Day of Judgement, and on this day a trumpet will be blown to announce its arrival. Everyone on Earth will cease to live. Then, the trumpet will blow again and all humankind will be standing present before God for His judgement.

> Quran 39:67-68 – They measure not God with His true measure. The earth altogether shall be His handful on the Day of Resurrection, and the heavens shall be rolled up in His right hand. Glory be to Him! High be He exalted above that they associate! For the Trumpet shall be blown, and whosoever is in the heavens and whosoever is in the earth shall swoon, save whom God wills. Then it shall be blown again, and lo, they shall stand, beholding.

On the Day of Judgement, the Earth will shake and then every person will be judged for all their good and bad deeds according to God. Muslims believe in Predestination (God knows everything that will ever happen) but Muslims also believe it doesn't stop people from having free will and making their own choices in life. So every action every person has ever committed in their lives has been recorded in 'the Scrolls' and this is what they'll be judged on. These 'Scrolls' contain all the deeds of humanity.

Quran 54:52-53 – Every thing that they have done is in the Scrolls, and everything, great and small, is inscribed.

Quran 99:1-8 – When earth is shaken with a mighty shaking and earth brings forth her burdens, and Man says., 'What ails her?' upon that day she shall tell her tidings for that her Lord has inspired her. Upon that day men shall issue in scatterings to see their works, and whoso has done an atom's weight of good shall see it, and whoso has done an atom's weight of evil shall see it.

Muslims who are God-fearing and worship Him devoutly will be rewarded with an eternity in Heaven.

Quran 39:73-74 – Then those that feared their Lord shall be driven in companies into Paradise, till, when they have come thither, and its gates are opened, and its keepers will say to them, 'Peace be upon you! Well you have fared; enter in, to dwell forever.' And they shall say, 'Praise belongs to God, who has been true in His promise to us, and has bequeathed upon us the earth, for us to make our dwelling wheresoever we will in Paradise.' How excellent is the wage of those that labour!

While the gates of Hell will open to those who don't heed God's warnings or signs; they will be punished there forever.

Quran 39:71-72 – Then the unbelievers shall be driven in companies into Gehenna till, when they have come thither, then its gates will be opened and its keepers will say to them, 'Did not Messengers come to you from among yourselves, reciting to you the signs of your Lord and warning you against the encounter of this your day?' They shall say, 'Yes indeed; but the word of the chastisement has been realized against the unbelievers.' It shall be said, 'Enter the gates of Gehenna, to dwell therein forever.' How evil is the lodging of those that are proud!

This is what all Muslims believe will happen to everyone that's ever lived when Judgement Day arrives. It's one of the main reasons people are Muslims in the first place: so that when they die or Judgement Day comes, God will not send them to Hell forever. The concept of Hell has allowed religions to thrive and sustain themselves for thousands of years; fear and uncertainty makes people cautious about not believing in religion or God. All around the world parents teach their daughters and sons the concept of Hell, and young children grow up believing it's a place they could potentially have to live in forever. That if they don't obey the rules, they'll go to this horrible place and suffer excruciating pain for eternity. Meanwhile, all their friends and family who were 'good' will enjoy Heaven forever without them.

The same impressionable children grow up to become adults who then repeat the pattern: indoctrinating their children with the same rhetoric they received when they were young. So the cycle continues, the fears of one generation of Muslims are passed on to the next generation.

There's no proof the place we know as Hell exists. In Islam, it's the Quran which tells us it exists. So Muslims give their entire lives over to this single point of failure. But no religion or ideology has a monopoly on the afterlife since they all claim to know what's going to happen after we die, yet they can't all know and they can't all be right.

All faiths also offer their own forms of worship and redemption to avoid their Hells. But no one can say for certain which, if any, are true because no one has better proof than anyone else. The only proof people have are 'holy' words in a number of different books thousands of years old, from ancient mythologies, from various tribes, and from different continents. All of which have been passed on for generations by the impressionable, irrational and unpredictable humans that we are. So with that in mind, let's begin to explore Hell to get a better understanding of what horrors the Quran says will await every non-believer.

Hell is known as 'Gehenna' and 'Jahannam' in Arabic, and the Quran does a good descriptive job of letting us know what's in store for us if we're disobedient. Shrewdly, it does this by describing the horrors of Hell alongside the wonders of Paradise. This allows the Quran to make the contrast between the two even more stark and compelling to readers, as we'll see examples of throughout this chapter.

> Quran 47:15 – This is the similitude of Paradise which the godfearing have been promised: therein are rivers of water unstaling, rivers of milk unchanging in flavour, and rivers of wine — a delight to the drinkers, rivers, too, of honey purified; and therein for them is every fruit, and forgiveness from their Lord — Are they as he who dwells forever in the Fire, such as are given to drink boiling water, that tears their bowels asunder?

As we may have already guessed, non-believers will reside in burning fires.

> Quran 3:151 – We will cast into the hearts of the unbelievers terror, for that they have associated with God that for which He sent down never authority; their lodging shall be the Fire; evil is the lodging of the evildoers.

> Quran 11:106-107 – As for the wretched, they shall be in the Fire, wherein there shall be for them moaning and sighing, therein dwelling forever, so long as the heavens and earth abide, save as thy Lord will; surely thy Lord accomplishes what He desires.

Their bodies will burn and their faces will scald with '*water like molten copper*'; while those in the Gardens of Eden will rest on thrones alongside flowing rivers draped in fine jewelry and garments.

> Quran 18:29-31 – Say: 'The truth is from your Lord; so let whosoever will believe, and let whosoever will disbelieve.' Surely We have prepared for the evildoers a fire, whose pavilion encompasses them; if they call for succour, they will be succoured with water like molten copper, that shall scald their faces — how evil a potion, and how evil a resting-place! Surely those who believe, and do deeds of righteousness — surely We leave not to waste the wage of him who does good works; those — theirs shall be Gardens of Eden, underneath which rivers flow; therein they shall be adorned with bracelets of gold, and they shall be robed in green garments of silk and brocade, therein reclining upon couches — O, how excellent a reward! And O, how fair a resting-place!

Hell has seven gates, complementing the seven levels Heaven also has in Islam. Non-believers are assigned a gate of Hell corresponding to the wickedness of their sins. In contrast, the god-fearing will be in peace and security amidst gardens and fountains.

> Quran 15:41-46 – Said He, 'This is for Me a straight path: over My servants thou shalt have no authority, except those that follow thee, being perverse; Gehenna shall be their promised land all together. Seven gates it has, and unto each gate a set portion of them belongs.' But the godfearing shall be amidst gardens and fountains: 'Enter you them, in peace and security!'

According to God, the people occupying the worst part of Hell are the hypocrites: those who pretended to believe in God when they did not.

> Quran 4:145-146 – Surely the hypocrites will be in the lowest reach of the Fire; thou wilt not find for them any helper; save such as repent, and make amends, and hold fast to God, and make their religion sincerely God's; those are with the believers, and God will certainly give the believers a mighty wage.

Hell is fueled by all the non-believing sinners who are in it.

> Quran 3:10-12 – As for the unbelievers, their riches will not avail them, neither their children, aught against God; those — they shall be fuel for the Fire like Pharaoh's folk, and the people before them, who cried lies to Our signs; God seized them because of their sins; God is terrible in retribution. Say to the unbelievers: 'You shall be overthrown, and mustered into Gehenna — an evil cradling!'

According to God, non-believers belong in Hell because they're Satan's friends. However, all of us do have something in common, we all have what God considers '*shameful parts*' (even though God made us this way and doesn't give a good reason as to why they're shameful).

> Quran 7:27 – Children of Adam! Let not Satan tempt you as he brought your parents out of the Garden, stripping them of their garments to show them their shameful parts. Surely he sees you, he and his tribe, from where you see them not. We have made the Satans the friends of those who do not believe.

Hell is below Heaven of course, but not so far away from Heaven that sinners can't beg for mercy and the saved reluctantly respond (which one would imagine would become quite annoying for those in Heaven).

> Quran 7:50-51 – The inhabitants of the Fire shall call to the inhabitants of Paradise: 'Pour on us water, or of that God has provided you!' They will say: 'God has forbidden them to the unbelievers who have taken their religion as a diversion and a sport, and whom the present life has deluded.' — Therefore today We forget them as they forgot the encounter of this their day, and that they denied Our signs.

When sinners are in Hell, they only have three things to eat for sustenance. First, cactus thorns which are painful to eat, fail to relieve hunger and can't sustain a person.

> Quran 88:1-16 – Hast thou received the story of the Enveloper? Faces on that day humbled, labouring, toilworn, roasting at a scorching fire, watered at a boiling fountain, no food for them but cactus thorn unfattening, unappeasing hunger. Faces on that day jocund, with their striving well-pleased, in a sublime Garden, hearing there no babble; therein a running fountain, therein uplifted couches and goblets set forth and cushions arrayed and carpets outspread.

The second thing to eat is 'ghislin' which Arberry has translated from the Quran to mean a *'foul pus'*.

> Quran 69:33-37 – Behold, he never believed in God the All-mighty, and he never urged the feeding of the needy; therefore he today has not here one loyal friend, neither any food saving foul pus, that none excepting the sinners eat.'

The third food is fruit from a tree called '*Zakkoum*' (or Zaqqum) which bubbles in the stomach like molten copper. Zakkoum has its roots at the bottom of Hell and its fruit is shaped like the devil's head.

> Quran 37:62-68 – Is that better as a hospitality, or the Tree of Ez-Zakkoum? We have appointed it as a trial for the evildoers. It is a tree that comes forth in the root of Hell; its spathes are as the heads of Satans, and they eat of it, and of it fill their bellies, then on top of it they have a brew of boiling water, then their return is unto Hell.

> Quran 44:43-48 – Lo, the Tree of Ez-Zakkoum is the food of the guilty, like molten copper, bubbling in the belly as boiling water bubbles. 'Take him, and thrust him into the midst of Hell, then pour over his head the chastisement of boiling water!'

The Quran personifies Hell since it describes it as '*sighing*'.

> Quran 67:6-11 – And for those who disbelieve in their Lord there awaits the chastisement of Gehenna — an evil homecoming! When

they are cast into it they will hear it sighing, the while it boils and wellnigh bursts asunder with rage. As often as a troop is cast into it, its keepers ask them, 'Came there no warner to you?'; They say, 'Yes indeed, a warner came to us; but we cried lies, saying, "God has not sent down anything; you are only in great error. They also say, 'If we had only heard, or had understood, we would not have been of the inhabitants of the Blaze.' So they confess their sins. Curse the inhabitants of the Blaze!

Hell also has a voice to speak with: in the Quran God asks Hell if it is full and Hell responds.

> Quran 50:30 – Upon the day We shall say unto Gehenna, 'Art thou filled?' And it shall say, 'Are there any more to come?'

Hell burns sinners' skins, only to replace the skin so they can be re-burned again.

> Quran 4:56 – Surely those who disbelieve in Our signs — We shall certainly roast them at a Fire; as often as their skins are wholly burned, We shall give them in exchange other skins, that they may taste the chastisement. Surely God is All-mighty, All-wise.

The non-believers faces and back are set on fire in Hell.

> Quran 21:39-40 – If the unbelievers but knew when that they shall not ward off the Fire from their faces nor from their backs, neither shall they be helped! Nay, but it shall come upon them suddenly, dumbfounding them, and they shall not be able to repel it, nor shall they be respited.

Chains on the necks of sinners drag them through boiling water, and then Hell throws them back into the fire.

> Quran 40:70-76 – Those who cry lies to the Book and that wherewith We sent Our Messengers — soon they will know! When the fetters and chains are on their necks, and they dragged into the boiling water, then into the Fire they are poured; then it is said to them, 'Where are those you associated, apart from God?' They shall say, 'They have gone astray from us; nay, but it was nothing

at all that we called upon aforetime.' Even so God leads astray the unbelievers. 'That is because you rejoiced in the earth without right, and were exultant. Enter the gates of Gehenna, to dwell therein forever.' How evil is the lodging of those that are proud!

Further punishment is inflicted by clothing sinners with '*garments of fire*', pouring boiling water over their heads, melting their skins and what's in their stomachs, and using hooked iron rods on them. In contrast, those who believe are in gardens with flowing rivers, dressed in silk and '*bracelets of gold and with pearls*'.

> Quran 22:19-24 – These are two disputants who have disputed concerning their Lord. As for the unbelievers, for them garments of fire shall, be cut, and there shall be poured over their heads boiling water whereby whatsoever is in their bellies and their skins shall be melted; for them await hooked iron rods; as often as they desire in their anguish to come forth from it, they shall be restored into it, and: 'Taste the chastisement of the burning!' God shall surely admit those who believe and do righteous deeds into gardens underneath which rivers flow; therein they shall be adorned with bracelets of gold and with pearls, and their apparel there shall be of silk; and they; shall be guided unto goodly speech, and they shall be guided unto the path of the All-laudable.

Anything would be better than the punishment mentioned, but the heavenly alternative of jewelry and clothes is quite superficial. Perhaps it met the desires of Arabian people 1,400 years, but gold and pearl bracelets won't satisfy everyone throughout human history.

In the end according to the Quran, the only people who can hope to escape such horrors are those who follow Islam: Muslims.

> Quran 5:55-56 – Your friend is only God, and His Messenger, and the believers who perform the prayer and pay the alms, and bow them down. Whoso makes God his friend, and His Messenger, and the believers — the party of God, they are the victors.

These are the descriptions of Hell found in the Quran. This is the fear instilled into young children which reads more like a horror story than a divine holy book. It's why critics of Islam consider it emotional child abuse (see chapter '*Children*').

But Islam is no different from many other religions in this regard. Religions need Hell, just like religions need Heaven. Because human beings respond to good incentives, whether it's by the carrot (Heaven) or by the stick (Hell), rather than good intentions. What motivation would people have to become servants to God if there was nothing at stake or nothing to gain?

This is how religion works to keep people ensnared: through fear. Fear of the unknown. Fear of uncertainty. Fear of eternal torture. It's this fear which continues to hold humankind back because it stops us from questioning the things which made us fearful in the first place: God, the Quran, our parents.

We must be braver to overcome the anxieties and worries we've inherited from our ancestors. We must break free from the chains of fear religion has wrapped around us for thousands of years. We need to be wary of these threats from ancient mythologies for the sake of our intelligence and the advancement of humanity. Making decisions on how we live our entire lives because we're scared, is no way to live. If the choices we make in life decide who we become, then let us make them reflect our hopes, not our fears.

42

Apostasy

"Let the human mind loose. It must be loose. It will be loose. Superstition and dogmatism cannot confine it" – John Adams

Apostasy for a Muslim is the conscious abandonment of Islam. It's carried out by an individual born to a Muslim family or someone who had previously accepted Islam. She or he may abandon Islam to convert to another religion or to no religion at all, both would be considered apostasy. The exact definition and the 'appropriate punishment' for apostasy varies among Muslim countries, but it's widely accepted as a grave sin and crime against Islam.

> Quran 9:66 – Make no excuses. You have disbelieved after your believing. If We forgive one party of you, We will chastise another party for that they were sinners.'

Muslims believe everyone in the world is born a Muslim. Some never find or accept Islam, while those who accept Islam later in life are said to revert to Islam, rather than convert, since they're returning to their original state.[1] Muslims encourage the 'reversion' of non-believers to Islam, but the conversion of a Muslim to anything else is a sin.

Muslims consider it blasphemy as it expresses contempt for Islam, which is a religious crime. There are 23 Muslim-majority countries in the world which still punish apostasy through their criminal laws and the punishment for this 'crime' can be as severe as the death penalty.[2]

To avoid the death penalty, apostates are given a chance to repent and

---

1. "1. Reversion versus Conversion." Islam Answering. Accessed November 28, 2016. http://www.islamanswering.com/subpage.php?s=article&aid=1249.

2. Goitom, Hanibal, and Global Legal Research Directorate. "Laws Criminalizing Apostasy." Laws Criminalizing Apostasy. June 30, 2015. https://www.loc.gov/law/help/apostasy/index.php.

return to Islam to save their lives. However, how sincere this would be is questionable and even the Quran expresses doubt about it.

> Quran 3:90-91 – Surely those who disbelieve after they have believed and then increase in unbelief — their repentance shall not be accepted; those are the ones who stray. Surely those who disbelieve, and die disbelieving, there shall not be accepted from any one of them the whole earth full of gold, if he would ransom himself thereby; for them awaits a painful chastisement, and they shall have no helpers.

Islamic religious authorities use the Quran to charge ex-Muslims with apostasy: condemning and punishing dissidents, skeptics and minorities in their communities.[3] Some Sharia courts also use their civil code to void a Muslim apostate's inheritance rights and marriage rights. Even child custody rights have also been denied to those who leave Islam.[4]

> Quran 16:106-107 – Whoso disbelieves in God, after he has believed — excepting him who has been compelled, and his heart is still at rest in his belief — but whosoever's breast is expanded in unbelief, upon them shall rest anger from God, and there awaits them a mighty chastisement; that, because they have preferred the present life over the world to come, and that God guides not the people of the unbelievers. Those — God has set a seal on their hearts, and their hearing, and their eyes, and those — they are the heedless ones; without a doubt, in the world to come they will be the losers.

Islam is more than a religion: it's a way of life. Islam doesn't just create a religious community but a polity, a form of civil government. So leaving a polity by apostasy is seen as treason. It's not just a denial of religious belief, it's a denial of allegiance and loyalty as well. But civil rights activists view the punishments for this 'treason' as violations of universal human rights: individuals choosing to leave Islam are denied their freedom of religion. Sharia law which prohibits apostasy directly conflicts with the United Nation's Universal Declaration of Human Rights. Article 18 of this Declaration states:

---

3. Campo, Juan Eduardo, and J. Gordon. Melton. Encyclopedia of Islam. New York: Fast on File, 2009. p.48, p.174.

4. Zwemer, Samuel M. "The Law Of Apostasy." The Muslim World 14, no. 4 (1924): 373-91. doi:10.1111/j.1478-1913.1924.tb00536.x.

"Everyone has the right to freedom of thought, conscience and religion; this right includes freedom to change his religion or belief, and freedom, either alone or in community with others and in public or private, to manifest his religion or belief in teaching, practice, worship and observance."[5]

Afghanistan, Egypt, Iran, Iraq, Lebanon, Pakistan, Syria and Turkey voted in favor of this Declaration in 1948 when it was adopted by the United Nations General Assembly.[6] But how well it's enforced in those countries is debatable. The countries who haven't voted in favor, such as Saudi Arabia who abstained, have had their Sharia law criticized for not recognizing this basic human right. Some of these Islamic nations responded by criticizing the Declaration. They see it as an attempt by the non-Muslim world to impose their values and codes onto Muslims thereby preaching a cultural superiority over the Islamic world.[7]

We've seen verses in the Quran which express God's dissatisfaction with apostates. Yet other Muslims and apologists of Islam will point to different verses which expresses the Quran's tolerance towards freedom of religion.

Quran 2:256 – No compulsion is there in religion. Rectitude has become clear from error. So whosoever disbelieves in idols and believes in God, has laid hold of the most firm handle, unbreaking; God is All-hearing, All-knowing.

This verse is popularly used to indicate Islam's tolerant view towards religion in general. But, it can also be interpreted in another way. It can be referring to people in other religions converting to Islam. It's letting Muslims know there's no need to compel people from other religions because Islam's proofs and evidence are plain and clear for all to see. Therefore it can be interpreted not as an ayah about freedom of religion, but an ayah about not proselytizing.

There's also an instance in the Quran where idolaters suggest to Prophet Muhammad he should worship their God for a year. In return, they will worship the Prophet's God for a year as a compromise. The Prophet responded to this suggestion.

5. "Universal Declaration of Human Rights." United Nations. Accessed October 18, 2016. http://www.un.org/en/universal-declaration-human-rights/index.html.

6. United Nations. Yearbook of the United Nations. Part 1, Chapter 5, Social, Humanitarian and Cultural Questions. 1948-49. Accessed November 28, 2016. https://web.archive.org/web/20130927221000/http://unyearbook.un.org/1948-49YUN/1948-49_P1_CH5.pdf. p.535

7. Monteiro, A. Reis. Ethics of Human Rights. Cham: Springer, 2014. pp.414-16.

> Quran 109:1–6 – Say: 'O unbelievers, I serve not what you serve and
> you are not serving what I serve, nor am I serving what you have
> served, neither are you serving what I serve. To you your religion,
> and to me my religion!'

This verse can be interpreted in a way which shows Prophet Muhammad
expressing religious tolerance: everyone to their own religion. It's a popular
verse with Muslims to demonstrate Islam's tolerance. But it's never as simple
as that with the Quran. Other Muslims argue it shows Prophet Muhammad's
revulsion to the idea of other religions. That to even compare another religion
with Islam is inappropriate. So while Muslims can view the verses in *Quran
2:256* and *Quran 109:1–6* as God expressing freedom of religion, the laws of the
majority of Muslim countries across the world would suggest otherwise.

The Quran doesn't help itself with its complexities of language. Muslims
and non-Muslims could all interpret the ayahs in this chapter about apostasy
in several ways depending on their disposition. This is what allows one group
of Muslims to dislike but permit apostasy, and/or be in favor of the United
Nations' Universal Declaration of Human Rights. While another group of
Muslims deny such rights are owed to anyone, claiming God's laws supersede
any man-made laws such as freedom of religion and freedom of thought. So as
a result they kill people who leave Islam.

These are two highly contrasting interpretations from the same book and
it's caused by the Quran's ambiguity. To add further uncertainty, God also states
that only He can make people believe. So if there are unbelievers in the world,
it's because God made them that way.

> Quran 10:99–100 – And if thy Lord had willed, whoever is in the
> earth would have believed, all of them, all together. Wouldst thou
> then constrain the people, until they are believers? It is not for any
> soul to believe save by the leave of God; and He lays abomination
> upon those who have no understanding.

Regardless of how we wish to interpret the Quran's religious tolerance, Muslims
do believe God will punish apostates after their death anyway. The Quran
reaffirms this.

> Quran 88:21–26 – Then remind them! Thou art only a reminder;
> thou art not charged to oversee them. But he who turns his back, and
> disbelieves, God shall chastise him with the greatest chastisement.
> Truly, to Us is their return; then upon Us shall rest their reckoning.

But this isn't satisfactory enough for some Muslims, they'd prefer if the punishment came in this lifetime. They may believe if punishment came to apostates sooner rather than later it would be a deterrent to other Muslims who had considered leaving Islam. This is what happened to 42 year old Avijit Roy, an atheist Bangladeshi-American writer. On 26th February 2015, on a public street in Dhaka, Bangladesh, he was hacked to death by machete-wielding attackers for his freedom of expression and critiques of Islam.[8]

Since Sharia law bases itself primarily on the Quran, then the decision to punish apostasy has come primarily from the Quran. Therefore we can't say punishing apostasy is merely a cultural decision and not reflective of the religion of Islam. Punishing apostasy is a religious decision from Islamic countries. So even though the Quran makes zero references to the death penalty for apostates, Islam's position on apostasy means it's one of the few (if not the only) religions in the world which practices the death penalty for followers leaving it.

Islam uses the fear of punishment in the afterlife to bring people into its religion, and it also uses the fear of becoming an apostate to keep people within its religion. But Sharia law's death penalties aren't a compelling way to engender true loyalty in one's faith. If anything, this show of insecurity is but one sign that the proofs and arguments for Islam are not strong enough to keep people believing in it. Personally speaking, punishing apostasy did not discourage me from consciously leaving Islam, rather, it reinforced to me that I was remaining faithful to the wrong ideals.

In modern society, it's strange how it's not taboo to discuss the Muslims who've become so alienated from western society that they prefer to live as fundamentalists; yet we have more trouble recognizing the Muslims who've become so alienated with their religion that they prefer to live as freethinkers. However many fundamentalists there must be, I believe there are just as many, if not more, Muslim freethinkers (there are 1.7 billion Muslims after all), and one of the main reasons we don't hear from them is because of the fear of persecution they would inevitably face. Insiders are too cautious to talk about it, and outsiders are too sensitive to ask.

Just like the gay liberation movement of previous generations, Muslim apostates like myself know that recognition of our 'status' would bring shame, rejection, threats and likely, family expulsion. Amal, a 32 year old from the UK, had to endure the latter:

8. Agence France-Presse. "American Atheist Blogger Hacked to Death in Bangladesh." The Guardian, February 27, 2015. https://www.theguardian.com/world/2015/feb/27/american-atheist-blogger-hacked-to-death-in-bangladesh.

"It was the hardest thing I've ever done – telling my observant family that I was having doubts. My mum was shocked; she began to cry. It was very painful for her. When she realised I actually meant it, she cut communication with me. She was suspicious of me being in contact with my brothers and sisters. She didn't want me to poison their heads in any way. I felt like a leper and I lived in fear. As long as they knew where I was, I wasn't safe."[9]

The isolation from leaving Islam can lead to depression and even worse, suicide. This is how Irtaza Hussain (originally from Pakistan and was living in the UK) felt about the family trauma he was suffering with from being an ex-Muslim. In one of his emails filled with pain and despair he wrote:

"I'm starting to lose it and I'm sick to death of my situation."

He hanged himself in September 2013. He was 22 years old.[10]

I've certainly felt the fear of what comes with leaving Islam for a long time and will continue to do so for the rest of my life. I fear for myself and I fear for my family's safety, which is why I choose anonymity. It's a concern that's been shared by other ex-Muslims such as Nasreen from London:

"I'm not so worried about the loonies because it's almost normal now to get threats. What worries me is that they go back to my parents and damage them, because that's not unheard of."[11]

But in a perverse way, like Amal mentioned earlier, I also fear for my safety *from* the threat of my own family. I don't know how many of them will react if they were to ever find out about how I feel about Islam. But when I read about what has happened to other people who have left Islam, like Yasmin from the UK, it makes me realize the gravity of the situation:

"My family completely disowned me. They thought I had

9. Morrison, Sarah. "Allah vs Atheism: 'Leaving Islam Was the Hardest Thing I've Done'." Independent, January 19, 2014. http://www.independent.co.uk/news/uk/home-news/allah-vs-atheism-leaving-islam-was-the-hardest-thing-i-ve-done-9069598.html.

10. "Remembering Irtaza." News release, September 24, 2013. Council of Ex-Muslims of Britain. http://ex-muslim.org.uk/2013/09/remembering-irtaza/.

11. Anthony, Andrew. "Losing Their Religion: The Hidden Crisis of Faith among Britain's Young Muslims." The Guardian, May 17, 2015. https://www.theguardian.com/global/2015/may/17/losing-their-religion-british-ex-muslims-non-believers-hidden-crisis-faith.

committed the biggest sin — I was born a Muslim, and so I must die a Muslim. When my husband found out, he totally disowned my sons. One friend tried to strangle me when I told him I was converting…We had bricks though our windows, I was spat at in the street because they thought I was dishonouring Islam. We had to call the police so many times. I had to go to court to get an injunction against my husband because he was inciting others to attack me."[12]

There's no morality in discriminating against people who choose to believe differently from others, especially not when death is considered to be the appropriate punishment for them. Apostasy as a sin, and the death penalty as its punishment, are not indicative of a fair and tolerant religion of peace, and since the Quran's words are eternal for Muslims, then Islam is in danger of being an unfair and intolerant religion forever.

12. Browne, Anthony. "Muslim Apostates Cast out and at Risk from Faith and Family." The Times, February 5, 2005. http://www.webcitation.org/query?url=http://www.timesonline.co.uk/tol/news/uk/article510589.ece&date=2011-09-18.

43

Censorship

"The mixing of government and religion can be a threat to free government, even if no one is forced to participate. When the government puts its imprimatur on a particular religion, it conveys a message of exclusion to all those who do not adhere to the favoured beliefs. A government cannot be premised on the belief that all persons are created equal when it asserts that God prefers some" – Harry Blackmun

Censorship has become an inherent part of modern day Islam, used by Islamic governments to eliminate any form of blasphemy. Many Muslims have tried to defend censorship, arguing if people were free to criticize Islam it would only create hostility among Muslims and non-Muslims. Muslim nations have even petitioned the United Nations to limit the freedom of speech on Islam. Naturally, many other nations view these 'blasphemy laws' as a human right violation against the freedom of speech.[1]

The punishment for challenging anything considered sacred in Islam varies by each country's Sharia law and whether the person who committed them is Muslim or non-Muslim. The Hadith collections suggest a various number of punishments for blasphemy and while the Quran also condemns blasphemy as well, it doesn't specify a punishment for it in this life, only the next.

> Quran 33:57-58 – Those who hurt God and His Messenger — them God has cursed in the present world and the world to come, and has prepared for them a humbling chastisement. And those who hurt believing men and believing women, without that they have earned it, have laid upon themselves calumny and manifest sin.

As a result, Islam takes blasphemy seriously with punishments ranging from fines to imprisonment, floggings, stonings, amputations, hangings and

---

1. Shea, Nina. "An Anti-Blasphemy Measure Laid to Rest." National Review, March 31, 2011. http://www.nationalreview.com/article/263450/anti-blasphemy-measure-laid-rest-nina-shea.

beheadings. In some instances, Sharia law allows individuals to escape their punishment if they convert to Islam.[2] But regardless of the offense committed, every Muslim country considers blasphemy a sin and a crime. Even if someone is not a Muslim and not living in a Muslim country, Muslims and Islamic governments can, and do, target blasphemers for the 'sin' they've committed against Islam.

These incidents are often intensified by Muslim clerics who call for a punishment to the alleged blasphemer by issuing a fatwa (a legal declaration). The most notable example was when writer Salman Rushdie was accused of blasphemy for his book '*The Satanic Verses*'. Mr Rushdie became the subject of a fatwa issued in February 1989 by the then Supreme Leader of Iran, Ayatollah Ruhollah Khomeini, calling for his execution.[3] This is how censorship in Islam now exists in the modern world: unfortunately, it applies to everyone, everywhere.

In recent times, the censorship of Prophet Muhammad has become a sensitive issue due to a number of high profile incidents causing public protests and violent retaliation by Muslims. These incidents include the derogatory cartoons of Prophet Muhammad published by the Danish newspaper *Jyllands-Posten* in 2005, and the derogatory cartoons of Prophet Muhammad published by the French satirical newspaper *Charlie Hebdo* in 2012.[4] On 7th January 2015, as a retaliation for the cartoons of the Prophet, two Muslim men armed with assault rifles and other weapons killed 12 people and injured 11 others in the offices of *Charlie Hebdo* in Paris.[5]

The Quran doesn't explicitly forbid images of Prophet Muhammad, however there are Hadith prohibiting his visual depiction. There's also no consensus on his authentic appearance, but oral and written descriptions of him have been readily accepted in Islam.[6] The majority of Sunni Muslims

2. Ernst, Carl. "Blasphemy: Islamic Concept." In Encyclopedia of Religion: Volume 2, edited by Lindsay Jones. Detroit: Macmillan Reference USA, 2005.

3. Murtagh, Peter. "Rushdie in Hiding after Ayatollah's Death Threat." The Guardian, February 15, 1989. https://www.theguardian.com/books/1989/feb/15/salmanrushdie.

4. Lichtenberg, Hans Henrik. "UN to Investigate Jyllands-Posten 'Racism'." Newspaperindex.com, December 10, 2005. https://web.archive.org/web/20080209153538/http://blog.newspaperindex.com/2005/12/10/un-to-investigate-jyllands-posten-racism/. See also Vinocur, Nicholas. "Magazine's Nude Mohammad Cartoons Prompt France to Shut Embassies, Schools in 20 Countries." National Post, September 19, 2012. http://news.nationalpost.com/news/magazines-nude-mohammad-cartoons-prompt-france-to-shut-embassies-schools-in-20-countries.

5. "French Terror Attacks: Victim Obituaries." BBC News, January 13, 2015. http://www.bbc.com/news/world-europe-30724678.

6. Bloom, Jonathan, and Sheila Blair. Islamic Arts. London: Phaidon, 2013.

believe visual depictions of any prophets of Islam should be prohibited, they just happen to be particularly adverse to those of Prophet Muhammad.[7] The concern among Sunni Muslims is that if all Muslims began visually depicting Prophet Muhammad, it would encourage idolatry within Islam in the same manner which Jesus is idolized in Christianity. The Quran explicitly forbids idolatry, and the comparison of anyone to God.

> Quran 4:48 – God forgives not that aught should be with Him associated; less than that He forgives to whomsoever He will. Whoso associates with God anything, has indeed forged a mighty sin.

This is why Islamic art is dominated with Islamic calligraphy and Islamic geometric patterns, rather than images of figures within Islamic theology (apart from the modern day Shia sect of Islam where images of Prophet Muhammad are quite common).[8]

More so than ever non-Muslims (and Muslims) have to think twice before publicly drawing on any aspect of Islam. This is because many Muslims become provoked and rise to anger quickly from any negative opinion on Islam or Prophet Muhammad, no matter how insignificant it may be. Some modern day Muslims see it as their duty to police other people, particularly online, when it comes to defending their faith and beliefs. It's the so called 'corruption done in the land' they're trying to inhibit (see chapter 'Terrorism').

> Quran 5:33-34 – This is the recompense of those who fight against God and His Messenger, and hasten about the earth, to do corruption there: they shall be slaughtered, or crucified, or their hands and feet shall alternately be struck off; or they shall be banished from the land. That is a degradation for them in this world; and in the world to come awaits them a mighty chastisement, except for such as repent, before you have power over them. So know you that God is All-forgiving, All-compassionate.

Modern society has now arrived at a place where it's as though Islam can't be questioned by anyone, and must be accepted by everyone. Everything else in the world (including other religions) can be openly-critiqued safely among civil

7. Larsson, Göran. Muslims and the New Media: Historical and Contemporary Debates. Farnham, Surrey: Ashgate, 2011. p.51.

8. McManus, John. "Have Pictures of Muhammad Always Been Forbidden?" BBC, January 15, 2015. http://www.bbc.co.uk/news/magazine-30814555.

adults, but not Islam. Those who choose to ask justified questions of Islam, must do so cautiously.

If someone criticizes a religious practice they don't agree with it doesn't immediately make it a form of bigotry. Yet if they do so about anything in Islam, even respectfully, both Muslims and non-Muslims become overprotective and too politically correct about it. This is all at the expense of living in a free world where we speak openly, share ideas and engage with each other respectfully.

It's not only non-Muslims who can benefit from freedom of speech, but Muslims too. There was a time between the 8th and 13th century when science, culture and economies thrived thanks to Muslims. Islam entered a renaissance period known as the Islamic Golden Age, and Muslims contributed substantially to the human collective knowledge. Advancements were made by Muslim engineers, scientists and scholars in the arts, agriculture, economics, industry, law, literature, navigation, philosophy, the sciences and technology. They all flourished thanks to Muslims who spoke freely, challenged pre-existing ideas, changed the world and made it a more conscious and informed place for all of us.[9]

But now, most Islamic countries violate freedom of speech. They also enforce laws restricting people to a rigid Islamic jurisprudence framework. This has all contributed to a stifling of the Muslim collective and the inhibition of the Muslim individual's mind in favour of obedience to ancient texts. This isn't a surprise though, it's against the Islamic establishment's interest to have well-informed and critical-thinking citizens. But Sharia law and freedom of speech don't have to be mutually exclusive. Reducing censorship could actually diminish all the weak, false and widespread accusations about Muslims and who they are as people.

How so many Muslim countries operate now is no different to regimes where dictators suppress the voice and the power of the people. But these kinds of administrations started to reach a breaking point in December 2010 when the Arab Spring began.

Revolutionary demonstrations, protests, riots and civil wars took place across the Arab world beginning in Tunisia with the Tunisian Revolution. It led to major insurgencies and civil wars in Iraq, Libya, Syria and Yemen as well as civil uprisings in Bahrain and Egypt. Large street demonstrations were carried out in Algeria, Iran, Jordan, Kuwait, Lebanon, Morocco, Oman

9. Khan, Adnan. "Islam, Science and Civilisation." The Khilafah, February 26, 2009. http://www.khilafah.com/islam-science-and-civilisation/.

and Sudan, with minor protests also taking place in Djibouti, Mauritania, the Palestinian territories, Saudi Arabia, Somalia and the Western Sahara.[10]

It was confirmation of the dissatisfaction Muslims had, and still have, with their Islamic governments. The dictatorships, human rights violations, political corruptions, unemployment, wealth gap and poverty finally led to a tipping point. It caused a large number of educated but dissatisfied Muslims to reject the status quo and say enough is enough; particularly the Muslim youth, who'd become disillusioned with their country's rule.

Muslims have already begun to break free of the limitations their Sharia-based governments impose on them. These Islamic governments have even tried to keep intelligence out of reach of the people, going as far as to block websites like Facebook and Twitter to stop Muslims communicating and organizing with each other.[11] We've seen how courageous Muslims must be if they're to live a more prosperous life, and just as important, we've also seen there's nothing wrong with questioning the status quo, especially if we have serious concerns about its benefits to us, our children, or our country. It's either that, or we continue to live in a totalitarian Islamic world. One where any form of dissent (religious or political) is treated with excessive punishments like stonings, floggings and hangings.

Questioning governments is one thing, but for Muslims to start asking questions about their religion is another. Islam is 1.7 billion people's entire lives. It's all they've ever known. But the answer isn't to reject it all in its entirety. It's to realize that it's unhealthy to be silenced just for having an opinion which conflicts with Islam. If this status quo remained it would be an impractical and futile way to advance humanity for the next 10, 100 or 1,000 years. Our children will wonder why we've left the world in this way for them.

It's censorship which maintains the closed information loop the Islamic world operates in, unbeknownst to many Muslims. It's the governments of Muslim countries like Iran and Saudi Arabia which the *Committee to Protect Journalists* say block millions of websites (particularly news and social networking websites) critical of the ruling regime.[12] It's why *Reporters Without Borders* ranks Muslim countries like Sudan, Syria and Yemen at the bottom of

10. Ruthven, Malise. "How to Understand ISIS." The New York Review of Books, June 23, 2016. http://www.nybooks.com/articles/2016/06/23/how-to-understand-isis/.

11. Stepanova, Ekaterina. The Role of Information Communication Technologies in the "Arab Spring". PONARS Eurasia Policy Memo No. 159. May 2011. http://pircenter.org/kosdata/page_doc/p2594_2.pdf.

12. "10 Most Censored Countries." Committee to Protect Journalists. 2015. https://www.cpj.org/2015/04/10-most-censored-countries.php.

their 2016 World Press Freedom Index since those countries suppress and jail journalists for publishing information on human rights crimes they commit.[13] It's also why *Freedom on the Net* ranks the internet freedom in other Muslim countries like Bahrain, Egypt, Pakistan, Turkey and the UAE as 'Not Free' since social media users continue to face unprecedented penalties for publishing, sharing or even 'liking' content challenging the religious and political status quo.[14]

All the censorship rife in the Islamic world means there is little to no spread of the necessary intelligence about the society or world we live in. Living in this bubble will only continue to foster ignorance and misunderstandings between Muslims and the rest of the world. It will lead to the Islamic Dark Ages, if we're not already in one.

13. "2016 World Press Freedom Index." Reporters Without Borders. 2016. https://rsf.org/en/ranking.

14. "Freedom on the Net 2016." Freedom House. 2016. https://freedomhouse.org/report/table-country-scores-fotn-2016.

44

Islamization

"Religious people claim that it's just the fundamentalists of each religion that cause problems. But there's got to be something wrong with the religion itself if those who strictly adhere to its most fundamental principles are violent bigots and sexists" –
David G. McAfee

Islamization is a society's shift towards Islam's codes and values when it already has a different political or social system established. Islamization is often wrongly used interchangeably with Arabization. This is a misnomer because Arabization is the spread of the Arabic language and culture onto a non-Arab area, it's not the spread of the Islamic culture and laws onto a non-Islamic area. The spread of Islam and the spread of Arabic culture are two very different things. Particularly since most of the 1.7 billion followers of Islam today aren't even Arab. They are mostly Indonesian (205 million Muslims), Pakistani (178 million Muslims), Indian (177 million Muslims) or Bangladeshi (149 million Muslims). This is in comparison to the 322 million Muslims in the Middle East and North Africa who identify as Arab.[1]

In the 20th and 21st century Islam and Islamization has spread considerably across the world. This is due to many factors such as the increasing growth of the world's population, the high birth rate of Muslims, more accessible travel capabilities and because Islam is a religion which can transcend national and ethnic customs.

This has begun to concern many people who consider Islam to carry practices which conflict with Western values. However, Islamic political parties also feel aggrieved. They view Westernization and the 'universal human rights' argument as the imposition of a Western culture on Muslims, and Muslims view this as disrespectful to the customary cultural practices of Islam.

1. Grim, Brian J., and Mehtab S. Karim. The Future of the Global Muslim Population. Report. January 27, 2011. http://www.pewforum.org/2011/01/27/the-future-of-the-global-muslim-population/.

But looking at some Islamic laws, like the legal inequalities of women (see chapter '*Women as unequals*') or the lack of freedom of speech (see chapter '*Censorship*'), it's clear why some non-Muslims are concerned about Islam's practices being enforced in their countries. They *are* at odds with many basic human rights.

Naturally Muslims will always look to protect their religion, but Islam isn't just a religion. Islam is also a governing system, and Sharia is a universal system of law deemed essential to be enforced to practice Islam. So to enforce it correctly, Muslim nations often restrict freedom of religious expression and suppress political dissent. If it's to protect Islam, then many Muslims see it as a necessity.

As a result, Islam has grown a reputation as an inflexible ideology, one carrying fewer values in common with secular democratic societies than other religions. This perception has led to the rise of Islamophobia in non-Muslim societies. The Islamophobic consensus is that Islam is inferior to Western cultures and ideals. It's seen as a barbaric, violent, primitive and sexist religion, which fosters terrorism, slows the adaptation of its migrants to other cultures and communities, and uses its ideology to its political advantage.

All this has made it harder to defend Islam in the 21st century and yet, most of a Muslim's life actually has little to do with politics. It centres around values that we all hold dear, such as family, community, education and charity. But the lack of freedom of speech and freedom of religion may be Islam's Achilles' heel for generations to come. At this moment in time, Islam simply does not tolerate any critique of its religion or its Prophet. But these criticisms aren't always raised to provoke Muslims, they're raised to help non-Muslims understand why Muslims believe what they believe. How else can we achieve tolerance and understanding if Islam isn't willing to listen to the other side speak?

We'll not see the 'full Islamization' of a non-Islamic state anytime soon. But fears exist that as Muslim populations grow, rights like freedom of speech, freedom of media or freedom of religion may become suppressed, before eventually, becoming forbidden. Most non-Muslim countries recognize the need to accommodate to different faiths. However, not many faiths are as strict and severe as Islam can be.

Islamization is a warranted concern, and those who fear it aren't necessarily racists or Islamophobes. They know the majority of Muslims in the world are not to be feared, and that Muslims can be flexible, relaxed, and cooperative. Therefore it's up to Muslims to listen to the concerns about Islamization and understand it's not always a personal attack on them or their religion. It's a plea for recognition, consideration and acceptance of the fears many people across the world have.

PART X

Life After Religion

People need religion because it gives them something they can't get from anywhere else. When religion is taken away, a gap appears. It can leave us feeling isolated and anxious. A sense of emptiness or disillusionment may surface. A loss of faith can feel like the loss of a loved one we've had with us our whole lives; or the separation from someone we were previously close to, but we know are no longer right for us anymore. Religions are more than an ideology. Religions are intertwined with a person's identity and understanding of the world. Take these things away from someone, and they're often lost.

Non-believers *and* believers need to know they can still be fulfilled outside of religion. Religion doesn't have a monopoly on living a rich and meaningful life. There are over 800 million non-religionists (atheists and agnostics) in the world and they've all decided they can live their life without religion.[1] We're not alone.

I thought the hard part would be leaving my faith but actually, the hardest part was yet to come. I had to figure out how I was going to make sense of the world I live in. I would have to start from the beginning, with no 'holy' book telling me what was right and wrong.

Suddenly the possibilities of the entire world opened up to me and it was a lot to take in all at once. But I knew before I could finish my journey, I had to start from first principles and reassess what I believed to be true about life and people. Only then would it be possible to complete the journey I started at the beginning, when I first started losing my religion.

It's here where I'll give a personal and subjective account of how I approach life without Islam. In addition, when I refer to religions in general, I speak

1. Johnson, Todd M., Gina A. Zurlo, Albert W. Hickman, and Peter F. Crossing. Christianity 2015: Religious Diversity and Personal Contact. Report. Vol. 39. Series 1. South Hamilton: International Bulletin of Missionary Research, 2015. Accessed October 18, 2016. http://www.gordonconwell.edu/ockenga/research/documents/2IBMR2015.pdf.

predominantly of the Abrahamic religions: Judaism, Christianity and Islam. However the same message can apply to many other religions too.

This book and this journey is still an experiment for me. It's a work in progress, just like my life. I hope I can remain flexible to new ideas as I continue to meet unique people and experience unfamiliar thoughts. I wouldn't say I feel all my internal conflicts have been resolved, but as I've started to live my life everyday in a way that is true to myself, my anxieties have slowly started to leave me. A pressure weighing my shoulders down has been slowly taken off, piece by piece, step by step. Now, I stretch. I release. Because I'm restored to my original state.

I'm blank canvas once more and the picture I paint will now be my own, not a religion's.

45

Atheism or agnosticism

"I contend that we are both atheists. I just believe in one fewer God than you do. When you understand why you dismiss all the other possible Gods, you will understand why I dismiss yours" – Stephen Roberts

Theism, atheism and agnosticism provide three different perspectives on the concept of God. For a theist, the answer to the question "Do you believe any gods exist?" is a "Yes". A theist can then be defined further as to which god or gods they believe exist.

For an atheist, the answer to the question "Do you believe any gods exist?" is "No". For an agnostic, the answer to the question "Do you believe any gods exist?" is "I don't know".

So an agnostic differs from an atheist by claiming the existence of a supernatural being is unknown and perhaps unknowable. But the spectrum on which theism, atheism and agnosticism lie can be defined even further. Evolutionary biologist and atheist Richard Dawkins popularized the idea of a spectrum of theistic probability. He claims there are seven positions one could hold:

1. **Strong theism** – The believer does not just believe God exists, they know without doubt God exists.
2. **De facto theism** – The believer is not entirely 100% confident God exists. But considers it very probable so lives their life as though He does exist.
3. **Weak theism** – The believer isn't completely certain in the existence of a God. But is inclined towards believing in God.
4. **Pure agnostic/completely impartial** – They hold God's existence is just as likely to be true as it is false, it is exactly 50%.
5. **Weak atheism** – The individual isn't certain whether God exists, it is lower than 50% but not very low. They are inclined to be skeptical.

6. **De facto atheism** – The individual believes there is a very low probability God exists. They consider it to be so improbable they live their life as though He does not exist.

7. **Strong atheists** – The individual knows with a 100% certainty God does not exist.[1]

If I had to place myself on this spectrum, I'd identify as a 'de facto atheist': I'm confident God doesn't exist. This is because with the information I've gathered from researching and writing this book, the probability He exists is extremely low in my opinion. Therefore I chose to live my life as though He doesn't exist at all. I wouldn't call myself a 'strong atheist' because I don't know with 100% certainty if God or gods don't exist as it hasn't been proven either way.

I also wouldn't call myself agnostic about the Abrahamic God of Jews, Christians and Muslims, for the same reason I'm not agnostic about the Norse god Thor, the Greek god Zeus or the Egyptian god Ra. I can't prove or disprove any of their existences but in my opinion all the evidence also points towards their non-existence even though entire civilizations believed in Thor, Zeus and Ra, just as devoutly as Jews, Christians and Muslims believe in their God today.

To express how I feel about the probability of God's existence, let me use an example. For me, trying to win the lottery is an example of long odds not worth investing in. The probability of winning the lottery (picking 6 correct numbers from a pool of 49) is so low (1 in 14 million) I may as well believe with confidence I won't win the lottery.[2] Though the odds are extremely low there's still a minuscule chance I may win the lottery, other people have certainly done so. I believe there's still a chance God may exist too, but in my opinion, the odds of God existing are even lower than my chances of winning the lottery. At least it has been proven the lottery can be won. Nothing has proven God's existence to me personally so it's not worth my time, energy and attention to say He does exist or live my life as if He does. But, this is a personal judgement, and everyone has to make their own assessment with the information they have at hand.

All religions with deities claim with too much certainty the existence of their God or gods but I personally believe they're human-created conceptions. I can't empirically prove this, but I also haven't seen any empirical evidence to suggest otherwise. As a result, I will side with the facts and laws of science

---

1. Dawkins, Richard. The God Delusion. Boston: Houghton Mifflin Company, 2006. p.50.

2. 13,983,816 and the Lottery - Numberphile. Performed by James Clewett. Numberphile. March 28, 2012. http://www.numberphile.com/videos/lottery.html.

to understand the universe and our place in it: physics, chemistry, biology, geology and astronomy. They've all been empirically tested, reproduced and proven, and as we advance further in each of their fields the likelihood of any God or gods existing decreases further and further.

However, I am agnostic about the idea of a higher power. I do believe there could be the existence of something bigger than all of us, a powerful force in the universe we're unaware of. I think this is likely because we're unaware of a lot that's happening around us. For instance, we can't hear all the sounds vibrating in our presence. We can only hear sounds within a specific spectrum due to the limitations of our ears, thus reducing our awareness of what's constantly happening in the world we live in. For example, we can't hear what dogs or whales hear, these mammals are more attuned than us to the sounds vibrating in the world. The same is true for sight: we're limited in our spectrum of what we can and can't see. We can't see infrared or ultraviolet light with the naked eye in the same way some snakes or fish can respectively.

These are things we're only aware of with the help of science and technology. Both are improving every year, but there are still many questions they're working on answering. There's an enormous amount happening around us everyday that we humans can't process or even acknowledge, and that's just on this one planet. We also have to consider the scale of the ever-expanding universe and everything that could be happening out there. It could be the things we don't know that we don't know which are the most exciting things left to be discovered. This is why I don't believe it's unreasonable to suggest something bigger than us is in effect, something we cannot, or may ever not, comprehend with our limited physical and mental capabilities.

But for the reasons I've explained in this book, I just don't believe this potential higher power is in the form of the God I previously worshiped. Nor is it likely to be in the form of any of the gods human religions have preached about for thousands of years. Therefore I have no reason to abide by their rules. I'm atheist about all human religions. But I'm agnostic about our existence and the existence of a higher power or being.

At the end of the day, it's up to us to decide what we believe the odds are God exists; we can then identify where we place on the spectrum of theistic probability. But, to maximize our chances of finding the truth, we can't assume everything we were taught about religion is true. Each of us have to define our own terms for what we believe constitutes the existence of God. Then, regardless of how we feel about God, we'll at least be living lives true to ourselves.

46

Morality

"A man's ethical behavior should be based effectually on sympathy, education, and social ties and needs; no religious basis is necessary. Man would indeed be in a poor way if he had to be restrained by fear of punishment and hopes of reward after death"
– Albert Einstein

The morals human beings have are deep-rooted. Our brains evolved over hundreds of thousands of years and during this time behavioral strategies developed which aided the survival of our genes. Having these innate behaviors is what has improved the survival of our species. Human beings behave in certain ways towards each other because our brains evolved to ensure not just our survival, but also the survival of our kin.

Humans are a unique species as they look to ensure the survival of their genes *and* abstract things like their nationality, their economy, and their religion. The abstract things people choose to 'save' in their lives are influenced by their environment: family, peers, and society. These external influences can cause behaviors to be shaped or manipulated in a way that appears rational to those in our environment, but erratic and dangerous to those outside our environment.

Religion exists to provide moral and righteous guidance on the best way to live our lives. Many people even claim religion is what makes people good, and without it we would live in a sinful and immoral world without rules. But first, even if religion does make people more ethical, it still doesn't prove the existence of God; and second, there are immoral and indecent religious people, just like there are immoral and indecent atheists.

Atheists don't have a religion for guidance, they don't have a God to hold them accountable, and they don't have Heaven and Hell as a carrot and stick incentive. So in theory yes, there's nothing to stop atheists from doing 'bad' things. Yet there are virtuous and principled atheists with integrity and morals, just like there are virtuous and principled religious people. The difference is these atheists didn't need a book to teach them how they ought to behave: they behave with virtue due to their own inner morals. After all, if someone is refraining from terrible deeds only due to the fear of God, what does it say about the morality and authenticity of that person?

The argument 'there can be no morals without religion' falls apart for many reasons but it essentially comes down to one realization: if God was proven not to exist beyond any doubt, all the people in the world who believed in Him wouldn't immediately turn 'evil' and start doing 'bad' things. They all know better than this, and it's due to the behavioral strategies our brains evolved with. This is what enables us to cooperate with each other, and on some level instinctively know right from wrong. The same way a baby knows seeing a smiling face is positive and seeing an angry face is distressing. It's innate in the baby, without it being taught any concepts of right or wrong.

If we're to believe some religious ideologies, a land ruled without religion would be one of lawlessness and wickedness, but we've seen the opposite materialize with several secular states across the world. Some of the most economically stable and socially accommodating countries in the world don't live by the rules of any holy scriptures: Australia, Canada, Japan, New Zealand, Singapore and Sweden to name a few.

Critics of atheism often counter-argue using examples of infamous political regimes: dictators like Stalin and Mao suppressed religion, advocated atheism, and committed mass murders. But the fact is these atrocities weren't influenced by atheism. Though Stalin and Mao were atheists, they didn't undertake their actions in the name of atheism, they did them in the name of dogmatic Marxism. Atheism is not a religion. It doesn't have a scripture to follow or a centralized organization to adhere to. It has no stories, dogmatic principles or core ideology. It is simply a lack of belief in gods.

But unfortunately a disbelief in God or gods is still considered taboo in many cultures around the world. So much so that a Gallup Poll in 2012 showed almost half of Americans are unwilling to vote for an atheist presidential candidate (only 54% said they would be willing). This is in comparison to a black candidate (96% said they would), a woman (95%), a Catholic (94%), a Hispanic (92%), a Jewish (91%), a Mormon (80%), a gay or lesbian (68%) and even a *Muslim* US presidential candidate (58%).[1]

It's important to keep in mind the USA is actually a secular state as well. It doesn't have an official religion at either the federal level or state levels so it's

1. Jones, Jeffrey M. "Atheists, Muslims See Most Bias as Presidential Candidates." Gallup. June 21, 2012. http://www.gallup.com/poll/155285/atheists-muslims-bias-presidential-candidates.aspx.

officially neutral in matters of religion, just like many other countries globally. However, this doesn't mean citizens don't favor certain people just because of their religion or non-religion.

The sentiment Americans share about atheists is likely true in several countries worldwide. Many people just aren't comfortable with the idea of someone who doesn't believe in God. It doesn't even have to be their God, it could be any god or gods in general. There's a disconnect and a lack of trust which comes from the perceived accountability atheists supposedly have.

However, it's atheists who'll probably have the most up to date morals about tolerance and civil rights in society. Human ethics evolves over time, just like humans and societies. What was once deemed moral, such as slavery or withholding women's rights, is now seen as immoral. Religion doesn't allow its morality to update with the times, it's stagnant since its codes of conduct are written in permanent holy ink which can't be questioned or altered. Religion is a belief system enamored with infallibility and this only encourages resistance to change.

A disbelief in God doesn't mean atheists are bad or they're going to do bad things if they're running a country. It doesn't mean they'll neglect the people who raised them, or raise their own children to be immoral. In reality, they'll feel more tolerant towards other people than the religious might. People who become atheists have often sat on both sides of the table since they've regularly come from a religious upbringing. Therefore they can sympathize with those who do and do not believe in God. Thankfully, they can even sympathize with people they previously distrusted as a result of their religious environment. For example, atheists may see people of other faiths and people in the LGBT community in a friendlier light without the prejudices their religion previously gave them.

Without religion, it's still possible to create a world where we treat all people equally and respectfully; a world in which everyone has the opportunity to live their lives the way they wish to, with or without God. If we strive for social justice and equality, if people are kind and tolerant of each other, then we have no reason to fear living in a multi-cultural, multi-ethnic world with people of different faiths.

These ideals tie closely with Humanism, which I would say is my philosophical life stance: my way of thinking about the world. The International Humanist and Ethical Union describes Humanism as:

> "a democratic and ethical life stance, which affirms that human beings have the right and responsibility to give meaning and shape to

their own lives. It stands for the building of a more humane society through an ethic based on human and other natural values in the spirit of reason and free inquiry through human capabilities. It is not theistic, and it does not accept supernatural views of reality."[2]

People who hold this set of ethics are called humanists. Humanists believe every human being deserves to be treated with respect and to have respect for others. Humanists also believe this respect extends to the choices people make on how they wish to live their lives.

Humanism is close to secularism since it refers to a non-theistic approach to understanding the world. Both humanism and secularism value looking to science instead of religious dogma for reason, ethics, decision-making, problem-solving and the basis of morality. By using non-dogmatic and non-violent ideals, humanists decide what choices are moral by whether those choices will help make human life better.

But how do we make human life better? As a species, human beings are where we are today through trial and error. We constantly make mistakes, then we do the best we can to learn from those mistakes in as few attempts as possible. My concern with religion is that history has shown people acting in its name with both positive and negative consequences, and so many of the negative consequences are still being repeated till this day. These negative consequences have been happening for thousands of years and by a multitude of different religions. It's said the definition of insanity is doing the same thing over and over again and expecting different results. When it comes to religion, I'm unsure if we're learning from our mistakes. If I may paraphrase essayist and religious critic Christopher Hitchens, I believe religion has made the same violent, intolerant and racist mistakes over and over again. Organized religion has proven itself over time to promote irrationality, tribalism and bigotry. It is hostile to free inquiry from science, which means it remains invested in ignorance. Since its origins it has been contemptuous towards women and coercive towards children. Using fear to maintain its vice grip, organized religion ought to have a great deal on its conscience.[3]

I don't believe God or any gods allowed or caused this to happen because I believe all the gods of religion are man-made. It's not any god's fault, it's men and our inability to tolerate and respect differences which causes so much strife

---

2. "What Is Humanism?" International Humanist and Ethical Union. Accessed December 01, 2016. http://iheu.org/humanism/what-is-humanism/.

3. Hitchens, Christopher. God Is Not Great: How Religion Poisons Everything. New York: Hachette Book Group - Twelve, 2009.

and division in the world. No two people's needs are ever in conflict, only the strategies for getting those needs met conflict. It's as if we're too familiar to ignore, but too different to tolerate. The religions we've followed for thousands of years have to accept their share of responsibility for this.

Even with the Golden Rule, maybe it's in our nature as Homo sapiens to act in an aggressive manner to outsiders, to 'them'. Perhaps we can't expect anything less from a fast-evolving young species of primitive biological animals. But this deep-seated aggression coupled with the stubbornness religion instills causes even worse immoral outcomes as history has shown time and time again.

Looking at the past, it's clear to see we've come a long way. Now we need to stop pointing the finger of blame at others all the time and look at ourselves. How we behave. What we believe. How we treat people who are different from us. There's still hope humankind will learn from the lessons of history, and not be bound forever more to repeat them.

47

Spirituality and growth

"All the world's major religions, with their emphasis on love, compassion, patience, tolerance, and forgiveness can and do promote inner values. But the reality of the world today is that grounding ethics in religion is no longer adequate. This is why I am increasingly convinced that the time has come to find a way of thinking about spirituality and ethics beyond religion altogether" – The 14th Dalai Lama

The words 'religious' and 'spiritual' have often gone hand in hand. They're used synonymously to describe various aspects of the concept of religion. But religion doesn't own spirituality, nor does any ideology, group or individual. Some go as far as to say organized religion isn't even authentic spirituality: that spirituality is a private reflection and a private experience, not a public ritual.[1]

Spirituality is a vague term and it can mean whatever you want it to mean. Personally, the best explanation of spirituality I've come across is this:

"Science is what we know, and spirituality is how we coexist philosophically, psychologically and emotionally with that knowledge. Science gives us the information; spirituality helps us wrap our heads around it. The two lead us as a tag team, each taking care of their critical halves of the "figuring it all out" puzzle—when science tells us something shocking, like "The Earth is revolving around the sun and not vice versa!" we turn, wide-eyed, to spirituality and ask, "How does that change things? How does that transform the way we should think about ourselves, about the world, and about life?""[2]

1. Kenneson, Philip D. "What's in a Name? A Brief Introduction to the 'Spiritual But Not Religious'." Liturgy 30, no. 3 (2015): 3-13. doi:10.1080/0458063x.2015.1019259.

2. Urban, Tim. "How Religion Got in the Way." Wait But Why. October 10, 2014. http://waitbutwhy.com/2014/10/how-religion-got-in-the-way.html.

If we tried to define spirituality we could say it's a focus on the human spirit or soul, and not on material or physical things. It's this increased focus on our spirit or soul which can help develop our personal growth and self-awareness.

Spirituality can be a source of inner peace, strength and optimism, leading to positive health benefits like increased morale, happiness, and life satisfaction.[3] Religious people often achieve this sense of inner peace when practicing their faith: by praying, fasting, or reciting from their holy book. Sometimes it can even lead to a blissful out-of-body experiences.

But spirituality can be achieved outside of religion and there's a term to define people who attempt to do so: spiritual but not religious (SBNR). Spiritual but not religious doesn't just imply the rejection of religion, but the need to not let it restrict us. Those who are spiritual but not religious don't believe organized religion is the sole or most valuable way of furthering one's spiritual growth. They value the importance of finding one's own individual path to spirituality.[4] People said to be spiritual but not religious are categorized into five distinct groups, though people can fit into more than one category:

1. **Dissenters** – individuals who make a conscious effort to stay away from organized religions
2. **Casuals** – individuals who see the religious and/or spiritual practices as mainly functional above everything else, it's used when needed
3. **Explorers** – individuals who are on a constant search of novel spiritual practices to try and satisfy their curiosity, with the comfort of having no spiritual destination in mind
4. **Seekers** – individuals looking for a spiritual home to commit to, but contemplate recovering earlier religious identities
5. **Immigrants** – individuals who are trying to adopt a completely new spiritual environment but are still struggling to feel integrated and settled within it[5]

If I had to select the SBNR categories I currently identify myself with, it would be Dissenter and Casual. I'm in a period of my life where I don't want

---

3. Ellison, Christopher G., and Daisy Fan. "Daily Spiritual Experiences and Psychological Well-being Among US Adults." Social Indicators Research 88, no. 2 (2007): 247-71. doi:10.1007/s11205-007-9187-2.

4. Erlandson, Sven E. Spiritual but Not Religious: A Call to Religious Revolution in America. San Jose: Writer's Showcase, 2000.

5. Mercadante, Linda A. Belief without Borders: Inside the Minds of the Spiritual but Not Religious. New York, NY: Oxford University Press, 2014. pp.35-67.

to associate with any organized religions but, I also see the value of spiritual practices to increase my sense of well-being.

Spirituality *can* be experienced in a secular way, one where we're still able to enjoy a sense of awe and wonder, far removed from all the trivialities of everyday life. Many people reach this other dimension when expressing themselves physically or artistically, for example, through yoga, tai chi and reiki or playing music, painting, writing and dancing.

Religion has influenced all these art forms, and religion has also lead to beautiful monuments, stunning temples and fascinating cultures across the world. But human beings are naturally creative creatures, we're not creative because of religion. Religion is just another art form our ancestors created, it's a muse we've used to help us express ourselves. So if religion hadn't influenced our language, music, literature or art, something else would have instead. When religion is removed, it doesn't leave a permanent gap. Human beings fill that gap with something else to inspire producing equally, if not more, beautiful expressions of the human mind, body and soul. There's more than enough beauty in this world to provide the non-religious with inspiration, we only have to give it a chance to be seen and heard over the blinding noise of religion.

To see a clearer picture and hear a purer sound, I personally find meditation to be great for my emotional, mental and spiritual health. There are several forms of meditation and if you're interested in it I'd recommend taking the time to find the one which suits you the most. I have a preference for Vipassana meditation as it can be taught in an entirely secular way if one wishes. This is one daily practice I adopt to help me become my most creative and expressive self outside of religion.

Meditation helps to slow everything down in the rushed, instant gratification, mobile phone addicted, world we live in. It's healthy for us to take some time and sit still as the world and everyone else in it keeps turning in circles. Neurological studies have shown meditation can increase productivity and increase the ability to focus. It can also increase blood flow to the brain, increase grey matter in the brain and decrease the rate the brain ages.[6] A simple guide to practicing meditation and mindfulness can be found in the footnote.[7]

But please note it's just one of many accessible practices we can adopt to keep our minds calm, our bodies healthy and our souls at peace. I believe nothing is more important than looking after our health and well-being. I also

6. Bailey, Chris. "Guide: Everything You Need to Start Meditating." A Life Of Productivity. May 17, 2013. http://alifeofproductivity.com/meditation-guide/.

7. Harris, Sam. "How to Meditate." Samharris.org. September 26, 2013. https://www.samharris.org/blog/item/how-to-meditate.

believe our bodies and minds are the greatest instruments we'll ever own, we must use them and enjoy them in every way we can. They're instruments which don't get worn down the more we use them, on the contrary, they get better, and our physical, emotional, mental and spiritual health flourishes as a result.

Spirituality is a unique and subjective experience for each of us, no two people will experience it in the same way. So there's no right or wrong answer when it comes to spirituality, there's only a right answer for you at this moment in time. Therefore whatever the answer is for you now, it will likely change in the future, because over time we all change who we are and this changes who we become. It's all a part of growing spiritually as human beings.

As we grow, we must also be mindful of the environments we find ourselves in. We must always look to surround ourselves with the energy and people we wish to emulate. When we do, it's a force-multiplier to get the best out of our minds and bodies. When we look after ourselves as best as we can, always seeking to achieve our full potential, then people around us reap the benefits too. Not only will people become inspired by our actions, but our loved ones will receive the best version of us. This can only be good for them. It's when we're the best version of ourselves that we'll be able to care for them to the best of our abilities, just as they've cared for us in the past. When we're secure in ourselves and with who we are, we're in the best possible position to help others.

It's difficult to become this self-reliant when all our lives we've leaned on something else to get us through tough times. But an important thing to remember about living without religion is that our lives are entirely our own. This means it's up to us to take complete responsibility for the choices we make and the consequences of those choices. We can't control a lot of the events which happen in our lives, but we can control how we react to them. There are no more supernatural beings to call on for help, nor are there any more supernatural beings to blame when things don't go our way. It's up to us to deal with life, and we'd better make the most of it since this is the only chance we get. It's now or never.

People who become spiritual but not religious don't want the restrictions organized religions places on them. They value intellectual curiosity, freedom of speech, and an open-minded approach to life. However, many people will decide they want and need a religious ideology for guidance. If that's the case, then they must also be free to follow the path they've chosen for themselves. As long as they're kind to themselves and kind to others, they must be given their basic human right (freedom of religion) to practice what they believe in.

Whether they're Muslim, Christian, Jewish, Hindu, Buddhist, Sikh or of any other faith.

But, without religion's taboos, I believe we can explore and fulfill our intellectual thirst for knowledge even further. We can absorb the intellect we wish to acquire about anything in the world and finally have nothing to hold us back, no matter how disapproving or prohibited it may be in the eyes of our religions. There's no way of knowing now just how useful the knowledge we acquire will be to us or to others in the future. We can't connect those dots looking forward, we can only do so after looking back. But regardless, if we enjoy the time we spend educating ourselves, adding value to the world and to other people's lives, then it's a wonderful life. It's time to take curiosity and fun more seriously.

48

Meaning of life

"Our job in this lifetime is not to shape ourselves into some ideal we imagine we ought to be, but to find out who we already are and become it" – Steven Pressfield

Many religious people feel sorry for atheists and agnostics. They think if someone doesn't have religion in their life then it must be empty and meaningless. They may believe atheists and agnostics have nothing to live for. They may believe without religion, there's no meaning to life.

Believers place their religion and God(s) at the center of their lives, everything revolves around their belief in Him. Everything good that happened, is happening, or will happen in their lives is a result of their faith. Many just can't imagine living a rich and rewarding life without their religious beliefs.

However, just because religious people can't imagine it, doesn't mean it can't be done. If someone's life is God-less, it doesn't mean it's without joy, love, purpose and meaning. Some of the highest achieving people in history didn't need the fear of God to donate generously to charity, have integrity, accomplish great things, and live happy meaningful lives. These include philanthropic magnates Carnegie and Branson. Physicists Feynman and Hawking. Philosophers Hume and Sartre. Artists Monet and Picasso. Novelists Orwell and Asimov. Actresses Hepburn and Mirren. Entrepreneurs Gates and Zuckerberg. All of them don't believe in God.[1]

It's human nature to seek out meaning, that's how our brains evolved. The more information our ancestors obtained, the greater their chances of survival were. When we can't find meaning, we add it to things which had none to begin with because our brains constantly want to understand what's happening in life and make sense of it. It's a survival mechanism innate in Homo sapiens.

---

1. "Celebrity Atheist List." Celebatheists.com. October 25, 2012. http://www.celebatheists.com/wiki/Main_Page.

We often involuntarily see patterns or shapes in things to connect the dots in our minds, like when we see the appearance of familiar objects made by clouds in the sky.

From a scientific standpoint, human life has absolutely no meaning to it, regardless of what any religion says. Homo sapiens are the outcome of blind evolutionary processes, and the universe appears to be operating without any goal or purpose. Certainly, without any of us in mind. There has been nothing to suggest we're a part of any grand cosmic plan. The planet Earth could explode tomorrow and the universe will likely continue to function as it always has done before Earth existed. The universe won't stop whatever it was doing, it'll be business as usual.

So from a scientific perspective, our human presence in this universe, or even on Earth, won't be missed. It was fine without us and it will likely be even better if we're gone considering the negative ecological impact we've made. Therefore, any meaning we give to our lives comes from us. Some decide to use religion to add the meaning and some do not. It's a personal decision because life is what we make it out to be.

But one may ask, can religions really give our lives meaning, can someone or something else impose meaning upon us? Or, is it only us who makes life meaningful? Let's try to answer this question with an analogy.

If we read a book which someone else says has meaning, the book doesn't necessarily have meaning to us. But if we read a book which has meaning to us and other people don't see the meaning, then it still has meaning to us because we gave it meaning. To us the book is still meaningful with or without the external influence. The meaning is created by us based on our values, it comes from within. So, it's not religion which gives us meaning, it's us that gives religion meaning. It's the other way around. We place value upon religion which is how it becomes important to us. Just like money or the borders of countries, they're constructs of the human mind we've given meaning to. If we decide money or borders don't carry any more meaning, then they would cease to exist. It's the same with religion, we can have meaning without religion, but religion can't have meaning without us.

So once we realize we have the power to give things meaning, we can decide how to use this power. We can either delegate it to a religion and let it decide for us what we should find meaningful in our lives. Or, we can use this power to pursue the endeavors we find meaningful, thus giving our own lives meaning. The argument can even be made that finding meaning in our lives outside of religion is more authentic. Instead of following what something else tells us to follow, we pursue what we find to be fulfilling, the things which match our inner values.

People find meaning in their lives in several different places. These include their children, partners, family, friends, careers, personal projects, hobbies, pets, learning, teaching or charities. Religion is not the only thing which can give purpose to someone's life. Worshiping a supernatural being and living to die in the hope of Heaven may be a meaningful life for some people. But if it's not for us, then we alone have the power to change that decision.

This isn't to say religious people don't live meaningful lives or pursue noble causes, they do. There are religious people all over the world who take care of their loved ones, help those in need, fight for justice, and strive for moral excellence. I would only say that this can all be achieved in the absence of religion too. People who don't believe in God can also make the world a better place for us all. People like us believe we only have one opportunity to live life to its fullest, we're not wanting for another life after death. This means we don't abide by questionable laws made thousands of years ago, and it also means we do good deeds out of the kindness of our hearts, not because of fear of punishment or a chance of reward after death. The here and now is what matters to us most, it's what we have the power to influence. All our energy must go towards creating value in this world, helping people, and making our societies a better place for future generations. There's no need to misplace any of our time, energy and attention on ancient religions which intellectually limit us and use fear to suppress us.

I also believe when we take away the idea of a life after death we're more compelled to live mindfully in the present. We're more attentive and focussed to live this one life we're fortunate enough to have to the best of our ability. Taking away a life after death provides an acute perspective on how fragile and fleeting our time on this floating rock in space is. We're less than a dot in the scale of time and everything that has come before us. So, we might as well get busy making the most of the time entrusted to us by the good fortunes of physics, chemistry and biology.

There's a certain clarity and elimination of waste that comes with the knowledge of a deadline. An adage which encapsulates this thought is called Parkinson's Law. It claims "work expands so as to fill the time available for its completion".[2] This behavior is noticeable in our everyday lives. It's why when given a month to complete a task, we often take the whole month. Or, why a student leaves a homework assignment to a Sunday night when they've had all

2. Parkinson, Cyril Northcote. "Parkinson's Law." The Economist, November 19, 1955. http://www.economist.com/node/14116121.

week to do it. It's a part of human behavior. Well, the same can be said about our lives.

But remember, it's all about perception and how we frame it. Only we can decide how to react to the events happening in our lives. No one else controls our thoughts, only us. So, we can decide to see our limited time in this one human life as a depressing realization. Or, we can see it as an opportunity not to waste a second more of our precious time, embracing the full precariousness of our own existence. It doesn't have to be demoralizing if we don't want it to be. It can be empowering and quite exhilarating. The deadline of death doesn't make our time on Earth pointless. It's quite the opposite. Death is essential because it makes life purposeful. If we lived forever, would we ever accomplish anything? Would we ever have the incentive or desire to? Remember Parkinson's Law.

Imagine if we 100% knew after death there'd be an amazing place waiting for us called Heaven and we'd be there for all eternity. Would it make us more or less motivated to accomplish all the things we want to do while we're still alive on Earth, to leave the world a better place than when we found it? There's a myth that people who don't have a religion have nothing to live for. But it's the opposite. We have nothing to die for. We have everything to live for. Life isn't too short, life is long enough to reach the things we want to achieve. The meaningful things people throughout human history have accomplished is a testament to this.

Though there's no God in our lives, it doesn't mean the non-religious take anything on this earth for granted. Personally, I feel immensely lucky to be alive in this moment of time, it's the greatest period of prosperity humanity has ever experienced. It's inspiring to know we are all made of the stars that we see in the sky, to know we're a group of atoms that can think about other atoms. There is plenty in this life to provide us with beauty, wonder and awe. Religion is not a necessity to have a full appreciation of it.

Life has so much to offer us, and as we grow what gives our life purpose will evolve with us. But there's no script to life, it doesn't always work out the way we'd like it to. The only thing we can do is decide how we're going to react to the challenges placed in front of us. We can become angry or depressed about the perceived injustices we're experiencing. Or we can view them as opportunities to build and strengthen ourselves.

The most we can do is stay true to what's in our heart and keep moving forward in that direction. Then we'll get the best out of ourselves and give the best of ourselves to others. It's rarely a straight line forward, it's often a lot of zigzagging and a couple of steps backward to take even more forward.

But as long as we know we are moving in the right direction in the long run, then we're making progress. We're setting the wheels in motion for personal greatness, and it's we who get to decide what personal greatness looks like in our lifetime. Because if we don't define it, then someone (parents, peers, God) or something (society, social media, religion) else will.

What would we do if we knew we couldn't fail? How would we live our lives differently if our parents were dead? How would the answers to these questions affect what personal greatness means to us? I believe it's best if we go through life minimizing the number of regrets we have. Only then can we be content in the knowledge that we're doing the very best we can to achieve our own personal greatness.

This universe has given us so much, it's unfair of us to ask anymore of it. We ask ourselves "What's the purpose and meaning of this universe? What can I get from it during my time here?" As if the universe owes us something. As if it hasn't already done enough for us. Instead, it's us who ought to be asking "What's the purpose and meaning of me?" We owe this universe and our small planet everything. We're infinitesimally lucky. The course of history had to happen exactly the way it did from 13.7 billion years ago up until today for us to be alive reading this book right now.

So let's stop asking "What's the meaning of life?" and "What's my purpose in this world?" Instead let's ask better questions like "How can I give back to the world after everything it has done for me?" and "How can I make the world a better place in a way which excites me?" This is how we find meaning in our lives without religion.

I wrote this book so I could organize and summarize important information about Islam. I also wished to discuss religions and our relationship with them, and I wanted to share it with my sisters and brothers around the world. I believe this information and my experiences could help them since I knew I couldn't be the only one going through this doubt and reflection. I hope the time I invested in this book will help others make more informed decisions about how they wish to live their lives, regardless of what they choose.

This book was a pleasure to write because it was important to me and it was in service of others. This is how you find meaning in your life after religion. Do what excites you to make the world a better place.

PART XI

Conclusion

To all my sisters and brothers; Muslim, Christian, Jewish, Hindu, Buddhist, Sikh, Agnostic, Atheist and more: I hope I've stayed respectful to you all and shared my journey in a way which portrays the sincerity of my thoughts and the best intentions of my heart. I've no issues with people deciding for themselves how they want to live their own lives. I hope to receive the same courtesy in return.

If another person were to challenge religion or the existence of God, as I've done in this book, please don't see this as an attack on you. We ask these questions to open up a dialogue about why you believe what you believe. For us the question isn't "Why don't we believe in God?", it is "Why would we believe in God?" When we explain our position, it's in the hope that you'll understand us better as well. It's an opportunity for a healthy and respectful discussion where both sides can learn more from each other.

Nonetheless, I know I've angered, insulted and disappointed many people with my words. For those who I've upset, I'm sorry, and I hope you understand why I wrote this book. But for those who've been through what I've been through, for those who've been feeling alone, worried and confused, and for those who now feel optimistic, energized and empowered, keep reading. Life is about more than just losing faith in God, it's about gaining faith in humanity.

With that being said, there are a few more things I'd like to share with you.

49

Science is life

"When something is important enough, you do it even if the odds are not in your favor" – Elon Musk

Education is good for everyone. It's difficult to disagree with this. But the effectiveness of the education is dependent upon what we decide to educate ourselves and others with. We need facts, we need it to be up to date, and we need to make sure if it's wrong then it's subject to change for the truth. This is where religion and science differ.

Science has its set of rules for physics, chemistry, biology, geology and astronomy. These are testable explanations about the universe, consistent for all humanity. Whereas religious ideologies have numerous sets of rules, in various books, given to different races of people, and at different periods of time, and all of this can happen even within the same religion.

Science admits there are many things out there still unknown. Scientists are aware there are things we know, things we don't know, and things we don't know we don't know. When verified new data is uncovered, science will always updates to correct its inaccuracies. It never claims it has all the answers we'll ever need. Science has led us to previously unimaginable advancements in our understanding of the world we live in, the space and stars that surround us, the technology we use everyday, and the medicine we all rely on.

But, religion does have an advantage over science. Religion is effective at persuading people through their storytelling, more so than science has been using its cold hard facts. Facts tell, but stories sell. So the reason people know and share accounts of Adam, Noah and Moses' lives aren't because they're necessarily true, but because they're instructive and have a memorable narrative. In the same way people know about Archimedes and his 'eureka' moment, Newton and his apple, or Benjamin Franklin and his kite experiment. Storytelling has been, and still is, one of the most important ways to transmit information and convince populations. Throughout history, religion has always told better stories than science, and whoever tells the best story wins. Science needs to influence and motivate people with the same fervor as religious dogma has done for thousands of years. Only then will science be able to compete alongside religion as a social movement and compel more people away from superstitions which defy the laws of the universe, and towards science which actually explains the laws of the universe.

Religion and science have both given us opposite accounts of the world we live in. It's almost impossible to fully believe in one as well as the other. Neither are the type of disciplines which would be happy for you to pick and choose from it as it suits you (though 'cafeteria Catholics' and other believers opt to do so). But science can't change something it has tested, proven and replicated the results for. Why would it? However, religion doesn't want to change its holy books because it can't admit fallibility. Admitting fallibility makes people lose faith.

All their life a believer's faith has given them a sense of certainty and security with the knowledge of God. They had answers to questions, and it comforted them. We humans desire this comfort and guidance a great deal. Even today there are still gurus, spiritual guides and mystics with thousands of followers existing all around the world.

Humans also desire the power and status having a following brings, so much so that we're still creating religions. One only has to see the rise of Scientology as an example, which claims it has around 10 million members worldwide (though the true number is unknown). It was founded less than 65 years ago in 1954. By a science fiction writer.[1]

This is how deep the human desire is to feel safe, in control and looked after. We'll follow a leader, a tribe, a religion, if they can give that to us. Yet no religion is better than the other. In fact, the moral teachings religions provide aren't even unique to any one faith or holy book. They're simply the culmination of principles humanity has conceived over millennia. It's not only Moses, Jesus and Muhammad who can be our teachers, but Aristotle, Buddha, Confucius, Descartes, Kant, Nietzsche, Plato, Socrates and many others as well.

But as science and technology develop, they raise uneasy questions for those who interpret holy books as the literal word of a supernatural being. Instead of science and technology liberating them, the religious may feel it's trying to take something away from them. This is a scary prospect to any religious person and it's understandable. I know having gone through the same fear and emotions. It's unsettling to question the entire way we've lived our

---

1. Reitman, Janet. "Inside Scientology." Rolling Stone, 2006. http://www.rollingstone.com/culture/news/inside-scientology-20110208?print=true.

lives and how our parents lived their lives. It would make anyone feel anxious or distressed. That's why it's simpler for many people to ignore, avoid or tune out these uneasy questions they're confronted with. The idea of change is scary because people fear the unknown, the uncertainty. But the single greatest constant of history is that everything changes, so we can't dismiss it forever.

As I've stated before, I don't believe the goal must be to rid the world of religion. That would be unrealistic as we're too far gone past the point of no religion. But more importantly, it's unnecessary to rid the world of religion. As long as we're tolerant, respectful and kind, we can all still co-exist with religion. The problem is that too many religious and non-religious people don't hold these qualities. In addition, there are some religions which make it harder to carry these attributes than others, particularly ones like Islam which withhold people's freedom of speech and freedom of thought. Religions which withhold such basic human rights make the world a less knowledgeable and tolerant place than it could be.

So while religion *may* be essential to people, science *is* essential to humanity. Without science humankind would still be in the dark ages. We'd have a lack of understanding on everything from gravity, to photosynthesis, to the periodic table. We don't need to debate which is more important, science or religion, but we do need to accept what we've proven to be true so humanity can progress. This information is the most important thing in the world. There needs to be universal education of sciences for children, and there needs to be the prevention of misinformation from parents, teachers and governments. This will result in enhanced decision making across endless fields of studies and it will not only be for the benefit of the Islamic world, but for all humankind.

The reason I explicitly mention Islam is because my own experience has led me to worry about it more than any other religion. I'm worried Islam restricts Muslims of their intellectual curiosity. I'm worried how defensive Muslims can get when they're exposed to new and challenging ideas which conflict with their beliefs. I fear a majority of the 1.7 billion Muslims in the world will be reduced to societal, technological and scientific stagnation.

Some Muslim intellectuals, scientists and economists are the brightest individuals humanity has to offer today. But this appears to be an underrepresented number of the Muslim community when we take its size into account. If we don't intellectually liberate millions more Muslims, it would be a catastrophic loss of some of the most brilliant and fantastic minds the world has ever seen. The global Muslim population is an intellectual sleeping giant waiting to be woken. Imagine the achievements Muslims could contribute to their families, societies, countries and humanity, if only they were to ask first principle questions of everything around them, including Islam.

I believe religions (like Islam) restrict intellectual curiosity. Throughout my life it never occurred to me to question Islam, and it never occurred to me to question anything my family ever said about Islam. As a result, I was stuck in an echo chamber. Everything I heard or learnt about Islam was reinforced by repetition in my family. This closed information loop censored, disallowed or underrepresented any different or competing views. My family and I did this consciously as well as subconsciously. Hearing our opinions constantly echoed back to us only reinforced our belief systems. This echo chamber effect prevented us from noticing changes in our attitude or behavior in comparison to other people's. Consequently, it narrowed my abilities for critical analysis and personal discovery. All because I took too many assumptions as truths. So, I know if it can happen to me when I was a Muslim, it can happen to other Muslims too.

I want my Muslim sisters and brothers to imagine the greatest challenges humankind currently faces. Now, I want them to imagine improvements and breakthroughs in all those humanitarian challenges. Finally, I want them to imagine what if it was them, people in the global population of 1.7 billion Muslims who were the ones to make those discoveries and developments? What if millions of Muslims had their ability to question everything finally unleashed once more?

Once Muslims break the biggest mental barrier holding them back (questioning Islam) then their minds are unrestricted. Muslims must practice asking questions of Islam from first principles. Because it will leave them in a stronger and healthier mindset to face the even bigger questions and challenges we face in our lifetime. Questions which if answered helps billions of lives around the world for generations to come. It's not about questioning Islam so we can rebel for the sake of rebelling. It's about Muslims questioning Islam so they can open their minds to the possibilities of different ideas and perspectives. This is bigger than any of us individually – it's for the greater good of humanity.

Imagine if we evolved to be the person we ought to become. Imagine if we evolved to become the person we want to be, rather than the person we're told we should be. Imagine if our global sleeping giant of a Muslim population tackled life through unfiltered eyes by not taking anything as an assumption, and taking nothing for granted. Imagine if they questioned everything they knew using reason, logic, and the instincts within their heart, all with the purpose of trying to understand the true meaning as to why things are the way they are. With this healthy disposition for solving challenges from first principles, imagine what more humankind can achieve. The world needs as many people as possible working on humanitarian opportunities such as:

Climate Change

- Environmental ecosystems
- Global warming
- Natural resources: deforestation and fossil fuels
- Pollution: air, light, noise, soil and water
- Species extinction
- Sustainable fishing
- Urban farming

Conflict Resolution

- Gender
- Nuclear weapons
- Organized crime
- Racism
- Religion
- Terrorism
- Transparent governments
- Wars

Economic Stability

- Distribution of wealth
- Employment
- Fair trade
- Overpopulation

Global Poverty

- Clean water
- Food
- Homelessness
- Infant mortality rate
- Low life expectancy: prevention, immunization and treatment of diseases
- New epidemics and pandemics

Health and Well-being

- Alcohol
- Cancer
- Exercise
- Food
- Free universal medical care
- Joy of living
- Porn addiction
- Sleep
- Tobacco
- TV and social media hypnosis

Renewable Energy

- Hydroelectric
- Solar
- Thermal
- Wind

Technology

- Artificial Intelligence
- Clean GM crops
- Cyber security
- Genome sequencing
- Innovative business models
- Nanotechnology
- Space travel
- Universal information and communication technologies
- Virtual Reality

What could we achieve if we worked together on these humanitarian opportunities? The global poverty rate can go further down, and wealth inequality can improve. We'll have finally weaned ourselves off of fossil fuels, everyone will be using clean renewable energy and the impact of climate change will be reduced by every nation, on and off of Earth. Conflicts will end and hopefully minimal new ones will have arisen, and who knows how virtual reality, nanotechnology and artificial intelligence will impact our everyday lives.

To my Muslim sisters and brothers, please don't deny us of your personal greatness, your world-changing potential. The world needs you, more than God needs you.

50

Life is beautiful

"The secret to happiness is freedom, and the secret to freedom is courage" –
Thucydides

We're all blessed because we're alive in this period of time of human history. Most of us have been given education, healthcare and love. Not everyone on this pale blue dot gets to experience and enjoy this. Round-the-clock media coverage may paint the picture we're living in a violent, confusing and crumbling world but in reality, we're living in the safest, most prosperous and most tolerant period of human existence. There are significantly less deaths and wars in the world, and advancements in medicine mean we're living longer and healthier lives than ever before. There are still many problems on our planet and it's impossible to predict what may come in the future, but I'm optimistic this upward trend in justice, liberty and prosperity will continue in the long run.

Reflecting on my life recently and the journey I've gone through to create this book, it was daunting for me to embrace this freedom and discard everything my family taught me about the world. But I knew once I'd acquired the information I've since put into this book, there was no way of going back. Even if I'd wanted to, I now knew too much. To go back to the way things were would make life much easier for me and less painful for those around me. But some things just can't be unlearned. I'd now taken the 'red pill' and seen reality for what it truly is. I may become an outsider as a result but I'm also excited. Because those who find themselves in unique and unusual positions are also the ones who'll encounter new and novel experiences no one else does.

So, with this liberation and opportunity to live my life the way I choose, I plan to keep exploring the world and growing as a person. I'll continue to respect my body and mind as well as others'. I will not feel ashamed for enjoying natural pleasures in life such as sex. I will continue to question conventional wisdom about the world and the way humans choose to interact on it and with it. I will continue to seek more answers to the questions I have, and I'll also do my best to share these experiences and contrarian thoughts with you.

I hope you'll also do the same for humanity's sake; our strength as a species is our ability to pass on knowledge to other human beings in the next generation. Our learning occurs slower if it's in isolation, we mustn't keep what we've learnt to ourselves if it can help humanity in the long run. Therefore the process of learning must be accompanied by teaching as well. We're all different: we each possess unique insights and perspectives about humanity and our planet. We all have something to offer to each other, we just have to figure out why we want to share what we've learned. What do we want to pass on?

Personally, I believe we needed religion in the past more than we do today. This is a message I wanted to pass on. Throughout history religion helped us to work together in larger and larger groups until eventually entire civilizations were kept together by the shared religious beliefs of the people. But now, I believe it's starting to hold us back more than progress us forward.

Traditions are important for all cultures, but the traditions we decide to keep alive says a lot about our values in life. As time passes, cultures evolve, and so must traditions, especially the religious ones. Because a hero in one era may become a villain in another. This always occurs since historical knowledge increases over time and the values our cultures hold evolves too. An example of this is the evolving (and deteriorating) relationship Americans have with Columbus Day, or Australians have with Australia Day.

The values I now hold help me to create meaning in my life and they give me fulfilling goals to aspire to. So I plan to keep working hard and smart towards the goals of improving my life and the lives of others. Life is too precious to do otherwise. I constantly ask myself to go through life with as little regrets as possible and I'd encourage you to do the same, even when it requires you to be braver than you think you are. A regretful life is not a life lived. We're going to be scared no matter what we do, so are we going to learn how to use that fear to be productive or not?

It's best if we use the unknown time we have on this world to do what excites us which helps other people. Not just for the benefit of our family and friends, but for strangers, the young and the old, and those less fortunate. We're all foreigners to someone else in the world and we're all neighbors at the same time. We must strive towards helping each other and treating each other with the same respect, kindness and patience we'd hope to receive in their country.

Please believe and practice whatever religion you wish to. I have said this before, I sincerely believe every human being has the right to live their life the way they wish to. I only hope people are kind to themselves and to others, regardless of what they believe. My intention with this book was not to convert people or to tell them what to believe. In reality, I'm quite conscious of the fact that you can't reason people out of something they didn't reason themselves into. I only wished to share information I'd come across on my journey and then use that information to explain to my parents why I feel the way I feel about Islam and God. So, as the reader, you are free to act upon this information in any way you wish.

We all have the free will and choice to think for ourselves and make our own decisions. I've made mine.

God, thank you and goodbye.

Bibliography

Introduction

Merriam-Webster. Accessed February 28, 2017. https://www.merriam-webster.com/dictionary/atheism.

How this book can help you

Johnson, Todd M., Gina A. Zurlo, Albert W. Hickman, and Peter F. Crossing. Christianity 2015: Religious Diversity and Personal Contact. Report. Vol. 39. Series 1. South Hamilton: International Bulletin of Missionary Research, 2015. http://www.gordonconwell.edu/ockenga/research/documents/2IBMR2015.pdf.

Before we begin

Kübler-Ross, Elisabeth, and David Kessler. On Grief and Grieving: Finding the Meaning of Grief through the Five Stages of Loss. London: Simon & Schuster, 2005.

Arberry, Arthur J. The Koran Interpreted. Oxford: Oxford University Press, 2008.

Mohammed, Khaleel. "Assessing English Translations of the Qur'an." Middle East Quarterly 12, no. 2 (Spring 2005): 58-71. http://www.meforum.org/717/assessing-english-translations-of-the-quran.

Part I – Why Religion Works

Merriam-Webster. Accessed February 28, 2017. https://www.merriam-webster.com/dictionary/religion.

Henig, Robin Marantz. "Darwin's God." The New York Times, March 4, 2007. Accessed October 31, 2016. http://www.nytimes.com/2007/03/04/magazine/04evolution.t.html.

1. People develop personal relationships with God

Swaab, D.F. "This Is Your Brain on Religion: Uncovering the Science of Belief." Salon, January 4, 2014. Accessed January 14, 2017. https://www.salon.com/2014/01/04/this_is_your_brain_on_religion_uncovering_the_science_of_belief/.

2. Religion fulfils basic human desires

Reiss, Steven. The 16 Strivings for God: The New Psychology of Religious Experiences. Macon, GA: Mercer University Press, 2015.

4. Religion provides social order

Shermer, Michael. "Why Are We Moral: The Evolutionary Origins of Morality." In The Science of Good and Evil: Why People Cheat, Share, Gossip, and Follow the Golden Rule. New York: Times Books, 2004.

Harari, Yuval Noah. Sapiens: A Brief History of Humankind. Random House UK, 2014.

Janis, Irving Lester. Groupthink: Psychological Studies of Policy Decisions and Fiascoes. Boston: Wadsworth, 2013.

Rossano, Matt J. Supernaturalizing Social Life: Religion and the Evolution of Human Cooperation. Report. Accessed November 2, 2016. http://www2.southeastern.edu/Academics/Faculty/mrossano/recentpubs/Supernaturalizing.pdf.

Epstein, Greg M. Good without God: What a Billion Nonreligious People Do Believe. New York: Harper, 2010. p.115.

Johnson, Todd M., Gina A. Zurlo, Albert W. Hickman, and Peter F. Crossing. Christianity 2015: Religious Diversity and Personal Contact. Report. Vol. 39. Series 1. South Hamilton: International Bulletin of Missionary Research, 2015. Accessed October 18, 2016. http://www.gordonconwell.edu/ockenga/research/documents/2IBMR2015.pdf.

6. God helps people

Griffin, Andrew. "What Happens to You Just before You Die? Chemists Explain Exactly How Death Feels." The Independent, October 27, 2015. http://www.independent.co.uk/news/science/what-happens-to-you-just-before-you-die-chemists-explain-exactly-how-death-feels-a6710551.html.

Cox, Jeffrey. "Secularization and Other Master Narratives of Religion in Modern Europe." Kirchliche Zeitgeschichte 14, no. 1 (2001): 24-35. http://www.jstor.org/stable/43100018.

7. God answers people's prayers

Kesvani, Hussein. "Why Are Some British Muslims Going To Faith Healers To Treat

Mental Illness?" BuzzFeed, December 11, 2015. https://www.buzzfeed.com/ husseinkesvani/why-are-some-british-muslims-going-to-faith-healers-to-treat?utm_term=.ugn9BgyyG#.ivMR7Nlle.

Wilson, Jason. "Letting Them Die: Parents Refuse Medical Help for Children in the Name of Christ." The Guardian, April 13, 2016. https://www.theguardian.com/ us-news/2016/apr/13/followers-of-christ-idaho-religious-sect-child-mortality-refusing-medical-help.

Elgot, Jessica. "What The Huffington Post UK's Beyond Belief Series Taught Us About Faith."The Huffington Post, December 1, 2014. http://www.huffingtonpost.co.uk/ 2014/12/01/beyond-belief_n_6248360.html.

8. Religions evolve by natural selection

Stearns, Beverly Peterson, and Stephen C. Stearns. Watching, from the Edge of Extinction. New Haven: Yale Univ. Press, 2000. pp 19-21.

Lipka, Michael, and Conrad Hackett. Pew Research Center. Why Muslims Are the World's Fastest-growing Religious Group. Report. April 23, 2015. http://www.pewresearch.org/fact-tank/2015/04/23/why-muslims-are-the-worlds-fastest-growing-religious-group/.

Johnson, Todd M., Gina A. Zurlo, Albert W. Hickman, and Peter F. Crossing. Christianity 2015: Religious Diversity and Personal Contact. Report. Vol. 39. Series 1. South Hamilton: International Bulletin of Missionary Research, 2015. Accessed October 18, 2016. http://www.gordonconwell.edu/ockenga/research/documents/ 2IBMR2015.pdf.

Pew Research Center. The Future of World Religions: Population Growth Projections, 2010-2050. Report. April 2, 2015. http://www.pewforum.org/2015/04/02/religious-projections-2010-2050/.

9. Everyone believes their God is the right God

Popkin, Richard H. "Blaise Pascal." In The Columbia History of Western Philosophy, p.353. New York: Columbia University Press, 2008.

Johnson, Todd M., Gina A. Zurlo, Albert W. Hickman, and Peter F. Crossing. Christianity 2015: Religious Diversity and Personal Contact. Report. Vol. 39. Series 1. South Hamilton: International Bulletin of Missionary Research, 2015. Accessed October 18, 2016. http://www.gordonconwell.edu/ockenga/research/documents/ 2IBMR2015.pdf.

10. Books and faith are enough

Henderson, Bobby. "About." Church of the Flying Spaghetti Monster. Accessed November 5, 2016. http://www.venganza.org/about/.

Russell, Bertrand. "Is There a God? [1952]." In The Collected Papers of Bertrand Russell, Vol. 11: Last Philosophical Testament, 1943–68, edited by John G. Slater, 547-48. London: Routledge, 1997. http://russell.mcmaster.ca/volume11.htm

Part II – The Quran

Brown, Daniel W. A New Introduction to Islam. Malden: Blackwell, 2005.

Leaman, Oliver. "Canon." In The Qur'an: An Encyclopedia. London: Routledge, 2010.

Ahmad, Abdul Basit, Aqeel Walkar, and Muhammad Ayub Sapra. Uthman Bin Affan: The Third Caliph of Islam. Riyadh: Darussalam, 2004.

11. Equals of the Quran

Foster, Benjamin R., and Karen Polinger Foster. Civilizations of Ancient Iraq. Princeton: Princeton University Press, 2009. p.6.

Dalley, Stephanie. Myths from Mesopotamia: Creation, the Flood, Gilgamesh, and Others. Oxford: Oxford University Press, 2008.

Flood, Gavin D. An Introduction to Hinduism. Cambridge: Cambridge Univ. Press, 2011.

Jones, Constance A., and James D. Ryan. Encyclopedia of Hinduism. New York, NY: Checkmark Books, 2008.

Chan, Alan. "Laozi." In Stanford Encyclopedia of Philosophy, edited by Edward N. Zalta. Stanford, CT: Stanford University, Metaphysics Research Lab., 2004. https://plato.stanford.edu/entries/laozi/.

Doniger, Wendy. "Bhagavadgita." Encyclopædia Britannica. Encyclopædia Britannica, March 5, 2015. https://www.britannica.com/topic/Bhagavadgita.

Minor, Robert Neil. Modern Indian Interpreters of the Bhagavadgita: Research

Conference on Modern Interpreters of the Bhagavadgita: Papers. Albany, NY: State University of New York Press, 1986. p.88.

Williams, Paul. Mahayana Buddhism: The Doctrinal Foundations. London: Routledge, 2010.

McAuliffe, Jane Dammen. The Cambridge Companion to the Qur'ān. Cambridge: Cambridge Univ. Press, 2014.

12. Inaccuracy of the Quran

Leaman, Oliver. "Canon." In The Qur'an: An Encyclopedia. London: Routledge, 2010.

The Editors of Encyclopædia Britannica. "'Uthmān ibn 'Affān." Encyclopædia Britannica. Encyclopædia Britannica, July 20, 1998. https://www.britannica.com/biography/Uthman-ibn-Affan.

Tabā tabā i, Sayyid M. H. The Qur'an in Islam: Its Impact and Influence on the Life of Muslims. London: Zahra Publ., 1987.

13. Ambiguity of the Quran

Robinson, Neal. Discovering the Qur'an: A Contemporary Approach to a Veiled Text. Washington, D.C.: Georgetown University Press, 2004.

Grim, Brian J., and Mehtab S. Karim. The Future of the Global Muslim Population. Report. January 27, 2011. http://www.pewforum.org/2011/01/27/the-future-of-the-global-muslim-population/.

Part III – Hadith

Brown, Jonathan. Hadith: Muhammad's Legacy in the Medieval and Modern World. Oxford: Oneworld, 2011.

Leaman, Oliver. "Canon." In The Qur'an: An Encyclopedia. London: Routledge, 2010.

Nasiri, Ali. An Introduction to Hadith: History and Sources. MIU Press, 2013.

15. The Quran does not mention Hadith

Hecht, Jennifer Michael. Doubt: A History; the Great Doubters and Their Legacy of

Innovation from Socrates and Jesus to Thomas Jefferson and Emily Dickinson. New York: HarperCollins, 2004.

Robinson, Neal. Islam, a Concise Introduction. Washington, DC: Georgetown University Press, 1999.

16. Unreliability of Hadith sources

Dugan, Emily. "Most Popular Baby Names: The Top 20 Boys and Girls Names in England and Wales." The Independent, August 15, 2014. http://www.independent.co.uk/news/uk/home-news/most-popular-baby-names-the-top-20-boys-and-girls-names-in-england-and-wales-9671635.html.

17. Prophet Muhammad the illiterate man

Al-Tabari. The Commentary on the Qur'ān. Edited by Wilferd Madelung and Alan Jones. Oxford: Oxford University Press, 1990.

Watt, W. Montgomery. Muhammad: Prophet and Statesman. London: Oxford University Press, 1961. p.19.

Freemon, Frank R. "A Differential Diagnosis of the Inspirational Spells of Muhammad the Prophet of Islam." Epilepsia 17, no. 4 (1976): 423-27. doi:10.1111/j.1528-1157.1976.tb04454.x.

Altschuler, Eric Lewin, Andreea S. Calude, Andrew Meade, and Mark Pagel. "Linguistic Evidence Supports Date for Homeric Epics." BioEssays 35, no. 5 (2013): 417-20. doi:10.1002/bies.201200165.

Fox, Robin Lane. The Classical World: An Epic History from Homer to Hadrian. New York: Basic Books, 2006. p.19.

Greenblatt, Stephen, and Meyer Howard. Abrams. The Norton Anthology of English Literature. New York: Norton & Company, 2013.

18. Prophet Muhammad's successor

Pew Research Center. Mapping the Global Muslim Population. Report. October 7, 2009. http://www.pewforum.org/2009/10/07/mapping-the-global-muslim-population/.

19. Prophet Muhammad's Night Journey

Martin, Richard C. Encyclopedia of Islam and the Muslim World. New York: Macmillan Reference USA, 2004.

Mahmoud, Omar. "The Journey to Meet God Almighty by Muhammad—Al-Isra." In Muhammad: An Evolution of God, p.56. Bloomington, IN: AuthorHouse, 2008.

Muslim, Sahih. Translation of Sahih Muslim. International Islamic University Malaysia. Sahih Muslim, Book 39: The Book Giving Description of the Day of Judgement, Paradise and Hell (Kitab Sifat Al-Qiyamah Wa'l Janna Wa'n-Nar). Translated by Abdul Hamid Siddiqui. November 17, 2005. http://www.iium.edu.my/deed/hadith/muslim/039_smt.html. Book 39, Number 6725

Mourison, Robert G. "The Portrayal of Nature in a Medieval Qur'an Commentary." Studia Islamica, no. 94 (2002): 115. doi:10.2307/1596214.

20. Prophet Muhammad's self-serving rules

"Marriages of the Holy Prophet." Al-Islam.org. Accessed January 25, 2017. https://www.al-islam.org/life-muhammad-prophet-sayyid-saeed-akhtar-rizvi/marriages-holy-prophet.

"List of Muhammad's Wives and Concubines." WikiIslam. February 28, 2016. https://wikiislam.net/wiki/List_of_Muhammads_Wives_and_Concubines.

Esposito, John L. Islam: The Straight Path. New York: Oxford Univ. Press, 1998.

Anwar Al-Awlaki. The Life of the Prophet Muhammad (Makkan Period). Enjoyislam.com. Accessed February 28, 2017. http://www.enjoyislam.com/lectures/AnwarAlAwlaki/LifeOfMohammad.html. CD 5 – Important Events

Watt, W. Montgomery. Muhammad: Prophet and Statesman. London: Oxford University Press, 1961.

21. Prophet Muhammad as a role model

Armstrong, Karen. Muhammad: A Biography of the Prophet. San Francisco: HarperSanFrancisco, 1993.

Brown, Jonathan. Misquoting Muhammad: The Challenge and Choices of Interpreting the Prophet's Legacy. London: Oneworld, 2014. pp.143-44.

Spellberg, Denise A. Politics, Gender and the Islamic Past: Legacy of A'isha Bint Abi Bakr. Columbia U.P., 1996.

Turner, Colin. Islam: The Basics. London: Routledge, 2011.

Armstrong, Karen. Muhammad: Prophet for Our Time. London: HarperPress, 2006. p.167.

"Highest and Lowest Ages of Consent." AgeOfConsent.net. Accessed November 21, 2016. https://www.ageofconsent.net/highest-and-lowest.

UNICEF. Media Centre. "In Mali, Child Marriage Is a Death Sentence for Many Young Girls." News release. Unicef.org. Accessed February 28, 2017. https://www.unicef.org/wcaro/english/media_5120.html.

"Deep Divisions over Child Brides." IRIN, March 28, 2010. http://www.irinnews.org/feature/2010/03/28/deep-divisions-over-child-brides.

"No Minimum Age for Marriage of Girls – Grand Mufti." Arabian Business, December 22, 2014. http://www.arabianbusiness.com/no-minimum-age-for-marriage-of-girls-grand-mufti-576044.html.

Barr, Heather, and Linda Lakhdhir. "Time to Ban Child Marriage in Malaysia." Human Rights Watch, April 29, 2016. https://www.hrw.org/news/2016/04/29/time-ban-child-marriage-malaysia.

23. Noah

Cline, Eric H. From Eden to Exile: Unraveling Mysteries of the Bible. Washington, D.C.: National Geographic, 2007.

Dalley, Stephanie. Myths from Mesopotamia: Creation, the Flood, Gilgamesh, and Others. Oxford: Oxford University Press, 2008.

Rosenberg, Donna. World Mythology: An Anthology of the Great Myths and Epics. Lincolnwood, IL: NTC Pub. Group, 1994. pp.196-200.

Finkelstein, J. J., W. G. Lambert, and A. R. Millard. "Atra-Hasis: The Babylonian Story of the Flood." Journal of Biblical Literature 88, no. 4 (1969): 477. doi:10.2307/3263801.

Bremmer, Jan N. The Strange World of Human Sacrifice. Leuven: Peeters, 2007. p.158.

Klostermaier, Klaus. A Survey of Hinduism. Albany, NY: State University of New York Press, 2007. p.97.

24. Abraham

"Mom Who Said She Killed on God's Orders Acquitted." CNN, April 3, 2004. http://edition.cnn.com/2004/LAW/04/03/children.slain/.

"God Told Me to Do It." The Huffington Post. Accessed January 25, 2017. http://www.huffingtonpost.com/news/god-told-me-to-do-it/.

25. Moses

Wheeler, Brannon M. Moses in the Quran and Islamic Exegesis. London: Routledge, 2009.

Marszal, Andrew. "Pakistani Social Media Star 'murdered by Her Brother' in Apparent Honour Killing." The Telegraph, July 16, 2016. http://www.telegraph.co.uk/news/2016/07/16/pakistani-social-media-star-murdered-by-her-brother-in-apparent/.

Brown, Jonathan. Misquoting Muhammad: The Challenge and Choices of Interpreting the Prophet's Legacy. London: Oneworld, 2014. p.180.

Esposito, John L. What Everyone Needs to Know about Islam. Oxford: Oxford University Press, 2011. p.177.

Chesler, Phyllis. "Worldwide Trends in Honor Killings." Middle East Quarterly 17, no. 2 (Spring 2010): 3-11. http://www.meforum.org/2646/worldwide-trends-in-honor-killings.

26. Jesus

Muslim, Sahih. Translation of Sahih Muslim. International Islamic University Malaysia. Sahih Muslim, Book 41: Book Pertaining to the Turmoil and Portents of the Last Hour (Kitab Al-Fitan Wa Ashrat As-Sa'ah). Translated by Abdul Hamid Siddiqui. November 17, 2005. http://www.iium.edu.my/deed/hadith/muslim/041_smt.html. Book 41, Number 7023

Part VI – Science in Islam

Gingerich, Owen. "Islamic Astronomy." Scientific American 254, no. 4 (April 1986): 74-83. doi:10.1038/scientificamerican0486-74.

Johnson, Todd M., Gina A. Zurlo, Albert W. Hickman, and Peter F. Crossing. Christianity 2015: Religious Diversity and Personal Contact. Report. Vol. 39. Series 1. South Hamilton: International Bulletin of Missionary Research, 2015. Accessed October 18, 2016. http://www.gordonconwell.edu/ockenga/research/documents/2IBMR2015.pdf.

27. Evolution

Urban, Tim. "Putting Time In Perspective – UPDATED." Wait But Why (blog), August 22, 2013. http://waitbutwhy.com/2013/08/putting-time-in-perspective.html.

Harari, Yuval Noah. Sapiens: A Brief History of Humankind. Random House UK, 2014.

Lewis, Mark Edward. China's Cosmopolitan Empire: The Tang Dynasty. Cambridge, MA: Belknap Press of Harvard University Press, 2012.

28. Origins of the universe

Dalal, Roshen. Hinduism: An Alphabetical Guide. New Delhi: Penguin Books, 2010. p.224.

Foster, Benjamin R., and Karen Polinger Foster. Civilizations of Ancient Iraq. Princeton: Princeton University Press, 2009. p.6.

Hetherington, Norriss S. Encyclopedia of Cosmology. Routledge, 2015.

Ceurstemont, Sandrine. "This May Be the World's Oldest Jurassic Dinosaur Fossil." New Scientist, January 20, 2016. https://www.newscientist.com/article/2074126-this-may-be-the-worlds-oldest-jurassic-dinosaur-fossil/.

Chow, Denise. "The Universe: Big Bang to Now in 10 Easy Steps." Space.com, October 18, 2011. http://www.space.com/13320-big-bang-universe-10-steps-explainer.html.

The Editors of Encyclopædia Britannica. "Big-bang Model." Encyclopædia Britannica. December 2, 2015. https://www.britannica.com/topic/big-bang-model.

Hawking, Stephen W., and Leonard Mlodinow. The Grand Design. London: Bantam Press, 2010.

29. The Quran's science

Touwaide, Alain. "GALEN, On Semen, Edition, Translation and Commentary by Philippe De Locy, Berlin, Akademie Verlag, 1992, 291 Pp. (= Corpus Medicorum Graecorum, V, 3, 1)." Nuncius 9, no. 1 (1994): 333-35. doi:10.1163/182539184×00171.

Dudek, Ronald W. High-yield Embryology. Philadelphia: Wolters Kluwer/Lippincott Williams & Wilkins, 2014.

Part VII – Women

"Female Infanticide." BBC. Accessed January 17, 2017. http://www.bbc.co.uk/ethics/abortion/medical/infanticide_1.shtml.

Lewis, Bernard. What Went Wrong?: Western Impact and Middle Eastern Response. Oxford: Oxford University Press, 2002. pp.82-83.

Watt, William Montgomery. "Interview: William Montgomery Watt." Interview by Bashir Mann and Alastair McIntosh. AlastairMcIntosh.com. 1999. http://www.alastairmcintosh.com/articles/2000_watt.htm.

30. Women as unequals

Esposito, John L. What Everyone Needs to Know about Islam. Oxford: Oxford University Press, 2011. p.76.

At-Tirmidhi, Abu `Isa Muhammad. "The Book on Virtues of Jihad – Jami` At-Tirmidhi." Sunnah.com. Accessed November 28, 2016. https://sunnah.com/tirmidhi/22/46. Vol. 3, Book 20, Hadith 1663

Muslim Women's League. "Islamic Inheritance." Muslim Women's League. September 1995. http://www.mwlusa.org/topics/rights/inheritance.html.

UNICEF. Regional Overview for the Middle East and North Africa MENA – Gender Equality Profile – Status of Girls and Women in the Middle East and North Africa. Report. October 2011. https://www.unicef.org/gender/files/REGIONAL-Gender-Eqaulity-Profile-2011.pdf.

Bhutto, Benazir. "Politics and the Muslim Woman." In Liberal Islam, edited by Charles Kurzman. New York: Oxford Univ. Press, 2011.

Kabbani, Muhammad Hisham., and Homayra Ziad. The Prohibition of Domestic

Violence in Islam. Washington, D.C.: World Organization for Resource Development and Education, 2011. pp.6-12.

Ennaji, Moha, and Fatima Sadiqi. Gender and Violence in the Middle East. New York, NY: Routledge, 2011. pp.162-247.

Jawad, Haifaa A. The Rights of Women in Islam: An Authentic Approach. IX, 150 S.: Palgrave, 2002.

Aleem, Shamim. Prophet Muhammad(s) and His Family: A Sociological Perspective. Bloomington, IN: AuthorHouse, 2007. p.130.

Goodwin, Jan. Price of Honor: Muslim Women Lift the Veil of Silence on the Islamic World. New York: Plume, 2003.

Eltahawy, Mona. Headscarves and Hymens: Why the Middle East Needs a Sexual Revolution. London: Weidenfeld & Nicolson, 2016.

Clarke, Lisa. "Sakdiyah Ma'ruf: The Muslim Comedian Using Punchlines for a Purpose."Australia Plus, November 15, 2016. http://www.australiaplus.com/international/in-person/the-fearless-muslim-comedian-pushing-the-boundaries/8026696.

Mackey, Robert. "Saudi Women Free After 73 Days in Jail for Driving." The New York Times, February 12, 2015. http://www.nytimes.com/2015/02/13/world/middleeast/saudi-women-free-after-73-days-in-jail-for-driving.html.

Galliot, Lorena, and Wajeha Al-Huwaider. "The Saudi Woman Who Took to the Driver's Seat." The Observers – France 24, May 23, 2011. http://observers.france24.com/en/20110523-saudi-woman-arrested-defying-driving-ban-manal-al-sharif-khobar.

"Iran: Serious Health Fears for Artist on Prison Hunger Strike." Amnesty International, March 2, 2015. https://www.amnesty.org/en/latest/news/2015/03/imprisoned-iranian-artist-atena-farghadani-on-hunger-strike/.

Cavna, Michael. "Cartoonist Atena Farghadani, Sentenced for Satirizing Government as Animals, Is Freed in Iran." The Washington Post, May 4, 2016. https://www.washingtonpost.com/news/comic-riffs/wp/2016/05/04/cartoonist-atena-farghadani-sentenced-for-satirizing-government-as-animals-is-freed-in-iran/.

The Norwegian Nobel Committee. Nobel Media AB. "The Nobel Peace Prize for 2011 to Ellen Johnson Sirleaf, Leymah Gbowee and Tawakkul Karman – Press Release."

News release, October 7, 2011. Nobelprize.org. http://www.nobelprize.org/nobel_prizes/peace/laureates/2011/press.html.

Karman, Tawakkul. "Yemeni Activist Tawakkul Karman, First Female Arab Nobel Peace Laureate: A Nod for Arab Spring." Interview by Amy Goodman. Democracy Now! October 7, 2011. https://www.democracynow.org/2011/10/7/yemeni_activist_tawakkul_karman_first_female.

Peer, Basharat. "The girl who wanted to go to school." The New Yorker, October 10, 2012. http://www.newyorker.com/news/news-desk/the-girl-who-wanted-to-go-to-school?currentPage=all

Associated Press. "Malala Yousafzai Becomes Youngest-Ever Nobel Prize Winner." People.com, October 10, 2014. http://www.people.com/article/malala-yousafzai-wins-nobel-prize.

31. Women's clothing

Khalid, Asma. "Lifting The Veil: Muslim Women Explain Their Choice." NPR, April 21, 2011. http://www.npr.org/2011/04/21/135523680/lifting-the-veil-muslim-women-explain-their-choice.

Ahmed, Leila. Women and Gender in Islam: Historical Roots of a Modern Debate. Philadelphia: University of Pennsylvania Pr., 2011.

(un)veiled: Muslim Women Talk About Hijab. Directed by Ines Hofmann Kanna. Produced by Ines Hofmann Kanna. Documentary Educational Resources. 2007. http://www.der.org/films/unveiled.html.

Khalid, Asma. "Lifting The Veil: Muslim Women Explain Their Choice." NPR, April 21, 2011. http://www.npr.org/2011/04/21/135523680/lifting-the-veil-muslim-women-explain-their-choice.

Anthony, Andrew. "Losing Their Religion: The Hidden Crisis of Faith among Britain's Young Muslims." The Guardian, May 17, 2015. https://www.theguardian.com/global/2015/may/17/losing-their-religion-british-ex-muslims-non-believers-hidden-crisis-faith.

"Islam: Hijab." BBC. September 3, 2009. http://www.bbc.co.uk/religion/religions/islam/beliefs/hijab_1.shtml.

Wadud, Amina. Qur'an and Woman: Rereading the Sacred Text from a Woman's Perspective. Oxford University Press, 1999. p.34.

Sanghani, Radhika. "Burka Bans: The Countries Where Muslim Women Can't Wear Veils." The Telegraph, July 8, 2016. http://www.telegraph.co.uk/women/life/burka-bans-the-countries-where-muslim-women-cant-wear-veils/.

Saul, Heather. "Men in Hijab: Two Men Explain Why They Are Covering Their Heads to Support Their Wives and Family in Iran." Independent, July 31, 2016. http://www.independent.co.uk/news/people/men-in-hijab-iran-solidarity-wives-family-veil-islam-muslim-womens-rights-a7164876.html.

32. Women and polygyny

"Marriages of the Holy Prophet." Al-Islam.org. Accessed January 25, 2017. https://www.al-islam.org/life-muhammad-prophet-sayyid-saeed-akhtar-rizvi/marriages-holy-prophet.

A., Abdel Haleem M. The Qur'an: English Translation and Parallel Arabic Text. Oxford: Oxford University Press, 2016.

"Dealing Justly with Wives and Orphans (Qur'an 4:3)." WikiIslam. July 9, 2015. https://wikiislam.net/wiki/Dealing_Justly_with_Wives_and_Orphans_(Qur%27an_4:3).

Ahmed, Leila. Women and Gender in Islam: Historical Roots of a Modern Debate. Philadelphia: University of Pennsylvania Pr., 2011.

Ali-Karamali, Sumbul. The Muslim Next Door: The Qur'an, the Media, and That Veil Thing. Ashland, Oregon: White Cloud Press, 2008. p.145.

Ibid., p.142.

Wadud, Amina. Qur'an and Woman: Rereading the Sacred Text from a Woman's Perspective. Oxford University Press, 1999. p.83.

Ali-Karamali, Sumbul. The Muslim Next Door: The Qur'an, the Media, and That Veil Thing. Ashland, Oregon: White Cloud Press, 2008. p.145.

Kusha, Hamid R. "Polygyny." In The Oxford Encyclopedia of the Islamic World, edited by John L. Esposito. Oxford: Oxford Univ. Press, 2009.

Part VIII – The Modern World

Johnson, Todd M., Gina A. Zurlo, Albert W. Hickman, and Peter F. Crossing.

Christianity 2015: Religious Diversity and Personal Contact. Report. Vol. 39. Series 1. South Hamilton: International Bulletin of Missionary Research, 2015. Accessed October 18, 2016. http://www.gordonconwell.edu/ockenga/research/documents/2IBMR2015.pdf.

The Future of World Religions: Population Growth Projections, 2010-2050. Report. April 2, 2015. http://www.pewforum.org/2015/04/02/religious-projections-2010-2050/.

33. Sharia law

Uddin, Asma, Religious Freedom Implications of Sharia Implementation in Aceh, Indonesia (March 7, 2011). University of St. Thomas Law Journal, Vol. 7, No. 3, 2010. https://ssrn.com/abstract=1885776.

"Iranian Chocolate Thief Faces Hand Amputation." BBC News, October 17, 2010. http://www.bbc.com/news/world-middle-east-11559750.

Abdorrahman Boroumand Foundation. "Cruel, Inhuman and Degrading Punishments." Human Rights & Democracy for Iran. Accessed November 27, 2016. https://www.iranrights.org/library/collection/142/amputation-and-eye-gouging.

The Associated Press. "Saudi Arabia Cuts Off Thief's Hand as Punishment." Haaretz, December 15, 2014. http://www.haaretz.com/middle-east-news/1.631994.

Bello, Ademola. "Who Will Save Amputees of Sharia Law in Nigeria?" The Huffington Post, May 25, 2011. http://www.huffingtonpost.com/ademola-bello/who-will-save-amputees-of_b_532949.html.

Mansfield, Katie. "Christians Sentenced to 80 Lashes by Sharia Court for Drinking Communion Wine." Express Newspapers, November 16, 2016. http://www.express.co.uk/news/world/733081/christians-sentenced-80-lashes-Sharia-court-drinking-communion-wine.

Spencer, Richard. "Saudi Arabia Court Gives Death Penalty to Man Who Renounced His Muslim Faith." Telegraph, February 24, 2015. http://www.telegraph.co.uk/news/worldnews/middleeast/saudiarabia/11431509/Saudi-Arabia-court-gives-death-penalty-to-man-who-renounced-his-Muslim-faith.html.

34. Homosexuality

Ali, Kecia. Sexual Ethics and Islam: Feminist Reflections on Qur'an, Hadith, and Jurisprudence. Oxford: Oneworld, 2012.

Carroll, Aengus. State Sponsored Homophobia 2016: A World Survey of Sexual Orientation Laws: Criminalisation, Protection and Recognition. Report. 11th ed. Geneva: International Lesbian, Gay, Bisexual, Trans and Intersex Association, May, 2016.   http://ilga.org/downloads/ 02_ILGA_State_Sponsored_Homophobia_2016_ENG_WEB_150516.pdf.

"No Gay Marriage for Albania." Pink News, February 5, 2010. http://www.pinknews.co.uk/2010/02/05/no-gay-marriage-for-albania.

"The BDP's Debate on Gay Marriage (Turkish Language)." Timeturk, May 15, 2012. http://www.timeturk.com/tr/2012/05/15/bdp-nin-escinsel-evlilik-istegi-tartisiliyor.html.

Kugle, Scott Siraj Al-Haqq. "Sexuality, Diversity, and Ethics in the Agenda of Progressive Muslims." In Progressive Muslims: On Justice, Gender and Pluralism, edited by Omid Safi, p.222. Oxford: Oneworld, 2010.

Sommer, Volker, and Paul L. Vasey. Homosexual Behaviour in Animals: An Evolutionary Perspective. Cambridge: Cambridge University Press, 2006.

AI International Secretariat. Love, Hate and the Law: Decriminalizing Homosexuality. Report. July 4, 2008. https://www.amnesty.org/en/documents/POL30/003/2008/en/.

United Nations. General Assembly. "UN: General Assembly Statement Affirms Rights for All." News release, December 18, 2008. Human Rights Watch. https://www.hrw.org/news/2008/12/18/un-general-assembly-statement-affirms-rights-all.

"Submission to the Church of England's Listening Exercise on Human Sexuality." Royal College of Psychiatrists. Accessed November 26, 2016. http://www.rcpsych.ac.uk/workinpsychiatry/specialinterestgroups/gaylesbian/submissiontothecofe.aspx.

American Psychological Association. Report of the American Psychological Association Task Force on Appropriate Therapeutic Responses to Sexual Orientation. Report. August 2009. http://www.apa.org/pi/lgbt/resources/sexual-orientation.aspx.

Archer, Elizabeth. "Young Gay Muslim on Cost of Coming Out: "It's Crushing That My Parents Don't Accept Me"." Mirror Online, March 31, 2016. http://www.mirror.co.uk/news/real-life-stories/young-gay-muslim-what-comin-7659452.

35. Drugs

"Islamic Finance | What Is the Difference Between Qimar and Maisir?" Investment and Finance. November 23, 2013. http://investment-and-finance.net/islamic-finance/questions/what-is-the-difference-between-qimar-and-maisir.html.

WHO Report on the Global Tobacco Epidemic, 2008: The MPOWER Package. Geneva: World Health Organization, 2008. p.14. http://www.who.int/tobacco/mpower/mpower_report_full_2008.pdf

"Tobacco." World Health Organization. June 2016. http://www.who.int/mediacentre/factsheets/fs339/en/.

"U.S. and World Population Clock." United States Census Bureau. Accessed March 01, 2017. http://www.census.gov/popclock.

"2.1 The Global Tobacco Epidemic." In World Cancer Report 2014, edited by Christopher P. Wild and Bernard W. Stewart. Lyon: International Agency for Research on Cancer, 2014. http://publications.iarc.fr/Non-Series-Publications/World-Cancer-Reports/World-Cancer-Report-2014

Ghouri, Nazim. "Influence of Islam on Smoking among Muslims." BMJ 332, no. 7536 (2006): 291-94. doi:10.1136/bmj.332.7536.291.

Hays, J. Taylor, MD. "Hookah Smoking: Is It Safer than Cigarette Smoking?" Mayo Clinic. June 17, 2015. http://www.mayoclinic.org/healthy-lifestyle/quit-smoking/expert-answers/hookah/faq-20057920.

Eissenberg, Thomas, and Alan Shihadeh. "Waterpipe Tobacco and Cigarette Smoking." American Journal of Preventive Medicine 37, no. 6 (2009): 518-23. doi:10.1016/j.amepre.2009.07.014.

Neergaard, James, Pramil Singh, Jayakaran Job, and Susanne Montgomery. "Waterpipe Smoking and Nicotine Exposure: A Review of the Current Evidence." Nicotine & Tobacco Research 9, no. 10 (2007): 987-94. doi:10.1080/14622200701591591.

36. Children

Dawkins, Richard. "The Future Looks Bright." The Guardian. June 21, 2003. https://www.theguardian.com/books/2003/jun/21/society.richarddawkins.

37. Sex

Al-Nafzawi, Muhammad. The Perfumed Garden of Sensual Delight. Translated by Jim Colville. London: Kegan Paul International, 1999.

Suad, Joseph, and Najmabadi Afsaneh. Encyclopedia of Women & Islamic Cultures. Leiden: Brill, 2007.

Brunschvig, R., "'Abd", in: Encyclopaedia of Islam, Second Edition, Edited by: P. Bearman, Th. Bianquis, C.E. Bosworth, E. van Donzel, W.P. Heinrichs. Accessed 01 March 2017. http://dx.doi.org/10.1163/1573-3912_islam_COM_0003

"Islam: Circumcision of Boys." BBC. August 13, 2009. http://www.bbc.co.uk/religion/religions/islam/islamethics/malecircumcision.shtml.

WHO and UNAIDS. "WHO and UNAIDS Announce Recommendations from Expert Consultation on Male Circumcision for HIV Prevention." News release, March 28, 2007. World Health Organization. http://www.who.int/hiv/mediacentre/news68/en/.

"Home." Doctors Opposing Circumcision. Accessed January 28, 2017. http://www.doctorsopposingcircumcision.org/.

Husain, Ed. The Islamist: Why I Joined Radical Islam in Britain, What I Saw inside and Why I Left. London: Penguin Books, 2007. p.244.

38. Slavery

Hellie, Richard. "Slavery." Encyclopædia Britannica. March 24, 2016. https://www.britannica.com/topic/slavery-sociology.

Okeowo, Alexis. "Freedom Fighter." The New Yorker, September 8, 2014. http://www.newyorker.com/magazine/2014/09/08/freedom-fighter?currentPage=all.

"45.8 Million People Are Enslaved in the World Today." Global Slavery Index. October 18, 2016. http://www.globalslaveryindex.org/.

"Islam: Slavery in Islam." BBC. July 7, 2009. http://www.bbc.co.uk/religion/religions/islam/history/slavery_1.shtml.

Lovejoy, Paul E. Transformation in Slavery: A History of Slavery in Africa. New York: Cambridge University Press, 2009.

Lewis, Bernard. Race and Slavery in the Middle East: An Historical Enquiry. New York: Oxford University Press, 1992.

Ali, Kecia. "Slavery and Sexual Ethics in Islam." In Beyond Slavery: Overcoming Its Religious and Sexual Legacies, edited by Bernadette Joan. Brooten, by Jacqueline L. Hazelton. New York: Palgrave Macmillan, 2010.

"Crime and Clarity." The Economist, September 1, 2012. http://www.economist.com/node/21561883.

Klein, Herbert S. The Atlantic Slave Trade. Cambridge: Cambridge University Press, 2010.

Lewis, Bernard. Race and Color in Islam. New York: Harper & Row, 1971. p.38.

Manning, Patrick. Slavery and African Life: Occidental, Oriental and African Slave Trades. Cambridge: Cambridge Univ. Press, 2006.

Part IX – A Religion of Peace

Pickett, Joseph P. "Entry for šlm." In The American Heritage Dictionary of the English Language. Boston: Houghton Mifflin, 2006.

Jewish Dictionary. Accessed January 30, 2017. http://www.jewishdictionary.org/hebrew-words/shalom.html.

39. Terrorism

"Islam: Jihad." BBC. August 3, 2009. http://www.bbc.co.uk/religion/religions/islam/beliefs/jihad_1.shtml.

Pew Research Center. The World's Muslims: Religion, Politics and Society. Report. April 30, 2013. http://www.pewforum.org/2013/04/30/the-worlds-muslims-religion-politics-society-app-a/. Appendix A: U.S. Muslims — Views on Religion and Society in a Global Context

Bergen, Peter. "Why Do Terrorists Commit Terrorism?" The New York Times, June 14, 2016. http://www.nytimes.com/2016/06/15/opinion/why-do-terrorists-commit-terrorism.html?_r=0.

Esposito, John L. Islam: The Straight Path. New York, NY: Oxford University Press, 2016.

Kumar, Arvind. Encyclopaedia of Human Rights, Violence and Non-violence. Lucknow: Institute for Sustainable Development, 1998. p.187.

Mohammed, Khaleel. "Assessing English Translations of the Qur'an." Middle East Quarterly 12, no. 2 (2005): 58-71. http://www.meforum.org/717/assessing-english-translations-of-the-quran.

Hathout, Maher, and Samer Hathout. Jihad vs. Terrorism. Los Angeles, CA: Multimedia Vera International, 2002. p.49.

Ali, Maulana Muhammad. "When Shall War Cease." In The Religion of Islam: A Comprehensive Discussion of the Sources, Principles and Practices of Islam. Lahore, USA: Ahmadiyya Anjuman Ishaat Islam, 1992.

Fadl, Khaled Abou El, Joshua Cohen, and Ian Lague. The Place of Tolerance in Islam. Boston: Beacon Press, 2002. p.21.

Shah, Niaz A. Self-defense in Islamic and International Law: Assessing Al-Qaeda and the Invasion of Iraq. New York: Palgrave MacMillan, 2008. p.20.

Obama, Barack. "Remarks by the President on a New Beginning." Speech, Remarks by the President at Cairo University, Cairo University, Cairo, Egypt, June 4, 2009. https://obamawhitehouse.archives.gov/the-press-office/remarks-president-cairo-university-6-04-09.

Ghamdi, Javed Ahmad. "The Islamic Law of Jihad." Translated by Shehzad Saleem. In Mīzā n. Lahore: Dar Ul-Ishraq, 2001. http://www.studying-islam.org/articletext.aspx?id=771.

The Editors of Encyclopædia Britannica. "Battle of Badr." Encyclopædia Britannica. May 13, 2009. https://www.britannica.com/event/Battle-of-Badr.

Harris, Sam. The End of Faith: Religion, Terror, and the Future of Reason. New York: W.W. Norton & Company, 2005. p.31, p.149.

Charities Aid Foundation. CAF World Giving Index 2016. Report. October 2016. https://www.cafonline.org/about-us/publications/2016-publications/caf-world-giving-index-2016.

40. Non-Muslims

Kohler, Kaufmann, and Ignatz Goldziher. "Islam." Jewish Encyclopedia. Accessed March 1, 2017. http://www.jewishencyclopedia.com/articles/8263-islam#anchor15.

42. Apostasy

"1. Reversion versus Conversion." Islam Answering. Accessed November 28, 2016. http://www.islamanswering.com/subpage.php?s=article&aid=1249.

Goitom, Hanibal, and Global Legal Research Directorate. "Laws Criminalizing Apostasy." Laws Criminalizing Apostasy. June 30, 2015. https://www.loc.gov/law/help/apostasy/index.php.

Campo, Juan Eduardo, and J. Gordon. Melton. Encyclopedia of Islam. New York: Fast on File, 2009. p.48, p.174.

Zwemer, Samuel M. "The Law Of Apostasy." The Muslim World 14, no. 4 (1924): 373-91. doi:10.1111/j.1478-1913.1924.tb00536.x.

"Universal Declaration of Human Rights." United Nations. Accessed October 18, 2016. http://www.un.org/en/universal-declaration-human-rights/index.html.

United Nations. Yearbook of the United Nations. Part 1, Chapter 5, Social, Humanitarian and Cultural Questions. 1948-49. Accessed November 28, 2016. https://web.archive.org/web/20130927221000/http://unyearbook.un.org/1948-49YUN/1948-49_P1_CH5.pdf. p.535

Monteiro, A. Reis. Ethics of Human Rights. Cham: Springer, 2014. pp.414-16.

Agence France-Presse. "American Atheist Blogger Hacked to Death in Bangladesh." The Guardian, February 27, 2015. https://www.theguardian.com/world/2015/feb/27/american-atheist-blogger-hacked-to-death-in-bangladesh.

Morrison, Sarah. "Allah vs Atheism: 'Leaving Islam Was the Hardest Thing I've Done'." Independent, January 19, 2014. http://www.independent.co.uk/news/uk/home-news/allah-vs-atheism-leaving-islam-was-the-hardest-thing-i-ve-done-9069598.html.

"Remembering Irtaza." News release, September 24, 2013. Council of Ex-Muslims of Britain. http://ex-muslim.org.uk/2013/09/remembering-irtaza/.

Anthony, Andrew. "Losing Their Religion: The Hidden Crisis of Faith among Britain's Young Muslims." The Guardian, May 17, 2015. https://www.theguardian.com/global/2015/may/17/losing-their-religion-british-ex-muslims-non-believers-hidden-crisis-faith.

Browne, Anthony. "Muslim Apostates Cast out and at Risk from Faith and Family." The Times, February 5, 2005. http://www.webcitation.org/query?url=http://www.timesonline.co.uk/tol/news/uk/article510589.ece&date=2011-09-18.

43. Censorship

Shea, Nina. "An Anti-Blasphemy Measure Laid to Rest." National Review, March 31, 2011. http://www.nationalreview.com/article/263450/anti-blasphemy-measure-laid-rest-nina-shea.

Ernst, Carl. "Blasphemy: Islamic Concept." In Encyclopedia of Religion: Volume 2, edited by Lindsay Jones. Detroit: Macmillan Reference USA, 2005.

Murtagh, Peter. "Rushdie in Hiding after Ayatollah's Death Threat." The Guardian, February 15, 1989. https://www.theguardian.com/books/1989/feb/15/salmanrushdie.

Lichtenberg, Hans Henrik. "UN to Investigate Jyllands-Posten 'Racism'." Newspaperindex.com, December 10, 2005. https://web.archive.org/web/20080209153538/http://blog.newspaperindex.com/2005/12/10/un-to-investigate-jyllands-posten-racism/.

Vinocur, Nicholas. "Magazine's Nude Mohammad Cartoons Prompt France to Shut Embassies, Schools in 20 Countries." National Post, September 19, 2012. http://news.nationalpost.com/news/magazines-nude-mohammad-cartoons-prompt-france-to-shut-embassies-schools-in-20-countries.

"French Terror Attacks: Victim Obituaries." BBC News, January 13, 2015. http://www.bbc.com/news/world-europe-30724678.

Bloom, Jonathan, and Sheila Blair. Islamic Arts. London: Phaidon, 2013.

Larsson, Göran. Muslims and the New Media: Historical and Contemporary Debates. Farnham, Surrey: Ashgate, 2011. p.51.

McManus, John. "Have Pictures of Muhammad Always Been Forbidden?" BBC, January 15, 2015. http://www.bbc.co.uk/news/magazine-30814555.

Khan, Adnan. "Islam, Science and Civilisation." The Khilafah, February 26, 2009. http://www.khilafah.com/islam-science-and-civilisation/.

Ruthven, Malise. "How to Understand ISIS." The New York Review of Books, June 23, 2016. http://www.nybooks.com/articles/2016/06/23/how-to-understand-isis/.

Stepanova, Ekaterina. The Role of Information Communication Technologies in the "Arab Spring". PONARS Eurasia Policy Memo No. 159. May 2011. http://pircenter.org/kosdata/page_doc/p2594_2.pdf.

"10 Most Censored Countries." Committee to Protect Journalists. 2015. https://www.cpj.org/2015/04/10-most-censored-countries.php.

"2016 World Press Freedom Index." Reporters Without Borders. 2016. https://rsf.org/en/ranking.

"Freedom on the Net 2016." Freedom House. 2016. https://freedomhouse.org/report/table-country-scores-fotn-2016.

44. Islamization

Grim, Brian J., and Mehtab S. Karim. The Future of the Global Muslim Population. Report. January 27, 2011. http://www.pewforum.org/2011/01/27/the-future-of-the-global-muslim-population/.

Part X – Life After Religion

Johnson, Todd M., Gina A. Zurlo, Albert W. Hickman, and Peter F. Crossing. Christianity 2015: Religious Diversity and Personal Contact. Report. Vol. 39. Series 1. South Hamilton: International Bulletin of Missionary Research, 2015. Accessed October 18, 2016. http://www.gordonconwell.edu/ockenga/research/documents/2IBMR2015.pdf.

45. Atheism or Agnosticism

Dawkins, Richard. The God Delusion. Boston: Houghton Mifflin Company, 2006. p.50.

13,983,816 and the Lottery – Numberphile. Performed by James Clewett. Numberphile. March 28, 2012. http://www.numberphile.com/videos/lottery.html.

46. Morality

Jones, Jeffrey M. "Atheists, Muslims See Most Bias as Presidential Candidates." Gallup. June 21, 2012. http://www.gallup.com/poll/155285/atheists-muslims-bias-presidential-candidates.aspx.

"What Is Humanism?" International Humanist and Ethical Union. Accessed December 01, 2016. http://iheu.org/humanism/what-is-humanism/.

Hitchens, Christopher. God Is Not Great: How Religion Poisons Everything. New York: Hachette Book Group – Twelve, 2009.

47. Spirituality and growth

Kenneson, Philip D. "What's in a Name? A Brief Introduction to the 'Spiritual But Not Religious'." Liturgy 30, no. 3 (2015): 3-13. doi:10.1080/0458063x.2015.1019259.

Urban, Tim. "How Religion Got in the Way." Wait But Why. October 10, 2014. http://waitbutwhy.com/2014/10/how-religion-got-in-the-way.html.

Ellison, Christopher G., and Daisy Fan. "Daily Spiritual Experiences and Psychological Well-being Among US Adults." Social Indicators Research 88, no. 2 (2007): 247-71. doi:10.1007/s11205-007-9187-2.

Erlandson, Sven E. Spiritual but Not Religious: A Call to Religious Revolution in America. San Jose: Writer's Showcase, 2000.

Mercadante, Linda A. Belief without Borders: Inside the Minds of the Spiritual but Not Religious. New York, NY: Oxford University Press, 2014. pp.35-67.

Bailey, Chris. "Guide: Everything You Need to Start Meditating." A Life Of Productivity. May 17, 2013. http://alifeofproductivity.com/meditation-guide/.

Harris, Sam. "How to Meditate." Samharris.org. September 26, 2013. https://www.samharris.org/blog/item/how-to-meditate.

48. Meaning of life

"Celebrity Atheist List." Celebatheists.com. October 25, 2012. http://www.celebatheists.com/wiki/Main_Page.

Parkinson, Cyril Northcote. "Parkinson's Law." The Economist, November 19, 1955. http://www.economist.com/node/14116121.

49. Science is life

Reitman, Janet. "Inside Scientology." Rolling Stone, 2006.

http://www.rollingstone.com/culture/news/inside-scientology-20110208?print=true.

Resources for ex-Muslims

Below is a non-exhaustive collection of organizations and groups for ex-Muslims. I'm still at the beginning of this part in my journey. So I don't feel as though I have enough experience to share how best to cope with any new decisions you may be making in your personal life. I'm not affiliated with any of the below communities, but I hope you find the help you need and comfort in the knowledge that you're not alone.

Organizations

- Belgium: Movement of Ex-Muslims of Belgium
- Germany: Central Council of Ex-Muslims
- Ireland: Ex-Muslims of Ireland
- New Zealand: Council of Ex-Muslims of New Zealand
- North America: Ex-Muslims of North America, Muslimish
- Pakistan: Atheist & Agnostic Alliance Pakistan
- Scandinavia: Council of Ex-Muslims of Scandinavia
- Singapore: Council of Ex-Muslim of Singapore
- United Kingdom: Council of Ex-Muslims of Britain, Ex-Muslims of Scotland, Faith to Faithless
- United States: Former Muslims United

Meetup.com

- Ex-Muslim Meetup Groups

Facebook

- France: Conseil des Ex Musulmans de France
- India: Ex-Muslims: India
- Morocco: Council of Ex-Muslims of Morocco
- Norway: Ex-Muslims of Norway
- North America: Ex-Muslims of North America
- Pakistan: Council Of Pakistani Apostates (murtadin) Infidels (kafirun), Pakistani Atheists and Agnostics
- United States of America: American Council of Ex-Muslims

Forums

- Council of Ex-Muslims
- Faith Freedom International

- r/exmuslim (reddit.com)
- r/atheismcomingout (reddit.com)

More groups can found by searching ex-Muslim, atheist, agnostic or related terms on Google and Facebook.

Acknowledgements

I don't want anyone to receive unwarranted negative attention on my behalf as I know this will be a controversial book to a lot of people and my own identity is not even disclosed. Therefore I have chosen not to name people, unless they had already chosen to speak publicly about organized religion.

First, thank you to A and D. Thank you both for supporting me even though you weren't sure if what I was doing was the right thing. R and I, thank you for making me feel normal despite the lack of faith in our religion.

Thank you A. You provided me with a sounding board and a fresh pair of eyes when I so needed one. This book would not be what it is without your time, skill and patience. I'm indebted to you and your contribution into making this book what it is today. You are the reason it is so much more than I hoped it could ever have been.

Thank you M. You helped me reach the tipping point about moving on from religion. You also provided me with new ideas and frameworks about life philosophies. I hope to educate and entertain people as you do one day.

Thank you O. I've absorbed your music for hundreds and hundreds of hours while researching, writing, editing, redrafting and formatting this book. You helped keep me sane. You helped keep me going. I cannot thank you enough.

Thank you N for inspiring me to think bigger than I've ever done before and letting me know it was actually possible to succeed as well. I'm just following in your footsteps, trying to make the world a better place in my own unique way.

Thank you L for giving me perspective and letting me know it's possible to accomplish big projects. Your contribution is more appreciated than you know.

Thank you Armin. Your book 'Why There Is No God: Simple Responses to 20 Common Arguments for the Existence of God' was critical for the part 'Why Religion Works' in this book. Your efforts to improve the lives of ex-Muslims around the world is so commendable and I hope you realize how much it has influenced us all.

Last but not least, I want to thank M. You have been the most important teacher I've had in my adult life. I literally can't imagine what my life would be like had you not entered it. You helped me see the world in a way I didn't know was possible. You told me it's OK not to settle, and it's OK to go a different path from everyone else, even if I didn't know where it would take me. I can't thank you enough for how much you've taught me and still continue to teach me. I hope this book is the start of me adding value to the world and into people's lives, just like you've been able to do. Thank you again M. Thank you.

For my Mother and Father

For my mother and father,

I hope throughout this book you'll have journeyed into my mind and now seen how I've become the person I am today. I know there's a lot here you won't have agreed with, but I'm not asking you to change who you are for me. I'm asking the opposite. I'm asking you to still see me as your son.

Someone you're proud to call your son. Someone who tries to do the best he can in everything he applies himself to. Someone who acts out of kindness and follows what he believes in his heart is the right thing to do. This book isn't just about you and I, it's about helping all the people who felt as confused, disillusioned and scared with Islam as I did. It's about giving them a voice. It's about giving them something to show their parents, something they too can give to their family which helps them understand why they feel the way they do.

I know I have many flaws. I'm doing my best to improve them and become the best possible version of myself, and I honestly believe this book is helping me to get there. You'll most likely disagree, and I respect that. It's what I expected. But if you're reading this, then it hopefully means you've read your way through the entire book, and for that, I'm eternally grateful. It's the most I could have hoped for when really, I have no right to be asking any more of you as my parents. You've done more than enough for me my entire life. Now, I only hope you'll still talk to me. You'll still welcome me into our home. You'll still be there for me, as you have always been since I was born.

I hope you understand and forgive me for what I've done. I love you Mama and Baba, and I'm sorry.

Adam

My request to you

1. When faced with challenges and opportunities in your life, start from first principles. Question all conventional wisdom. Your intellectual curiosity could help more lives in the next thousand years than you possibly know.

2. I would love to see, hear or read the contents of this book presented as a narrative. Stories transcend time. A graphic novel, podcast, youtube video, film or any other form of media with the information from *Atheism for Muslims* or any kind of 'atheist confessional' from other religions would be joyous to absorb. You have my permission to use the contents of this book for your project if you wish to do so. If you have any questions (or have yet to tell me how the weather is where you are) let me know at adamwadi@protonmail.com

3. If you found this book helpful, could you please leave an Amazon review? The number of reviews a book gains on Amazon has a direct impact on how it sells. So leaving a review, **no matter how short**, helps get the book's message out to more people, and, makes it possible for me to produce more books like this for you. I've put a lot of myself into this book; I've loved writing it and I'd love to continue writing more books for you.

As an artist, I truly care about what I can do to improve and what you think. So if you found this book helpful, **it would mean the world to me if you could leave an Amazon review.**

Made in the USA
Middletown, DE
11 December 2022

18015590R00224